Visual Basic® 6: Error Coding and Layering

ISBN 0-13-017227-8

90000

9 780130 172273

PRENTICE HALL PTR MICROSOFT® TECHNOLOGIES SERIES

PRENTICE HALL PTR MICROSOFT® TECHNOLOGIES SERIES

Tyson Gill

Visual Basic® 6: Error Coding and Layering

PH
PTR

Prentice Hall PTR, Upper Saddle River, NJ 07458
www.phptr.com

Library of Congress Cataloging-in-Publication Data

Gill, Tyson.
    Visual Basic 6: error coding and layout / Tyson Gill.
       p. cm. -- (Prentice Hall series on Microsoft technologies)
    ISBN 0-13-017227-8
    1. BASIC (Computer program language) 2. Microsoft Visual BASIC. I. Title: Visual
Basic 6: error coding and layout. II. Title. III. Series.
QA76.73.B3 G55 2000
005.26'8--dc21

                                       99-056391

Editorial/Production Supervision: Precision Graphics
Acquisitions Editor: Jill Pisoni
Editorial Assistant: Linda Ramagnano
Cover Design Director: Jerry Votta
Cover Designer: Anthony Gemmellaro
Manufacturing Manager: Maura Goldstaub
Marketing Manager: Lisa Konzelmann
Art Director: Gail Cocker-Bogusz

© 2000 by Prentice Hall PTR
Prentice-Hall, Inc.
Upper Saddle River, New Jersey 07458

Prentice Hall books are widely used by corporations and government agencies for
training, marketing, and resale. The publisher offers discounts on this book when
ordered in bulk quantities. For more information, contact:

    Corporate Sales Department
    Prentice Hall PTR
    One Lake Street
    Upper Saddle River, NJ 07458
    Phone: 800-382-3419; FAX: 201-236-7141
    E-mail (Internet): corpsales@prenhall.com

Printed in the United States of America

10 9 8 7 6 5 4 3 2 1

ISBN 0-13-017227-8

Prentice-Hall International (UK) Limited, *London*
Prentice-Hall of Australia Pty. Limited, *Sydney*
Prentice-Hall Canada Inc., *Toronto*
Prentice-Hall Hispanoamericana, S.A., *Mexico*
Prentice-Hall of India Private Limited, *New Delhi*
Prentice-Hall of Japan, Inc., *Tokyo*
Pearson Education Asia Pte. Ltd., *Singapore*
Editora Prentice-Hall do Brasil, Ltda., *Rio de Janeiro*

CONTENTS

v

ABOUT THE AUTHOR

Tyson Gill is Senior Solutions Developer at WinResources Computing, Inc. in Carlsbad, California. He also teaches Visual Basic at the University of California San Diego. Prior to joining WinResources, he spent six years as an independent consultant, producing applications for a wide variety of clients in Southern California. Before coming to California, Tyson was Associate Scientist at the ICI Research Center in Ohio, where his software innovations earned him formal recognition as a "Key Corporate Asset." He holds a Master's degree in Chemistry from the University of Wisconsin.

Tyson has contributed to books on Visual Basic and makes numerous presentations on Visual Basic program design, architecture, and error coding. He is active in the San Diego Visual Basic User's Group and has authored over a dozen technical articles. He also loves creative writing and has authored an unpublished novel and two screenplays. Tyson lives with his wife, Marcie, and teenage son, Rossen, near the ocean in Carlsbad, California.

LIST OF FIGURES

....

Coding Smarter

This book will help you improve the quality and productivity of your software development effort. By the time you finish reading it, you will know how to code smarter and to participate in a team effort to code smarter. You will have a better appreciation of the problems and pitfalls associated with Visual Basic programming and the common causes of project failure. You will also have a clear understanding of how to avoid those problems and to ensure the success of your project in the long term as well as in the short term.

This Book Is for You

If you have anything to do with computer programming, this book is for you. Whether you are an analyst, a programmer, a manager, or a related professional, you will find value in this book. Regardless of your experience level, from student to senior developer, this material is at the appropriate level for you. No matter what type of project you are involved in, this book will be applicable.

The scope of this book is broad, from general philosophies to specific lines of code. While many of the general approaches and attitudes presented in this book hold true no matter in what language you are developing, the specific problems and solutions detailed in this book are designed for Visual Basic development.

This is not another "learn Visual Basic" book. It does not simply rephrase and repackage information found in help files and computer books. It presents new and uniquely valuable strategies to overcome coding problems that plague virtually all Visual Basic programs. While it is not a programming book, it does teach programming techniques. It deals with the process of Visual Basic programming as opposed to the language details.

While this is not a management book, it does discuss management issues. While it is not a book about testing, it does deal with testing issues. In short, this book covers all the topics that are vital to a successful team program development effort. It sets an ambitious new standard of excellence for Visual Basic applications, and provides simple (and, in retrospect, obvious) techniques for achieving that new standard of productivity and quality.

This is not a neutral book detailing a specific technology or documenting the latest API or object model. On the contrary, it is a passionate book dealing with both technical and nontechnical issues. Sometimes, it may hit close to home. It may expose flaws in the attitudes and techniques that you may have been using for years. If it does, it will have succeeded in half its mission. If it succeeds in showing you how to overcome those flaws, then it will have succeeded completely.

Getting the Most from This Book

To get the greatest benefit from this book, it is essential that you read it straight through as though you were reading a novel. If you are used to reading technical books by browsing the contents or index and jumping from topic to topic, that approach will not work. Both the conceptual and the practical ideas build progressively through the course of the book, each flowing from previous material. Like a novel, it builds to a climax, at which point you may wonder how you can possibly improve your coding practice in spite of all the formidable antagonists. In the end, it reaches resolution, however, and shows you how you can overcome all obstacles by adopting relatively simple coding approaches.

It is also recommended that you read it at least twice. During the first reading, you may come across suggestions that you question. That is good, but file them away and continue reading. Then go back and read it again. Suggestions that you might reject or question during the first reading may seem more appealing after you see how they fit into the complete picture. During the second reading, you can selectively incorporate the suggestions into your own work, adapting them if necessary to your particular situation.

Acknowledgments

Thanks to J. Kevin Meadows, Ed Stegman, Edward Michelic, Marcie Gill, and Bill Munro for reviewing the manuscript. Thanks also to David Johnson for contributing illustrations. A big group thanks to the entire staff at WinResources for their support and encouragement. Finally, thanks to Waterside Productions and Prentice Hall for making this book a reality.

Your Software Development Mission

It is possible to improve the quality and productivity of your software development effort. This book will show you how. It will provide you with both the high-level strategy and the low-level implementation details you need to accomplish this.

Software development is especially vulnerable to quality and productivity issues. Given the unique, customized nature of software products, even two comparable efforts can produce two widely varied levels of quality. Programming is both a technical craft and a creative endeavor. Different personnel, architectures, tools, and coding practices and a variety of subtle nuances can all affect quality and productivity dramatically.

Software is your product, whether you are an independent consultant or part of a large contract firm. You would undoubtedly like to increase both the quality and productivity of your software development effort.

When you increase the quality of your product, it creates greater demand and in turn commands a higher price. When you decrease the cost to produce your product, you become more competitive. Improved quality and productivity translate directly into higher profitability.

Don't let promises of increased profits make you too impatient to tackle the nitty-gritty details. It is critical to understand the strategic battle plan of your process improvement campaign before digging into the trenches with tactical details. Without clear strategic goals, the campaign is reduced to isolated skirmishes. The rest of this chapter provides that strategic overview.

1.1   Drafting Your Mission

Quality and productivity are critical properties of any software development process. Unfortunately, both quality and productivity can be dramatically altered by seemingly minor changes to the development process. Even very subtle changes can seriously undermine your effort. But if you are able to make the right subtle changes, you can substantially improve your effort.

While a number of metrics and tools are available to help you, it is still difficult to characterize, quantify, or improve the software development process. Software development is unlikely to turn into an assembly-line process any time soon.

To tackle these issues, we need a clear mission. Let's begin to draft a mission statement and refine it as we go along.

> **Your Mission Statement (First Draft)**
> To achieve a measurable improvement in our software development process.

This is a good starting point. You want to improve your software development process, and it is always a good idea to specify that those improvements must be measurable. But what specifically do you intend to improve? Quality and productivity come to mind. They are the key attributes having an impact on success.

Should you try to improve one or both? Improving both quality and productivity can be difficult. It is easy to improve one at the expense of the other. You can usually increase productivity by lowering quality, or increase quality at the expense of productivity. It is the net increase that counts! Productivity improvements that sacrifice quality may not be desirable. Likewise, quality improvement benefits may not be worth their cost.

You enjoy the maximum benefit only by increasing both quality and productivity.

Therefore, you need to refine your mission statement to specify that both quality and productivity must be improved.

> **Your Mission Statement (Second Draft)**
> To achieve a measurable improvement in both the quality and productivity of our software development process.

This revised mission statement is a step in the right direction. You have gotten more specific about what you intend to improve. When people promote strategies for improving some aspect of quality or productivity, they are quick to show you the benefits of their new ideas. However, they are not as quick to discuss or fairly represent the costs associated with these new strategies. Every change has potential benefit, but the critical question is, what is the cost of that benefit? Practically speaking, no such thing exists as benefit without cost. We should always talk about the cost/benefit ratio rather than only considering the benefits.

A benefit with a high cost may not be a benefit at all. A benefit with a low cost may still not represent a good cost/benefit bargain if other approaches have even lower costs. Many software development improvement strategies fall into this category. Management strategies that are essentially high-overhead administrative processes may not be worth their cost. They may produce net loss and can even be counterproductive.

You need to add some recognition of cost effectiveness to your mission statement.

Your Mission Statement (Third Draft)
To achieve a highly cost-effective and measurable improvement in both the quality and productivity of our software development process.

The third draft is better. You can improve your mission statement still further, however. Any discussion of product and process improvement is shortsighted if it fails to consider the nature of the improvement. Are the benefits short-term, long-term, one-time, ongoing, or cumulative?

Too often, we look at quality or process improvement as a one-time event. We commission a team to conduct a study, offer recommendations, and implement improvements. Total Quality Management and similar efforts by different names make a commitment to ongoing process improvement. TQM efforts may only result in a series of short-term improvements that do not necessarily result in improvements of a permanent and cumulative nature.

Cumulative process improvements are those that provide a permanent, growing return on investment. They represent improvements that make all subsequent efforts easier. It is not easy to achieve this kind of process improvement in most businesses.

In software development, it is possible to implement process improvements that are both permanent and cumulative. By adding a requirement that your improvements be cumulative in nature, you will complete your mission statement.

Your Mission Statement (Final Draft)
To achieve a highly cost-effective, cumulative, and measurable improvement in both the quality and productivity of our software development process.

Now you have a worthy mission, but how do you complete your mission? The first step is to determine what components are critical to success. In order to realize cumulative benefits, the first, most essential component must be the retention of corporate knowledge.

1.2   Retaining Corporate Knowledge

The success of software firms is tied tightly to the experience and talent of their developers at any given moment in time. Training is the typical approach to improving the quality and productivity of the development effort. Companies invest in training courses, expecting that the productivity of their staff will increase and that the quality of work will increase as well.

Training is mainly a short-term process improvement. It can increase the experience and knowledge of employees. However, for a company, obtaining knowledge is much easier than holding onto it. In today's highly fluid job market, the success of a software firm may be as transitory as its personnel roster. Of course, companies must train their staff to build skills. At the same time, they must realize that personnel come and go. Although they do everything possible to retain their human resources, they know personnel changes are beyond their control. Corporate expertise and programming experience depart with the employee who moves on.

ANECDOTE: The Problem of Retaining Corporate Knowledge

Retaining corporate knowledge is a problem facing all companies, no matter what their size and no matter what business they are in.

When I worked for a chemical research firm providing technical software solutions, accessibility to corporate knowledge was of critical concern. Tremendous amounts of vital technical knowledge were held by a handful of senior researchers. Loss of any of these people, either to competitors or by attrition, had a devastating effect on the company.

In our information systems group, we wrestled with solutions—including text search and retrieval, expert systems, and neural networks—to extract, retain, and share that experience and expertise. Some of those efforts were successful, some not so successful. One of the biggest obstacles was extracting the knowledge of the experts, some of whom were not able to organize such a wealth of information in their minds, let alone articulate it.

Software companies have an almost unique advantage in this regard. The knowledge of their experts is potentially directly reusable. Unfortunately, most software developers do not fully exploit this to their advantage.

The fleeting nature of corporate knowledge is just as vital to software developers as to persons in any other business. The loss of corporate knowledge not only diminishes productivity and level of quality, but it is a measurable loss of corporate investment. In order to enjoy ever-increasing quality and productivity, it is essential that software developers capture, retain, and reuse their corporate knowledge without depending on any particular employee. This includes experience and expertise as well as actual code knowledge.

In software development, retaining knowledge should be easier than in most other industries. The talent and experience of developers is manifest in their work in that it can easily be *reused*. Code can be reused and expanded indefinitely. While we can develop knowledge bases, web sites, and chat forums to make our knowledge permanently accessible, it is infinitely more efficient simply to create reusable code.

Before you dismiss the idea of "reusable code" as a mere platitude, think about this: how many industries have the fantastic advantage that software developers have? It would be like an automobile company creating only one steering wheel and digitally cloning it freely in every vehicle it makes. Imagine enhancing that same steering wheel with a new air bag feature and instantly updating all previous cars with the new steering wheel. That is the kind of magical benefit we could enjoy in the software business. For the most part, unfortunately, we don't exploit it.

Despite the fantastic theoretical benefits of code reuse and all the talk about it, in fact the vast majority of developers reuse very little of their code. Most of the talk about code reuse focuses on the use of a few third-party controls and never scratches the surface of the tremendous benefits of true code reuse. Of course, many developers are reluctant to rely even on third-party controls for which they have no source code and no assurance of long term maintainability.

When we talk about code reuse, the concepts of components, COM objects, class-based programs, and true object-oriented programming come to mind. As you will see, these architectures can facilitate code reuse, but they do not *guarantee* it. As a matter of fact, even though Visual Basic is object-based, not object-oriented, it is nevertheless possible to develop Visual Basic programs with a very high level of code reuse.

> *It is possible to retain corporate knowledge in a highly accessible fashion through code reuse.*

1.3   Standardizing the Creative Process

We all hear talk about code reuse, but we hardly ever see a living, breathing specimen of it. Everyone agrees that it is a good practice, but hardly anyone effectively reuses code. The code we produce is the most enduring and directly applicable form of our corporate knowledge. Without reuse, we simply cannot retain and reapply our corporate knowledge efficiently. Without reuse, we cannot accomplish our mission to produce higher quality products and become more productive at the same time.

While software development is a highly technical process, a great deal of creativity is also involved. Developers use whatever creative magic it takes to write routines to do what they want them to do. Master programmers develop programs just as master chefs create tasty dishes. A bit of this, a dash of that, take a taste, and add some more secret sauce. Each dish may look and taste great, but no two dishes ever come out quite the same. This may work for chefs, but software developers need to reuse what they make if they are to be competitive. Chefs can't very well do that, nor is it a desired business model for them. Chefs don't attempt to compete in productivity, nor is that expected of them. They also don't have to worry as much about users finding "bugs" in their dishes.

How can software developers share their work with other members of their team and with other teams? If they don't all follow the same development standards, they cannot share their code effectively. You may think that standards are not important in code reuse with interface-based programming. However, standards apply to interfaces as well. Standardized interfaces are more user-friendly. Also, the expected maintainability of reusable routines is a major consideration. Users are much more likely to want to use routines when they are confident they follow a maintainable internal architecture.

Lack of standardization is one of the major reasons code reuse is so under exploited. If code is not standardized, it cannot be effectively reused, since programmers would spend more time trying to understand and adapt nonstandard routines than the time they would spend simply rewriting them. They know this. Only when standards are adopted and adhered to can code reuse become a reality.

Clearly, if code reuse is to work, development standards must be adopted. Once you adopt a solid programming standard, you may be amazed to realize that you don't feel restricted at all. Instead, you will feel free from the day-to-day overhead considerations of deciding how to implement this or understand how that works. All the code you work with will be so consistent, so understandable, and so much more solid that you will feel at once relaxed and creative in your coding.

Standardization applies not only to the external interfaces of shared routines but also to the internal code. In reality, code needs to be continually enhanced and expanded. If it is not maintainable, it will not be reusable for long. Programmers will find it easiest to start from scratch if changing requirements necessitate making any enhancements to the code. In our ever-evolving world of software technologies, this is most often the case.

Failure to establish and maintain coding standards results in lower short-term and long-term productivity, since code must be repeatedly reinvented. Adopting coding standards not only provides direct short-term and long-term productivity benefits, but it also enables you to accomplish additional key components of your mission strategy, such as effective error coding.

It is possible to establish coding standards that do not inhibit the creative process and do not reduce short-term productivity.

1.4   Error Coding

Standardization is critical to code reuse and the retention of corporate knowledge. It helps to make the code familiar and understandable to anyone who will look at it. Standardization alone, however, is not enough to make code reuse a reality. The code must also be both versatile and robust.

If the code is not 100 percent standardized, not everyone will understand it. If the code is not flexible enough to meet varied situations, not everyone will be able to use it. If the code is not 100 percent solid and reliable, no one will *want* to use it. Too many efforts to promote code reuse focus on the mechanics of code sharing, neglecting to address the more difficult and important issue of the quality of the shared code.

To create solid code that is worthy of reuse requires effective error coding. As in all things, quality at the highest levels builds on quality at the lowest levels. If you expect to practice code reuse as a means to realize your larger goals, you must expect to perform complete error coding. Further, complete error coding must be implemented in standard fashion, and enforced and verified in every routine you write.

Complete error coding is essential to creating reusable code. As mutually supportive processes, reuse is essential to accomplishing complete error coding. One is not possible without the other.

It is possible to write reusable, standardized, completely error-coded code with no more effort than you are currently expending to write nonstandard, buggy custom code.

1.5   Coding Smarter

To accomplish our mission of a cumulative increase in quality and productivity, you must retain corporate knowledge through code reuse. In order to maintain and reuse code, you must adopt coding standards and enforce complete *error coding*.

How do you achieve those goals? How do you put systematic coding *and error coding* in place? How do you establish standards that have a high cost/benefit ratio? How do you communicate and promote those standards? How do you verify and enforce them? How do you accomplish all this without adversely affecting productivity and morale?

Substantial technical and nontechnical barriers are blocking your way. Programmers—even the most experienced ones—are not used to following detailed coding standards. Few companies have defined comprehensive, practical coding standards. Fewer companies have the mechanisms in place to promote or monitor the adherence to standards. Even fewer developers take a rigorous, systematic approach to error handling.

This book provides many specific strategies for overcoming these barriers and achieving your mission. The general answer is simple: "Work smarter." Working smarter means accomplishing more with less effort. It means achieving higher productivity, producing higher quality, and enjoying more vacation time. This whole concept seems as though it must violate some fundamental law of physics. It would seem that less effort can never result in greater benefits.

However, working smarter does work. No matter how much talent and experience you have, chances are good that you can be more productive if you work smarter. You will most likely have much more fun to boot.

In order to work smarter, you must unlearn your old ways of doing things, break existing habits, and no longer accept prevailing methods and practices as "good enough." Working smarter demands that you improve on commonly accepted standards and practices, and that you develop new ways to organize and systematize your work to make it more efficient.

The classic "efficiency experts" show companies how to work smarter. They study current business processes, analyze modes of inefficiency or failure, and envision a higher standard. They then break existing paradigms and expectations with a new set of strategies and measures of achievement. Efficiency experts are usually outside consultants because outsiders can look at the existing expectations and processes from a clearer vantage point. Their vision is not obscured by politics, habits, or history.

Think about the simple task of cleaning your garage. Once a year that simple task probably becomes a daunting one as you watch the garage get so cluttered, so messy that it is barely usable. You cannot find any of your tools. Dust and leaves are scattered everywhere. Boxes teeter precariously on top of wobbly stacks of supplies. You have no room for even one more lawn chair along the wall.

One day each spring you put aside an entire Saturday for the task and set to work. You start to clean and organize but quickly realize it is hopeless. You end up taking everything out onto the driveway, cleaning the garage, and then hauling everything back in. A couple hours after dark, in the light of the garage door opener, you finally get everything perfect.

You start out with the best of intentions to keep your overhauled garage neat and tidy for the remainder of the year. For the first week, it is a joy to be in, but soon you stick that carton on a shelf where it does not belong when you are in a hurry. You use one organizational system for your tools but organize your garden supplies differently. Different family members implement their own organizational ideas. Before you know it, you are pleased if you can just find a "temporary" spot to stick that surfboard. Eventually you abandon all attempts at organization, and the garage starts to degenerate rapidly toward the point next year when you will have to start over again.

In the same relentless way, we end up with "garages" full of fragmented Visual Basic code. We cannot remember where we put that routine, so we just write a new one. One developer may see clear logic in his or her naming conventions, but it may make no sense to the rest of the team. A program architecture may exist under the rubble somewhere, but it cannot be seen. Eventually, we are satisfied if we can fix only one statement without causing our stacks of code to fall over. Long before the program has lived out its product life cycle, we have to abandon it and start over with a major rewrite. It is the "spring cleaning" approach to code maintenance.

When you use your garage smarter, you make it more adaptable, maintainable, and useful. It is an asset, not a barrier to getting your household tasks done. Likewise, by coding smarter, you can develop Visual Basic code so that it is infinitely maintainable. You can quickly find the software components to get the job done and use them effectively. It is not hard. Actually, it is fun. All you need to do is break out of old paradigms and expectations.

Coding smarter means writing tighter, clearer, and more robust code with less effort. This book shows you techniques for smarter coding to develop standardized, fully error-coded, reusable routines with less effort, as well as methods for coding smarter by *layering* your program architecture. Layering means untangling spaghetti into clear, manageable, maintainable layers. You will see that layering is an important part of your overall strategy for coding smarter.

It is possible to achieve your mission by coding smarter.

1.6   Identifying the Possible

This chapter has started to identify achievable goals that are vital to accomplishing your overall mission. It has set a higher level of expectations for your development efforts and has created new expectations of what is possible. Here is a summary of your new vision of the possible:

- You can code smarter.
- You can accomplish complete error coding.
- You can standardize your development processes.
- You can reuse a growing inventory of code.
- You can retain and leverage your corporate experience.
- You can make improvements that have a growing, cumulative benefit.
- You can achieve higher quality and productivity.

Remember your mission?

Your Mission Statement (Final Draft)
To achieve a highly cost-effective, cumulative, and measurable improvement in both the quality and productivity of our software development process.

Is there room to improve both the quality of your software and the productivity of your development process? The answer is probably yes. Is it possible to substantially increase both productivity and quality? The answer again is most certainly yes! It is possible to achieve your mission.

1.7   Achieving the Possible

How then do you achieve your new vision of the possible? What steps must you take to reach your goal?

1. Understand existing programming paradigms.
2. Analyze the flaws and inefficiencies in those paradigms.
3. Envision methods to overcome those flaws and achieve your enhanced expectations.
4. Put those methods in place and generate a buy-in by all those involved.

These are the steps I have followed over the years to achieve the recommendations presented in this book. The concepts presented are the result of many years of effort to produce quality software. They are based not on academic theory but on trial-and-error experience. The conclusions and recommendations presented are the winners in an evolutionary survival-of-the-fittest process.

ANECDOTE: How I Got Here

In my 16 years as a software developer and programming instructor, I mastered the programming techniques that are commonly accepted as the standard of excellence. Having started programming in languages such as Assembler, C, Forth, and Fortran, I developed rigorous discipline. Working in a scientific research environment only helped to encourage that programming rigor.

When Visual Basic 1 was released, I adopted it immediately. Even though most projects could not be accomplished using that limited first version, for simple Windows applications it was a miracle. Today, Visual Basic can be and is used for virtually any type of application.

Since Visual Basic was so easy to use, my programming rigor relaxed somewhat. Though not as demanding as other languages, I did adopt all the best programming practices that are expected of quality Visual Basic programming.

I first began to suspect that these commonly accepted programming practices were lacking rigor when I started consulting. As a consultant, I was called on to save many projects threatened with failure. Some were years overdue and still far too unstable to ship. Others were existing products that needed updating but were too fragile to touch. It seemed to me that this situation was not the exception but the rule. This assessment was supported by the commonly cited statistic that over 90 percent of software projects fail to meet their goals.

Before I could determine how to save these projects, I first had to study the existing architecture and code to determine what the problems were. As one might imagine, some were cases of incredibly bad programming. However, I was surprised to discover that most of these failing programs were well-written in accordance with commonly accepted programming standards. Despite the best efforts of experienced and talented programmers, they still failed to meet their goals or were in danger of collapsing under their own weight.

Still, that observation did not really hit home until a project of my own started to stress. It kept growing in complexity until I became afraid to touch it. That was the moment of revelation. It was inescapable that commonly accepted programming standards were simply not adequate to develop high quality, robust, and scalable applications. There had to be a better approach.

I set about purposefully analyzing why projects fail or, at the very least, become more difficult to maintain than expected. Of course, many of these technical and nontechnical reasons are beyond the control of the developer or the development team.

It became clear to me that two root causes give rise to most programming problems and limitations. These are inadequate error coding and inadequate layering. To overcome these deficiencies, I developed error-coding and layering techniques that are simple to understand, easy to implement, and produce dramatic results. The resulting programs are far more scalable, maintainable, efficient, and robust than typical programs.

Since developing my error-coding and layering strategies, I have worked to find effective ways to implement them. I have lectured in many companies and user groups and have taught these techniques in my classes. Without exception, these principles resonate with audiences. Even novice programmers instantly recognize the problems and pitfalls I describe. They tell me that the solutions presented are startling in their simplicity and power. Senior programmers often express regret and embarrassment for not having implemented similar techniques in the past. None of the techniques are magical, and all seem simple and obvious in retrospect.

The good thing for you is that you don't need to struggle through all of those years of trial-and-error to reap the benefits. This book will bring you to the same point much faster. One of the most important of these concepts is the *Smart Coding Triangle*.

1.8   The Smart Coding Triangle

The Smart Coding Triangle (see Figure 1.1) is made up of error coding, standardization, and reuse. The three make up a mutually supportive whole. If any one of the sides is missing, the remaining two cannot easily succeed. Together they represent a practical, comprehensive package for development process improvement.

Error coding cannot be effectively implemented without coding standards, and it cannot be practically implemented without substantial reuse. Code will

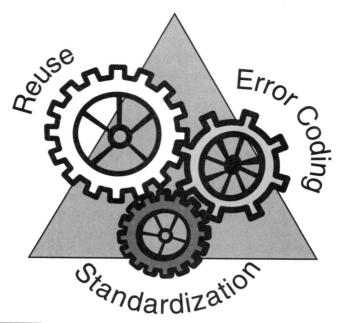

FIGURE 1.1   The Smart Coding Triangle

not be reused unless it is fully error coded and standardized. Standardization cannot have a net benefit unless it involves both error coding and reuse.

Adopting the Smart Coding Triangle will not only increase productivity and quality, but it will have additional benefits as well. By implementing the Smart Coding Triangle in a comprehensive manner, you will be able to leverage the experience of talented and experienced developers and allow junior developers to produce a higher quality product. You will experience not only greater customer satisfaction but greater employee satisfaction as well. Sensibly implemented, your developers will find that this process improvement trio will make their jobs much more fun.

Developers will find it easier to develop code when they can follow a standard and not have to think about how to reinvent code in each situation. They will find it a relief to leverage previous effort to reuse sophisticated, comprehensive error coding without having to rethink and recode for each possible error situation from scratch. Finally, they will feel a sense of satisfaction and pride in knowing that their code will "live long and prosper."

1.9   Barriers to Your Mission

Numerous barriers exist to accomplishing the mission of improved productivity and quality. The next chapter identifies and explores these barriers so that we can understand and ultimately overcome them.

Understanding the Barriers to Your Mission

Many barriers stand in the way of your goal of increased productivity and quality: barriers to implementing effective error-coding, barriers that make code reuse a rarity, barriers that make it difficult to standardize your programming methods. Understanding the barriers to creating your Smart Coding Triangle is the first, essential step toward overcoming them. Some barriers are technical; some are nontechnical. In this chapter, we identify and discuss a number of these barriers.

2.1 Visual Basic Error Coding

Visual Basic is the most widely used programming language in the world. The success of Visual Basic is largely due to its ability to shield the programmer from many low-level tasks that make programming difficult. By providing a complete programming framework and a rich library of functions, the programmer can work at a higher level and not deal with the complex details of developing a Windows program.

However, Visual Basic programs do have bugs. In fact, many Visual Basic programs are infested with them. Even programs that seem to work well may have hundreds of bug eggs waiting for the right conditions to hatch. Every veteran Visual Basic developer has fought desperate battles to keep program bugs under control. Too often, this is a losing battle.

Ironically, the simplicity that makes Visual Basic so attractive also makes it susceptible to bugs. Most new Visual Basic programmers have not learned the more careful and rigorous programming practices that come from struggling first in lower-level languages. Even experienced programmers quickly tend to become complacent about bugs after using Visual Basic for any length of time.

Visual Basic makes it fun to design new forms and features. This is the creative and exciting part of Visual Basic programming. It brings the joy of playing with form layouts, of implementing new functionality, and showing off fast and impressive results. Most new programmers quickly build such confidence in using Visual Basic that they naturally get the impression they can simply jump in and code new features.

The Visual Basic honeymoon can end when new developers start to encounter bugs. This leads some programmers or managers to overreact. They may conclude that Visual Basic is not a "professional" quality development tool. While it is undeniable that bugs plague many Visual Basic programs, it is wrong to conclude that the fault lies within Visual Basic. It is an unfortunate mistake to abandon the tremendous productivity benefits that Visual Basic has to offer. It would be tragic to do so when it is actually quite easy to write nearly bug-free programming.

ANECDOTE: Visual Basic Isn't the Problem

I was called in to assist one client after the company's Visual Basic project had failed to meet its goals. It was buggy, slow, and far behind schedule. Before I arrived, the management had concluded that Visual Basic was simply not a professional-quality development product. They had already begun to rewrite their project in C++. They simply wanted me to get the Visual Basic version limping along while waiting for the C++ version.

In a few short weeks, I tightened up several modules, reducing their code size by one-third while adding more features and the error coding. Those modules became very stable and responsive, so much so that the management was forced to admit that perhaps Visual Basic was not the problem. Their coding practices had failed them.

Using Visual Basic, programmers can efficiently develop professional applications that are both feature-rich and robust. However, because Visual Basic does not require rigorous programming practice, it is imperative that developers impose their own rigor. Visual Basic is not at fault if programs are coded haphazardly. While Visual Basic does not prevent sloppy programming, neither does it in any way inhibit excellent programming.

Solid error coding is an essential part of solid Visual Basic applications. It may be fun and easy to program new features in Visual Basic, but features without adequate error coding suffer in many ways:

- Features that fail quickly frustrate the user and undermine confidence in the application.
- Buggy features kill profits and reputation.

- Features with inadequate error coding are difficult to maintain and enhance. They may work for a while, but as soon as requests for enhancements or bug fixes come in, they can start to unravel.
- The product lifetime of applications with poor error coding is limited.
- Having to support programs that are buggy or hard to maintain destroys the morale of the development staff.

In order to avoid these negative consequences, it is important to understand why good error coding is so seldom achieved.

2.2 Why Good Error Coding Is Seldom Achieved

Despite the obvious importance of error coding, good error coding is seldom achieved. Even experienced and talented programmers who can produce great forms and features often fail to produce even barely adequate error coding. Many reasons for this exist. Some are inescapable qualities of error coding; others are attitudes and perceptions. The following items identify some of these reasons.

2.2.1 Sample Code Focuses on Functionality

In books, magazines, and course materials, sample code tends to show functionality only. It does not often present any significant error coding. This is perfectly understandable. Error coding obscures the functionality being demonstrated; it makes the functionality look complicated when the authors are attempting to convey simplicity and simply because space in publications is very limited.

2.2.2 Error Coding Is Not Glamorous

Everyone wants to know how to make features work. Implementing new features is sexy. No one shows off one's programming machismo by demonstrating cool error handling code.

2.2.3 Error Coding Is Difficult to Learn

While training can bring new programmers up to speed on the latest technologies, it does not usually include much information on error coding. New programmers cannot anticipate most bugs because they have never encountered them. Only bitter experience teaches how to predict, prevent, and handle error situations, because that is how programmers encounter bugs and learn techniques to prevent them.

2.2.4 Error Coding Is Difficult to Do

It takes considerable skill and experience to understand how to design comprehensive error coding. It also takes determination and meticulous attention to detail to implement those designs in a comprehensive and maintainable manner.

2.2.5   Error Coding Is Seen as Ancillary

Coding features is the primary emphasis of most programming efforts. Error coding is nice to have, but it is not usually thought of as critical to the effort.

2.2.6   Error Coding Is Taken for Granted

When a programmer is commissioned to implement a new feature, it is taken for granted that he or she will include all necessary error coding to protect it. This is usually a dangerous assumption. By placing all the emphasis on features, error coding is often neglected.

2.2.7   Error Coding Takes a Large Amount of Code

It may take 10–40 lines of error code to support one line of feature code. A fully error coded program can be mostly error code. Depending on how you implement complete error coding, it might increase your code size by an order of magnitude. With that much error code, you have far more code to write, to support, to document, and to debug. This is a disincentive from including large amounts of error code.

2.2.8   Error Coding Cannot Be Properly Implemented Separately

The "debugging phase" of a project is a myth. It almost never happens. Even if some attempt at a debugging pass is made, error coding that is performed late cannot achieve the same level of quality as error coding that is implemented simultaneously with feature coding.

2.2.9   Error Coding Is Not Visible in Final Product

Features cannot be left out, even if they are not 100 percent solid. Error coding is not a visible part of the feature list, so it doesn't get the same amount of attention.

2.2.10   Error Coding Is the First Place to Skimp

Projects are almost always rushed by deadlines. Error coding is the easiest, most natural place to skimp since error coding is not visible in the final product.

2.2.11   If We Do Skimp on Error Coding, So What?

Programs without complete error coding may work well at first. They may never fail. The client will sign off on features and pay the bill. The recipient may possibly never notice a lack of error coding.

2.2.12   Even If Errors Appear Later, They Can Always Be Fixed as They Appear

Why spend a great deal of time preventing potential bugs when we can simply fix the bugs that actually appear? Some developers feel they can't afford to prevent every potential bug. They fear that they would never complete the project on time and within budget. They feel it is more efficient to fix them if and when they appear.

   This belief is the root of many problems. Many authors cite estimates that errors cost 3 to 30 times as much to fix late in the process as at the point of introduction.

2.2.13   Management Creates Disincentives

Managers focus on a feature list, deadlines, and productivity. Most managers are not well-prepared to create environments that emphasize, promote, and ensure quality error coding.

   In performance reviews, it is easy to remember and evaluate how many features the developer was able to move out the door. It is much more difficult to evaluate the long-term benefits of the developer's efforts. Two developers may appear to have produced an equal amount of work. One developer may have produced code that is buggy and destined to cost the company a fortune to maintain over the lifetime of the product. The second developer may have produced code that a future developer could inherit and maintain without any difficulty. Most companies would have trouble evaluating and rating the great performance disparity between these two developers. In fact, the developer who produces buggy code may quickly receive the higher performance evaluations!

2.2.14   Code Is Viewed as Disposable

Complete error coding is essential to code reuse. Most developers don't think constantly of code reuse, and most companies don't have the infrastructure in place to facilitate reuse. They may not literally think of their code as disposable, but this is, in effect, the result of *not* thinking of it as reusable.

2.3   "We Will Adapt"

Thinking of code as disposable is a fundamental problem. Earlier it was suggested that a tight interrelationship exists between code reuse and error coding. Code that is viewed as disposable cannot be effectively error coded and reused.

   We write a program to meet our current needs as quickly as possible. When we do so, we implicitly assume that, when necessary, we will scrap it and start over again. We have come to accept our code as custom, disposable.

In doing so, we also tend to put little time into robust error handling. As long as it holds together for this particular situation, that is sufficient. We don't expect our code to endure.

As a result, since we don't write the code to be reusable, it is not reused. It is too poorly error coded to survive a wide range of environments. Without good error coding, no one reuses. Without reuse, we end up reinventing *code-wheels*. A code-wheel is what I call any block of code that would not otherwise need to be reinvented. A code-wheel should provide flexible and error-coded functionality so that programmers need never think about how it works again.

This acceptance of code as disposable has severe implications for our system of retaining corporate knowledge. It results in a limited amount of reusable code and therefore a limited amount of shared corporate knowledge. When the programmers who solved problems in disposable code move on, their solutions must be relearned and recoded. Obviously, this practice is not only inefficient, but it yields much lower quality products at higher costs.

These costs go far beyond individual projects. Coding that is not systematic and not fully error-coded cannot be effectively reused. Without code reuse, software development firms continually reinvent code-wheels and fail to retain and apply knowledge gained from past experience.

Similarly, since our code is not designed to be reused, it can survive neither reuse nor changing needs. Program revisions, enhancements, repairs, and maintenance are, in effect, changing environments. Our code can break if not designed to be reusable. This means, in essence, that disposable code is of limited usefulness not only over multiple projects but also over the life cycle of the product for which it was designed.

"We will adapt." If you are a Star Trek fan, you will immediately recognize this as a favorite line of the Borg. The Borg have a great outlook: they have recreated their entire race to be adaptable and reusable. They are not content to merely "get by for now" as humans do. Instead, they demand that every part of their "collective" contribute to a singular mission: to adapt to any changing situation that may arise.

Most programmers are merely human. They write disposable code in order to just get by the immediate, short-term requirements. It may be helpful to take a lesson from the Borg and think instead of every line of code as an enduring entity contributing to the whole "collective." Think of each reusable "Borg" code unit as enduring and adaptable to any future need.

In truth, if you do not write your code to be reusable, it will be reused anyway. The lifetime of any particular line of code or routine can be amazingly long. It gets cut and pasted into places it was never intended. If this code is not fully error-coded and robust, it becomes equivalent to viruses spreading throughout the code population.

2.4 Achieving Good Error Coding

If we accept long-held perceptions about error coding, and if we view our code as disposable, then we cannot achieve good error coding. If we shift our paradigm slightly, however, complete error coding is possible

- *With less work than you are currently expending.* It is possible to include complete error coding without creating additional work. The first time that a code-wheel is created takes longest. By reusing that fully error-coded code-wheel, subsequent features are implemented faster without having to recreate all the additional error coding.

- *With junior developers.* By reusing fully error-coded wheels, junior developers inherit the experience of senior programmers who have preserved their expertise in reusable code. New programmers do not need to learn the same hard lessons and develop the same error-handling solutions.

- *Without greatly increasing the amount of code.* Since the code-wheels are reused efficiently within the same application, the total amount of code need not increase greatly.

- *Without adding cost.* By reusing error coding, it takes no additional; time and effort to produce fully error-coded applications. The cost/benefit ratio improves as more code-wheels are produced and reused.

- *Without endangering deadlines.* It should not take significantly longer to produce fully error-coded programs. As the amount of reuse increases, time spent coding can actually decrease.

- *Without making programming less fun.* Once programmers start to reuse their error coding, the burden of recreating code-wheels whenever they are needed vanishes. Programmers can actually feel less concerned and worried about error coding while producing much more solid applications. They feel less as though they are doing the same tasks over and over again.

All of this is possible if we reuse error code, if we follow consistent standards in our error-coding, and if we use effective error coding techniques.

2.5 Barriers to Error Coding

It is not enough to develop standardized, reusable, error coding. To be successful, the error coding must be written using effective techniques. Effective error-coding techniques are not generally practiced for many reasons:

- *Lack of rigor in coding.* Error coding is not generally approached with the high degree of attention to detail that it requires and deserves.

- *A lack of training in error-coding techniques.* Most courses and educational materials focus on methods to implement details, but these fail to place enough effort into teaching the error-coding methods required to fully protect those features.

- *Lack of thought and planning for error coding.* Since error coding is seen as ancillary and sometimes applied in a cursory second pass, it is not integrated well into the feature code and is implemented in a haphazard manner.

- *A lack of standardization and organization of the error coding.* Not only is the error coding integrated with features in a haphazard manner, but the error coding itself is not standardized and organized in a systematic fashion.

- *Error coding that is limited to simple error trapping.* Error trapping is the least useful error-coding technique. Yet the error coding in many programs is limited to crude error trapping.

- *A lack of appreciation of error prevention as an error-coding technique.* Error prevention is the most important error-coding technique, an idea seldom appreciated or emphasized by developers.

- *Poorly constructed error messages.* Error messages are generally inaccurate, arcane, or too generic. They don't often anticipate the needs of the users who will be confronted with them.

- *Lack of reuse.* Again, without effective reuse of error-coding code-wheels, it is not feasible to implement complete error coding.

In the next few chapters, you will see how to overcome each of these common problems and implement effective error coding techniques in your applications. Once you do implement a new set of error coding techniques, though, you will need to know how to evaluate and quantify the effectiveness of those techniques. It is difficult to evaluate error coding, and it is not something that programmers normally do well.

2.6   Evaluating Error Coding

Typical code testing procedures do well at turning up bugs. Testing is well-equipped to identify bugs that derive from operating the application as designed and expected. Testers are good at stretching the bounds of normal operation to identify ways to break the program. However, if the goal is to evaluate the effectiveness of code-wheels for long-term robustness and reliability, normal application testing is not designed to accomplish that.

It is difficult to evaluate error coding because:

- *Testing is geared to test current application functionality.* It is not intended to exercise and test the robustness of low-level code as it may be reused in unanticipated future situations.

- *We don't see it functionally.* Application testers see features directly. Error coding is hidden within the programming of specific features. They can't visualize and test it directly, only indirectly through the functionality that it supports.

- *It is difficult to simulate a wide range of error conditions.* The range and type of error conditions that can be tested are normally limited by those conditions allowed by the current user interface. Again, if the goal is to provide more flexible and reusable code, testing cannot expose the code to the complete range of conditions. *Unanticipated errors are hard to test for.*

- *No good way exists to quantify effectiveness.* While testers can check off the operation of features on a checklist, no direct ways have been formulated to quantify the effectiveness of error coding. All our information about error coding is indirect at best.

- *Code review is a time-consuming process.* It is not feasible to perform a low-level inspection and code review of every line of functionality. Even more impractical is to think about independently testing code-wheels and revising them beyond the requirements of the current application.

Error coding is only tested indirectly at best. Testing may turn up errors in error coding as it tests features, but the error coding itself is not subject to the full spectrum of testing. It is only subject to the portion of testing that the feature permits. The underlying error coding may break if the feature changes.

Since error coding is not tested directly, only a very weak feedback mechanism exists for ensuring that it is robust and solid.

2.7   Barriers to Code Standardization

Standardization is also a critical part of our Smart Coding Triangle. Without standardization of both the feature coding and error coding, we cannot achieve our long-term goals. Many barriers stand in the way of standardizing our code:

- *A lack of a sensible, practical standard.* We cannot adopt a standard that does not exist. This book will present a good working standard.

- *A lack of determination and resolve to follow standards.* This arises partly out of a lack of appreciation of the benefits and importance of standardization, and partly out of the mistaken impression that the costs incurred would be too high.

- *A lack of team thinking.* Most developers think independently, at least as far as their particular areas of responsibility are concerned. They follow their own conventions and don't appreciate the importance of following team conventions.

- *Unrealistic timelines.* If timelines are too demanding, then developers may feel that they do not have time to implement standards. They are prevented from adopting a key solution to improve their productivity.

- *The mistaken impression that standards impose on the developer.* The imposition of a standard can be seen as insulting. It might seem that adhering to one would restrict creative and efficient program development. None of these impressions is necessarily true. The standard presented in this book is not limited by any of these concerns.

The barriers to standardization are largely nontechnical. The mindsets and attitudes of people normally tend to be resistant to the very suggestion of restriction. But standardization need not be restricting. Developers must understand and really believe this in order for them to buy in.

The technical barriers can be overcome more easily. The main barrier is the creation of a standard. One such standard is provided for you later in this book. The second technical barrier is disseminating and communicating the standard. This point will also be addressed later.

2.8   Barriers to Code Reuse

The third part of our Smart Coding Triangle is code reuse. Without effective reuse of code, you cannot achieve your goals of knowledge retention or complete error coding. Of course, barriers exist to effective code reuse.

One barrier to code reuse is bad experience with the reuse of internal or external code that did not follow standards for feature and error coding. Another barrier is design; most routines are not designed to be reusable, so they lack flexibility and robustness. A third barrier is a lack of sufficient external and internal documentation to allow developers to easily find, understand, and modify the code they need.

The bottom line is that reuse is usually the first victim in the war of short-term realities versus long-term benefits. This is a tragedy because it kills the very best chance for meeting short-term deadlines and constraints in the future. It is also a tragedy because it is quite possible to develop reusable code *and* meet short-term deadlines.

When we think of code as enduring, we are forced to take a different perspective. We are forced to think about maintainability, flexibility, standards, error coding, reuse, understandability, and other considerations that are normally neglected.

Clearly, powerful factors make it difficult to implement our Smart Coding Triangle. Many of the barriers to effective error coding boil down to one: short-term thinking. Most developers strive to get the code out the door so that it works today, often in response to demanding or unrealistic schedules. By coding smarter, we can implement strategies that benefit us in the long-term, and even very near term, without requiring a prohibitive investment.

2.9   Eliminating the Barriers

Despite all the barriers standing in the way, it is possible to do better. The barriers impeding progress can easily be eliminated, making our goals of improved productivity and quality possible. It is possible to produce:

- Programs with fully reusable, error-coded features.
- Programs with virtually no bugs.
- Code that can be reused in almost any similar situation.
- Programs that can be maintained and expanded indefinitely.
- Code-wheels that are improved and that become more robust with every project, enhancing the quality and improving the productivity of every project.

Now that we have discussed the barriers to achieving our mission, we can discuss strategies for overcoming these problems. The next chapter presents specific strategies and techniques for producing effective error coding.

Implementing Effective Error Coding

In the first chapter, we established that effective error coding is critical to the larger goals of higher productivity and quality. In the second chapter, we identified some of the barriers to implementing effective error coding. This chapter offers a discussion of techniques to achieve an improved standard of error coding.

3.1   Raise Your Expectations

The first step in standards improvement is to enhance your expectations. You must no longer accept old standards of error coding as satisfactory. You must demand more effective, more complete error coding from yourself and from your staff. The following are some of the raised expectations you should set for your development process:

- *Handle errors early.* When errors are dealt with early, less work is required to handle them. Early error management also results in a better user experience.

- *Error code as you go.* You must code each feature completely as it is written. Going back later to error code usually never happens. If it does actually happen, it takes more time and yields poorer results.

- *Avoid assumptions.* Assumptions are the bane of good error coding. Later in this chapter, we look at specific assumptions to avoid.

- *Design all routines to be reused.* By viewing all code as reusable, you automatically apply a higher standard of error coding and consistency. Your mind-set must be that every routine may be reused. You cannot apply one standard for reusable code, and another for "one-time only" code.

- *Never code for the same error twice.* If you don't reuse your error coding, it will not be feasible to apply it universally. You will simply have too much error coding to complete the project.

- *Develop a systematic error-coding methodology.* If error coding is not implemented in a systematic, standardized fashion, it will not be easily reused and maintained.

3.2   Manage Errors Early

To create the most satisfying user experience, it is critical to manage errors as early as possible. From the user's perspective, the earlier an error is corrected, the better. Let's imagine, for example, a typical data entry form with a number of text entry fields. We will examine several possible points at which to apply error coding in this typical situation.

1. The user enters all values and presses a "Save" button. The application attempts to save the values, and errors are returned from the database. The user is informed of a database error.

2. The user enters all values and presses a "Save" button. At that point, the application validates all values and informs the user that a field entry was incorrect. The user corrects the error, then clicks "Save" again. The application now informs him or her that a second field has an invalid value.

3. The user enters one field and presses tab to move to the next field. The application validates that field and informs the user of an error. The application does not allow the user to leave the field until a valid entry is made.

4. The user presses a key and the application detects that the key press is invalid. It cancels the key press and the user is not allowed to enter the invalid character.

When we examine these error-coding strategies, we see that they are obviously ordered by increasing effectiveness. However, the least effective of these examples is the most likely to actually be implemented in most applications. We will examine the reasons for this shortly.

The earlier the error is handled, the better. Errors handled early are less aggravating for the user because they can be handled more precisely and effectively. If the error is not handled immediately, then every step the user is allowed to make after the error is input results in more wasted effort for him or her.

Imagine pressing an invalid key but not being informed of it immediately. You continue working, thinking everything is fine. Then suddenly the program tells you that you made a mistake much earlier. All your subsequent effort was a waste of time. How would you feel? Wouldn't you much rather be told immediately that you pressed the wrong key so you don't go on needlessly? Even better, wouldn't you much rather be simply prevented from pressing that wrong key in the first place?

The secret of good error coding is simple: handle errors early. The following Golden Rule encapsulates this practical philosophy:

> ***The Golden Rule of Error Coding***
> *Prevent all errors that can be anticipated and prevented.*
> *Handle all errors that can be anticipated but not prevented.*
> *Trap all errors that cannot be anticipated.*

Errors fall into two general types: those that can be anticipated, and those that cannot be anticipated. The response of an invalid key can normally be anticipated. The application can recognize ahead of time what is valid and what is not. This error should be *prevented* from happening in the first place.

An example of an error that can be anticipated but not prevented is the reading of a file. All sorts of potential errors—such as a file being corrupted—can be anticipated, but these cannot normally be prevented. Therefore, the best we can do is handle them. To handle errors means taking corrective action, with or without user intervention. Prompting the user to repair the corrupted file and try again is an example of *handling* that particular error.

Some errors cannot be anticipated. Since the developer does not know the nature of the error ahead of time, these errors cannot be prevented, nor can they be handled. The best that can be done is to trap the errors. *Trapping* simply means making sure that the error does no damage, then reporting it to the user or the system administrator.

Note that error suppression is not error trapping. Suppressing an error is a form of error handling. We discuss this in greater depth later.

The Golden Rule of Error Coding prevents errors as early as possible.

3.3   Code Errors as You Go

The concept of early error management has important implications for the development process as well as for the user experience. The earlier error coding is put into place in the development cycle, the better. Let's examine several common scenarios for error coding during development.

1. The user entry form goes to the testing department. As their team attempts to save the fields, a database error occurs. It goes back to the development team. Rather than fix many input controls and risk introducing errors, it is more expedient to trap the database error and display a message, clearing the form of any potentially erroneous entries.

2. While unit testing a data entry form, the developer realizes that when the "Save" button is pressed, errors can occur because of invalid entries. He or she places code in the Save Click event to check for these errors and to alert the user of the first one encountered.

3. The programmer adds a large number of new text boxes to a form. He or she realizes later that he must protect these text boxes from invalid entries. He or she adds code to the LostFocus event to alert the user if the entry is invalid.

4. The programmer puts a new text box on a data entry form. He or she immediately adds code to the KeyPress event to filter user key presses so that no invalid keys can be entered. (Note that pasting text into the text field would not fire a KeyPress event. This must be handled separately.)

Which of these items is the most effective? Clearly, they are presented in order of increasing effectiveness, so the last approach, utilizing earlier error prevention, is certainly the most preferable. By preventing errors rather than responding to them, both the user experience and the coding efficiency are greatly enhanced.

Notice that these examples parallel the examples shown in the previous section. This is no coincidence. The development examples in this section could have resulted in the different user experiences from the previous section. These scenarios illustrate the general rule that the later at which errors are coded in the development process, the later they will also appear in the user experience. If you think about this a bit, you can see why it is natural and inevitable. The later errors are coded, the less likely that the solution will be a well-implemented and satisfying one.

Postponing error management in development has many other ramifications as well. An error is really more like a weed than a bug (see Figure 3.1). It starts with one seed but quickly winds through the ground. If you catch it early, it is easy to yank it out. But if you wait, its tendrils take hold in every part of the application. It pokes above ground in many places. The task of removing it can be formidable. It can be very difficult to find all the underground tendrils and even more difficult to remove them without causing damage.

One error can send many vines up into the user interface, giving the impression of an extremely buggy application. As another side effect, branching errors are caught late in the development process. The solution to them is likely to be a snipping at the buds, not a removal of the roots. This kind of error-snipping fragments the project and makes it more difficult to maintain. It

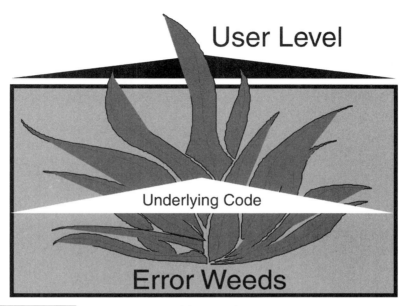

User Level

Underlying Code

Error Weeds

FIGURE 3.1   Bugs are more like weeds

requires much more testing and development time to find and snip each one, and it demoralizes the staff late in the project development cycle.

Another problem exists with thinking about errors late in the development cycle: if you don't code for errors as you code features, this procedure will probably never get done. You can be honest here—it's just us. Have you ever really gone back and added good error coding to your application? It almost never happens. Projects always run out of time, money, or both before error coding ever gets done. When the deadline has passed and the budget is dry, the manager will always decide to ship. When that happens, what should have been error coding gets pushed into the testing and debugging cycles. Worse yet, the errors force users to request support. This is not a profitable situation.

Even in those rare cases when enough time is given to go back for that "error-coding pass," it cannot be well implemented in a second pass. By the time you return to error code those features, you will have forgotten all the subtle error-coding requirements and the effective responses to them. Worse yet, a different programmer who never coded the features is often asked to error code them. The likelihood of introducing errors in a second error-coding pass is sometimes greater than the errors that would have been fixed.

For greatest effectiveness and efficiency, errors must be dealt with early in both the user experience and in the development cycle.

As each line of feature is coded, it must be 100 percent error coded before moving on.

Now, if you are wearing your management hat as you read this, you may be thinking that this sounds like ivory tower programming. In a perfect world maybe this could be done, but in reality, we could not meet our deadlines if we spend a lifetime error coding.

That would be true if you continued to program as usual. However, this book presents error-coding techniques in conjunction with standardization guidelines and reusability strategies that make it possible. The Smart Coding Triangle makes it possible to fully error code every feature and still meet deadlines.

A program that is feature complete with partial error coding is far less desirable than an application that is partly feature complete but completely error coded (see Figure 3.2). No one can predict how long it will take to make the first program stable. You have a very good idea how long it will take to complete the second one. Additionally, you can ship the second program at any time, with its completed functionality 100 percent solid. You cannot test or ship the first.

Your goal should be that your applications are 100 percent solid and shippable after each new feature is completed.

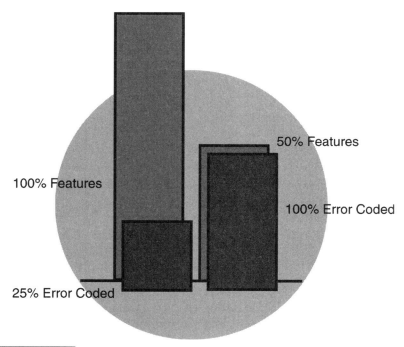

100% Features

50% Features

100% Error Coded

25% Error Coded

FIGURE 3.2   Complete error coding is more important than having complete features

3.4   Anticipate Errors

Anticipating errors is one of the most important keys to effective error coding.

Errors that can be anticipated can be coded much earlier in the development process and resolved earlier in the user experience. But how do we anticipate errors? Which errors can be anticipated and which cannot?

In truth, there is no such thing as unanticipated errors, only errors that you have not yet learned to anticipate. Some talented programmers have a "sixth error sense" that allows them to anticipate errors they have never encountered personally. The rest of us generally learn to anticipate errors only from experience. We have to be burned by them at least once to learn to avoid them. At best, we don't have to be burned too many times before we learn to avoid them.

Therefore, I would argue that a programmer's ability to anticipate errors is at least as important as his or her ability to implement new features. Here experience counts. A computer science degree does not guarantee a keen error sense, nor does it provide a great deal of experience. As I said earlier, most training emphasizes features and technology, not error coding. Experienced, battle-worn developers have probably seen it all and have been bitten by bugs often enough to know how to anticipate them. Better yet, they know how to prevent or handle them.

Some companies focus on new technologies in their hiring practices, so why not hire a newly trained programmer for a fraction of the cost of that battle-scarred veteran? Experience with error-coding situations is usually not factored into this evaluation. Rather than discussing the long-term economic impact of hiring practices, I am providing techniques that allow junior programmers to utilize the talent and experience of the veterans without having to learn the same hard lessons.

Anticipating errors is the result of experience. That experience can be effectively shared and reused.

3.5   Prevent Errors

The ability to anticipate errors is extremely important, but it is merely a necessary prerequisite to our real goal of preventing them.

Error prevention is the most important part of error coding. It eliminates much of the need for error handling and trapping. Additionally, it dramatically reduces the amount of code required for a robust application, resulting in the most maintainable applications. Finally, it is the most satisfying form of error coding from the user's perspective.

Why, then, is it almost universally overlooked? It is practically never discussed in technical literature. Instructional courses don't normally emphasize it. Discussions of error coding neglect error prevention completely. They discuss error trapping and some error handling, but never include error prevention in the discussion. It is like writing a book on lung cancer that talks about care and treatment without mentioning smoking habits. It focuses on how to deal with horses after they have left the barn, instead of discussing how to keep them from escaping in the first place.

Error prevention is the first and strongest line of defense in the war against bugs.

3.6   Handle Errors

Error prevention is the diplomatic arm of error coding, nipping problems in the bud. Error handling is the main fighting force, resolving errors when they occur. It comprises the bulk of error coding. In fact, without effective prevention and reuse, complete error handling could comprise 90 percent of all code in a project. Since it is so time consuming and difficult to produce, error handling forces are typically mobilized quite inadequately.

Error handling should be used to correct errors that can be anticipated but not prevented. Obviously, if you cannot anticipate an error, you cannot handle it. Handling implies that something intelligent is done specifically to correct a particular error situation as soon as it occurs. Simply recovering from an unanticipated error situation is not handling the error. That is error trapping. Error handling, like error prevention, is most effectively implemented as each new feature is being added.

Error handling is the second and most code-intensive line of defense against bugs.

3.7   Trap Errors

Error Trapping is the most commonly practiced form of error coding. It is the only defense against unanticipated bugs. Without error trapping, unanticipated bugs can result in program crashes, loss of data, and system failures.

Although important, error trapping is both overused and misused. It does not prevent errors, so error trapping effectively locks the barn door after all the horses have run out. This is not a very satisfying response for the user. Also, error trapping does not handle errors. Since it only traps unanticipated errors, it cannot do anything intelligent with each specific error. It merely takes a safe, generic action, such as reinitializing the program. Last, it does not really fix the specific problem. It merely recovers from the problem.

This is not to minimize the importance of error trapping. It is essential for handling unanticipated errors, but when error trapping is used to manage errors that could be prevented or handled, then it is being misused.

Error trapping is over-emphasized for many reasons. To name one of the biggest, it is extremely easy to do. This form of error coding can be added without any knowledge of the specific errors trapped or the correct responses to them. It adds a relatively small amount of code to the application. It also requires only modest programming skill to implement. In fact, a number of third party products that will automatically add error trapping code to your application.

Error trapping does not need to be implemented with each feature, as do error prevention and handling. It can be added at any time, even just prior to shipping. This means that development groups who failed to code error prevention or error handling as they created any features can tack error trapping on as an afterthought. They tell everyone that they did complete error coding. This is not the case, however. Again, the later in the development cycle that error coding is added, the less effective and useful it is. The attractiveness of error trapping is also its weakness.

If you have included error trapping in your application during development, you can use it to diagnose error conditions. If an error is trapped during development or testing, prevent or handle that error so it is never trapped again. An error should never be trapped twice.

As more errors are prevented and handled, the need for error trapping decreases. Again, theoretically no errors exist that cannot be anticipated, only errors that we have not yet learned to anticipate. As we anticipate and prevent or handle more errors, the need for trapping decreases. That is not to recommend completely dispensing with error trapping. Instead, this book will present a Safe Programming Framework that will allow you to code a majority of your application safely without any error trapping. The Safe Programming Framework will encourage you to use error trapping when it is legitimately required in localized circumstances, not as a catch-all approach to error coding.

Error trapping is the last, impenetrable line of defense against bugs.

3.8   Report Errors

Another essential component of error coding is reporting. Though not often treated as a separate topic, it really does deserve independent consideration. How will errors be presented to the user? How will diagnostic information be communicated to the developers?

As a user, how often have you seen programs display cryptic error details that make sense to no one except perhaps one or two developers? As a developer, how often have you been asked to respond to bug reports with only the sketchiest of high-level user information?

Clearly, error reporting has two important goals. One is to report errors to the user. The second is to provide diagnostic error information to the developer. The two should not be confused. It is probably best not to accomplish both in a single message.

User error reporting should:

- Be presented in language that the user can understand.
- Not confuse the user with unnecessary details.
- Be as specific as possible regarding the particular error that occurred.
- Clearly communicate the reason for the error.
- Clearly communicate how the user can correct the error, or the response the application is taking to correct it.
- Reassure, rather than frighten, the user.
- Tutor and mentor the user.
- Be presented to the user as soon as possible after the error occurs.

Diagnostic error reporting should:

- Provide the developer or support staff with all information necessary to reproduce the error.
- Not be shown to the user.
- Be easily accessible by support staff.

What do you think of the following typical error message (Figure 3.3)? What would you do if this error message suddenly popped up on the page as you were reading and did not allow you to continue?

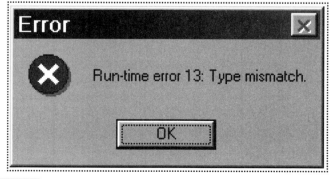

FIGURE 3.3   Typical user error reporting

What does this message mean, especially to a non-programmer? What was the cause of the error? What do you need to do to correct it? Figure 3.4 shows a better example of error reporting.

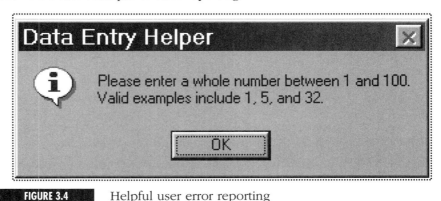

FIGURE 3.4   Helpful user error reporting

The message box displayed in Figure 3.4 is a great improvement over the one in Figure 3.3. It clearly communicates, in nontechnical terms, the cause and nature of the error. It also tells the user clearly what needs to be done to correct the error. As an even more subtle improvement, the second message box does not even appear to be an error. The first message is clearly an error, signaling a problem to the user and making the program look buggy. The second message is presented as more informational. It makes the users feel that the program is intelligently helping them rather than frustrating them. The attitude shown in your error coding can have a powerful effect on the perceived friendliness of your application.

The internal mechanism by which errors are generated, diagnosed, and communicated is a determining factor in achieving the goals of good error reporting. The error reporting mechanism not only determines the content but also the timing of error reporting.

A good error-coding scheme must integrate reporting into the coding standard.

3.9   Avoid Assumptions

Anticipating errors may be the means of achieving good error coding, but avoiding assumptions is the essential quality and technique vital to anticipating errors. Assumptions are the breeding ground of bugs. Ask any programmer how or why any particular bug was introduced, and he or she will almost always begin the answer with, "I assumed that . . ."

An assumption is a condition or fact that will or may be invalid in the future. Sometimes it manifests as one that the programmer feels is or will be obvious. Assumptions come in many forms, but most boil down to wishful thinking. One of the most common types of wishful thinking are short-term thinking. The following are some typical assumptions made by programmers and their managers. Look for underlying themes of wishful thinking.

3.9.1 *I Won't Ever Need to Use This Code Again*

This is the main assumption that undermines reuse. It results in the belief that disposable code does not require the same standard of error coding. One standard is applied to "one-time" coding and another to code designed specifically for reuse. It is usually only an excuse for not taking the time and effort to make it fully error coded. It takes the pressure off the programmer to attain a "reuse" level of quality. This point is discussed in the next section.

3.9.2 *I'm the Only One Who Will Touch This Code*

This belief is a variant of the previous assumption. Both are based on short-term thinking. This one rationalizes and attempts to excuse inadequate error coding and rationalizes poor coding in general. For example, if no one else will use this code, then why bother with detailed internal documentation? The programmer may say, "I know what I did," which is almost always a bad assumption. In the first place, if code is successful, others will almost certainly need to modify it later. Second, even when the original programmer returns to the code, it will be difficult to recall what was done and why without the proper level of commenting.

3.9.3 *I Only Designed It for a Particular Situation*

Here is yet another standard programmer disclaimer. By not attempting to make the code robust, the programmer accepts no responsibility for future maintenance. It is short-term thinking to develop any code for a particular purpose only. All code should be potentially reusable in a wide variety of situations.

3.9.4 *General Coding Assumptions*

The following are some general coding assumptions based on wishful thinking:

- *External variables.* When writing a function, it is dangerous to assume that external variables will be provided as globals. It is much better to make each routine self-contained by passing variables as arguments or by setting class properties. Avoid using globals.
- *Arguments.* When passing arguments, it is a poor assumption to expect that the calling routine will provide a valid argument. Each routine should validate any argument passed to it rather than place the burden of responsibility on the calling routine.

- *I can trust this function.* This is a system function, so can we assume it is robust? Don't trust built-in functions. Even though built-in Visual Basic methods are intended to be optimized for speed, they are not robust with regard to errors. Almost all built-in Visual Basic functions, statements, and methods must be protected with error coding.

- *Implicit behavior.* This is the type of assumption in which we believe that a certain behavior will remain the same. The next chapter looks at assumptions of this type in detail.

- *User behavior.* Assuming that the user will behave in a certain way is usually a recipe for a bug report.

We will refer to these general assumptions throughout the rest of the book with specific examples.

3.10 Design Functions for Reuse

This point was made during the discussion of assumptions, but it is important enough to deserve its own section. In order to accomplish effective error coding, each function must be designed to be reused *by someone else.* Without this mind-set, assumptions and compromises are justified that undermine effective coding practices. Consistent standards are not imposed on the code.

Implicit in the argument that code will not be reused is the assumption that you can predict future needs. In truth, none of us can really predict how or when some code might need to be reused, no matter how specific it may seem at the time. It is wishful thinking to assume that no situation will arise in the future in which this code will be needed again.

Further, it is wasteful for your business to write "one-time only" code. The higher the percentage of code that is designed for reuse, the more effective your future programming efforts will be.

3.11 Reuse Error Coding

In order to write good error coding, we must take the position that all our code might be reused in the future. There is another side to the relationship between code reuse and error coding. In order for error coding to be economically and consistently applied, the error coding itself must be designed for reuse—and then actually be reused.

When programmers are asked to improve their error coding, their first tendency is to add a great deal more error coding. They tend to cut and paste error handling code liberally and end up tremendously swelling the amount of code in their projects. This sometimes results in a situation opposite to the desired effect. With all the additional code, the likelihood of errors increases and the amount of code becomes more difficult to maintain.

This does not need to be the case. By coding smarter, you can add complete error protection to every line of feature code without bloating your application. To do so requires highly reusable error-coding routines that can be easily added and maintained, without adding a significant amount of code or code maintenance, and without introducing new errors into the error coding itself.

3.12   Systematic Error Coding

In order to reuse your error coding efficiently, it must be written in adherence to clear standards and conventions. This is not usually the case. Error coding, like feature coding, is typically written with a bit of this and a dash of that. When it is implemented, error coding is typically redesigned specifically for each situation. And no two developers on a team follow the same approach to error coding. Individual developers do not normally even follow consistent standards from one situation to another.

Without a coding standard, it is unlikely that error coding will be reused and easily maintained, or that it will mesh seamlessly into a cohesive application. The Safe Programming Framework presented later in this book provides one good systematic approach to integrated application and error coding.

One of the goals of the Safe Programming Framework is to avoid assumptions through good, explicit coding practices. Before describing the Safe Programming Framework, we discuss the importance of explicit coding and provide some specific recommendations to eliminate implicit assumptions from your code.

The next chapter describes implicit coding practices and suggests ways to eliminate them from your Visual Basic applications.

Explicit Coding

Visual Basic offers many shortcuts by allowing implicit behaviors. Microsoft's rationale is most likely that these features make it quicker and easier for new programmers to develop applications. The learning curve is reduced in comparison to languages such as C and Pascal, since Visual Basic makes assumptions that the other languages force the user to explicitly define.

However, the designers of other languages have good counterarguments why they have chosen to enforce explicit practices. An implicit behavior makes a type of assumption. Any initial benefits that these assumptions offer usually come at a greater cost in long-term maintainability. Since solid code should contain no assumptions, implicit language features should be avoided.

Fortunately, Visual Basic does not force you to accept implicit behaviors. In most cases, you can either direct Visual Basic to avoid assumptions or you can impose your own programming rigor. This does not mean that Visual Basic programming must become as difficult as more restrictive languages are, but it does mean that it can be made just as rigorous.

The risk of errors will be reduced and clarity increased if you avoid any implicit behaviors. The following discussion covers specific implicit coding assumptions that are made either by Visual Basic or in the typical practices used by programmers.

4.1 Explicit Variable Usage

Visual Basic offers programmers a great deal of flexibility in variable use. It allows the programmer to be very loose in defining variables by providing a variety of implicit behaviors. These implicit behaviors open the door to a variety of errors, however, and so they should be avoided. This section identifies some of the implicit behaviors in variable use.

4.1.1 Always Use Option Explicit

Option Explicit should be the first line you write in any new module. This statement directs Visual Basic to require explicit variable declarations. If Option Explicit is set, you will not be able to compile or execute your code when variables are left undefined.

By default, modules without this directive allow implicit typing. This means that any new variable referenced by your code is automatically dimensioned by Visual Basic as a variant data type. This option can be convenient because it allows you to create variables on the fly without having to declare them. Since the default data type is variant, you can use these variables to store any type of data.

Nevertheless, this convenience is not worth the risks inherent in using implicitly defined variants. You can easily take advantage of the flexibility of variants simply by explicitly declaring a variable as a variant. However, if you leave Option Explicit off, then you can create variables by mistake. Consider the example in Listing 4.1:

LISTING 4.1

```
Sub DisplayName()

    strUserName = "mjones"
    Msgbox "My name is " & strUsrName

End Sub
```

If you have a very good eye, you might have noticed that the variable strUserName is spelled incorrectly in the second line. Since Option Explicit is not set, this code will compile and run without error. However, the name will not display correctly. Visual Basic has actually created two separate variables. Of course, it is easy to see the mistake in this simple example. But in a real program, with many lines of code and many similarly named variables, this error could go undiagnosed for a long time. If the mistake is, for example, one variable in a long equation, it can cause the wrong answer for many years before it is detected and fixed. A simple typographical mistake can turn into a very nasty bug.

As a better alternative, consider the code in Listing 4.2:

LISTING 4.2

```
Option Explicit

Sub DisplayName()

Dim strUserName As String

    strUserName = "mjones"
    Msgbox "My name is " & strUsrName

End Sub
```

The code in Listing 4.2 will not run. Because the Option Explicit statement was added, it will generate a "Variable not defined" error as soon as Visual Basic tries to compile the line with the mistyped variable.

Hint—Never Forget Option Explicit
There is a way to be sure you never forget to use Option Explicit. In Visual Basic 6, go to "Tools|Options . . . " and click on the Editor tab of the Options Dialog. Make sure that the "Require Variable Declarations" item is checked. This item is normally not checked. When checked, Visual Basic will automatically add the "Option Explicit" statement to every new form or code module. If you set this Visual Basic option, you don't have to remember to set Option Explicit every time you create a new module.

Use Option Explicit in every Visual Basic code module.

4.1.2 Explicitly Type Variables

Even if you use Option Explicit, you must still beware. Visual Basic makes another assumption that can create typing errors. If you do not explicitly type a variable when you create dimensions for it, then it is automatically assumed to be a variant. Consider the example in Listing 4.3:

LISTING 4.3

```
Option Explicit

Sub ShowFirstInitial()

Dim strName

    strName = "mjones"
    MsgBox "First name starts with " & Left$(strName, 1)

End Sub
```

The strName variable is automatically declared as a variant since no variable type was specified. This should cause no problem, right? Wrong. You should not assume that implicit rules will always stay the same. If a new version of Visual Basic were to make a new variable type its default, your code could break.

That may seem like paranoia, but it reflects a healthy mind-set to eliminate assumptions. We can easily envision a more likely problem. Consider the following minor—and seemingly innocent—code modification in Listing 4.4:

LISTING 4.4

```
Option Explicit
DefInt I

Sub ShowFirstInitial()

Dim Name, Initial

    Name = "mjones"
    Initial = Left$(Name, 1)
    MsgBox "First name starts with " & Initial

End Sub
```

Note—Highlighted Lines

Notice that the examples in Listings 4.2 and 4.4 have highlighted lines. In the example in Listing 4.4, the line is highlighted to show that the DefInt statement has been added to the code. This convention is used in examples throughout the book to draw attention to key lines and to point out changes from previous examples.

Notice that a DefInt statement has been added ahead of the subroutine. This could be a reasonable change. A programmer may decide that he or she likes the convenience of the DefInt statement, which automatically sets the default data type of any variable starting with the letter "i" to Integer, but this breaks the ShowFirstInitial routine. When the code attempts to assign the Left$ return string to an integer variable, it generates a "type mismatch" error.

This point illustrates one of the worst assumptions that a programmer can make. Simply because the programmer cannot anticipate a potential error at the moment, he or she might feel justified in skimping on good preventative measures. If the first programmer were to explicitly type the variables, there would be no possibility of an error, whether or not it was anticipated.

You might argue that the second programmer was at fault. Perhaps it was naive to add the DefInt line. I argue that the original programmer was more naive to leave his or her code vulnerable. Simply because a programmer cannot predict any way that an error can be introduced, does not mean he or she should not prepare for it.

Always explicitly type your variables.

4.1.3   Avoid Deftype Statements

The example in Listing 4.4 illustrated another dangerous implicit coding feature of Visual Basic: the Deftype family of statements. These statements allow you to define a range or ranges of letters for a default data type for all implicitly typed variables, arguments, and functions in a module. The following is a list of the variety of Deftype statements:

- DefBool
- DefByte
- DefInt
- DefLng
- DefCur
- DefSng
- DefDbl
- DefDec
- DefDate
- DefStr
- DefObj
- DefVar

We saw in Listing 4.4 how the use of these statements can cause bugs to appear in the program. More generally, they will cause routines to be less self-contained and more dependent on external settings. When you consider the long term, this technique is unacceptable.

HORROR STORY: Deftype Statements

Jimmy developed a great routine for computing the remaining balance on a home loan, never considering that it could be useful outside his program. A few years later, another team required the same computation and asked Jimmy for his. Jimmy was busy with another project, but he dug up the code, copied it, and sent it to them. The new team added the routine to their application, and it seemed to work beautifully. They shipped their application.

Several months later, they received a bug report. Users determined that the application was returning slightly incorrect loan balances. After a lengthy debugging operation, the problem was traced to Jimmy's routine. It turned out that Jimmy's routine assumed that all variables starting with "c" were implicitly typed as double precision variables. In the new application, "c" was implicitly defined as a Currency type variable. The use of the Deftype statements made this routine less portable and resulted in errors that were difficult to diagnose.

Avoid using the Deftype family of statements.

4.1.4 Use Specific Data Types

Avoid the nonspecific Variant and Object data types whenever possible. By using the appropriate specific data type, you remove ambiguity and make the code not only more maintainable but more efficient.

Variants can be very useful in special situations, such as when you want to hold variable types of data. However, making them all variant is ill-advised. All variables should be explicitly typed unless you have a very good reason why they need to be generic. Use the most specific data type possible for all variables. Use a Boolean rather than an integer if possible. Use specific object types rather than the generic Object data type.

Use variant and object type variables only when specifically required.

4.1.5 Initialize All Variables

Never assume implicit initial values. When you declare a numeric variable, its initial value is normally zero. When you declare a string type variable, its initial value is an empty string. What, though, is the starting value of a variant? How will an uninitialized variant behave in different situations? How about a date type variable—what is the value of an uninitialized date? What about arrays?

There are answers to these questions, but why learn them? Why trust that they will not change? What if the VB code is exported to VB Script or another language? Will it behave in the same way? It is prudent practice to explicitly initialize all variables. This practice results in more clear and unambiguous code, and it results in more robust code in the long term.

Let's look at another example (see Listing 4.5):

LISTING 4.5

```
Option Explicit

Function strConcatStrings(str() As String) As String

Dim i As Integer
Dim s As String

  'Concatenate the strings
    For i = LBound(str) To UBound(str)
    s = s & str(i)
  Next
  strConcatStrings = s

End Function
```

This function works well. We all know that Visual Basic will initialize the "s" variable with an empty string, so what is the problem?

Let's look ahead again. This code actually has many potential errors, but for the moment let's focus on the initialization of "s." Imagine that our hypothetical second programmer is asked to modify this code by doing some preprocessing of the strings. He adds this (see Listing 4.6):

LISTING 4.6

```
Option Explicit

Function strConcatStrings(str() As String) As String
Dim i As Integer
Dim s As String

    'Pre-process each string
    For i = LBound(str) To UBound(str)
    s = strProcessString(str(i))
    If Len(s) > STR_MAX Then
        str(i) = Left$(str(I, STR_MAX))
     End If
    Next

    'Concatenate the strings
    For i = LBound(str) To UBound(str)
      s = s & str(i)
    Next
    strConcatStrings = s

End Function
```

Notice that our second programmer has used "s" as a temporary variable, which means that the concatenation block now has a bug. Again, it is easy to notice the error in this simple example, but in a long, complicated routine it would be very easy to introduce this kind of error without noticing it. The code shown in Listing 4.7 is recommended to avoid this kind of error:

LISTING 4.7

```
Option Explicit

Function strConcatStrings(str() As String) As String

Dim i As Integer
Dim s As String

    'Pre-process each string
    For i = LBound(str) To UBound(str)
    s = strProcessString(str(i))
    If Len(s) > STR_MAX Then
       str(i) = Left$(str(i), STR_MAX)
       End If
    Next

    'Concatenate the strings
    s = ""
      For i = LBound(str) To UBound(str)
      s = s & str(i)
    Next
    strConcatStrings = s

End Function
```

Notice that the "s" variable is initialized *within the block in which it is used*. This procedure is better than initializing it at the top of the routine. In our example in Listing 4.7, if the variable had been initialized at the very beginning, the error would still have been introduced. Initialization that appears at the top of the routine makes it easy for this kind of error to appear, especially in much larger routines. Each code block should be self-contained, including all initialization.

Note that you should also initialize new objects by explicitly setting them to Nothing immediately after you create them.

Initialize all variables near the point of use.

4.1.6   *Use One Variable per Line*

Visual Basic allows you to declare more than one variable per line. The example in Listing 4.8 works well:

LISTING 4.8

```
Sub ShowUsers()

Dim UserMin, UserMax As Integer

Exit Sub
```

However, you should recognize that in the example in Listing 4.8, UserMin may be a Variant, whereas UserMax is definitely an Integer. This may be a bug. The programmer probably meant to make them both Integer variables. We cannot be sure since UserMax is not explicitly typed in this dimension statement. It defaults to variant, or to whatever the Deftype statement may have defined for the letter "u."

The better way to define this statement is as shown in Listing 4.9:

LISTING 4.9

```
Sub ShowUsers()

Dim UserMin As Integer, UserMax As Integer

Exit Sub
```

This approach is still not preferred. It is even better to declare only one variable per line, as shown in Listing 4.10:

LISTING 4.10

```
Sub ShowUsers()

Dim UserMin As Integer 'The min User ID to show
Dim UserMax As Integer 'The max User ID to show

Exit Sub
```

Notice that not only does this approach make it easier to read and edit the code, but it also allows you to enter comments clearly on each line to internally document your variables.

4.1.7 Use TypeName, VarType, and TypeOf

Three Visual Basic functions can greatly assist when working with the generic Variant and Object data types. TypeName is used to determine the type of object stored in a Variant or in an Object type variable. VarType is used to determine the type of variable that is stored in a Variant. TypeOf is a related Visual Basic command, one used within If statements to determine the types of Object variables. You should become comfortable using all these statements as part of your effective coding practice (see Listings 4.11, 4.12, and 4.13):

LISTING 4.11

```
Sub ShowUsers(User As Object)

    If TypeName(User) = "UserObject" Then
        MsgBox "The User Name is: " & User.Name
    End If

Exit Sub
```

LISTING 4.12

```
Sub ShowUsers(UserName As Variant)

    If VarType(UserName) = vbString Then
        MsgBox "The User Name is: " & UserName
    End If

Exit Sub
```

LISTING 4.13

```
Sub ShowUsers(User As Object)

    If TypeOf(User) Is UserObject Then
        MsgBox "The User Name is: " & User.Name
    End If

Exit Sub
```

4.1.8 Use Enumerations

Enumerations greatly improve both the readability and maintainability of your code. Anytime a variable can take on only certain discrete values, consider using an enumeration.

4.2 Arguments

In using function arguments, Visual Basic offers a great deal of implicit flexibility. Arguments, like other variables, should be handled explicitly without relying on implicit behaviors. The following suggestions relate to the use of arguments in Sub or Function declarations.

Note—Arguments and Parameters

Note that the term *argument* is sometimes used almost synonymously with the term *parameter*. Strictly speaking, a parameter is a less specific term than argument, which can be used in a number of technical contexts. This book uses the term *argument* exclusively. In your other reading, you may see the term *parameter* used in similar contexts.

4.2.1 Always Use ByVal or ByRef

In Visual Basic, arguments can be passed either by reference (ByRef) or by value (ByVal). The default is by reference. When passed by reference, changes made to the argument in the function carry back into the calling function. There is only one variable, and it can be modified by the called function.

When passed by value, a copy of the variable is made and the copy is passed. Changes made to the argument do not affect the variable that was passed by the calling function.

Passing values by reference is necessary at times. In some situations, you will need to return a modified value of an argument to the calling function. There is a danger in passing values by reference, however. If the argument is inadvertently changed, then this can cause an error in the calling function. This type of error is very common.

To avoid this error type, always pass arguments ByVal unless you have a good reason to pass them ByRef. Listing 4.14 shows an example of passing an argument ByVal:

LISTING 4.14

```
Sub ShowUsers(ByVal UserCount)
```

However, if you have a good reason to change the value of UserCount, then it should be passed explicitly by reference, as shown in Listing 4.15:

LISTING 4.15

```
Sub ShowUsers(ByRef UserCount)
```

Another reason some programmers pass variables by reference is that this operation is slightly faster than passing them by value. Passing by value takes longer because a copy of the variable must be made. The performance gain can be significant if you are repeatedly passing large strings, for example. However, the added performance benefit is normally undetectable and does not outweigh the risk of passing arguments by reference. Further, when passing arguments to DCOM objects, ByRef can actually be up to three times slower than ByVal.

In isolated cases this performance optimization may be justifiable, but optimizations should always result in exceptions, not rules. You should avoid basing your standard on performance optimizations. If you do so, then you justify numerous practices that make your code less understandable and maintainable.

Here is an implicit behavior to avoid as well. If you do not specify the passing method as ByVal or ByRef, then the default ByRef is used. It is good programming practice to consistently and explicitly declare the passing method rather than rely on the implicit default method. The example in Listing 4.16 works, but it does not use good explicit programming technique:

LISTING 4.16

```
Sub ShowUsers(UserCount)
```

The example in Listing 4.16 is not recommended. By not specifying the passing method, the dangerous ByRef is automatically used. Programmers may think it is safe to modify the passed argument value when it is not.

You must remember to type each argument individually. You must always explicitly set the passsing method for each argument individually. In the example in Listing 4.17, the first argument is passed ByVal, but the second is passed implicitly ByRef:

LISTING 4.17

```
Sub ShowUsers(ByVal UserCount As Variant, _
        MaxUsers As Variant)
```

Note that if you pass a constant, this value must be passed ByVal to avoid errors. Although objects must be passed by reference, ByRef should still be explicitly declared.

ByVal should always be explicitly declared unless there is clear reason to declare ByRef.

4.2.2 Explicitly Type Arguments

In Visual Basic, the procedure declaration in Listing 4.18 is legal:

LISTING 4.18

```
Sub ShowUsers(ByVal UserCount)
```

In this example, the argument UserCount will *probably* be a variant type, since this is the default for Visual Basic. Of course, we cannot be sure because a DefType might be active, which could specify a different default data type for variables beginning with the letter "u."

For sound coding practice, it is recommended that you always explicitly declare the type of each argument. Listing 4.19 offers a better practice:

LISTING 4.19

```
Sub ShowUsers(ByVal UserCount As Variant)
```

This example explicitly defines the argument type. Future addition of a DefType statement cannot break this code. If the code is exported to another platform or maintained by another developer, the type is explicitly documented.

4.2.3 Set Explicit Default Values for Optional Arguments

Just as you should always set the initial value for variables explicitly, you should also always set an explicit default value for optional arguments. For example, in the procedure declaration in Listing 4.20, the value of the optional argument is not defined:

LISTING 4.20

```
Sub ShowUsers(Optional ByVal UserCount As Variant)
```

The initial value of UserCount in this example is not explicitly set. Since it is optional, it could even be missing. If an optional argument is omitted from the argument list, then the constant vbMissing is returned by the VarType() function. A better practice is to explicitly set a default value for optional arguments in the declaration. The code sample in Listing 4.21 illustrates this practice:

LISTING 4.21

```
Sub ShowUsers(Optional ByVal UserCount As Variant = 0)
```

Now if the user does not pass a UserCount, the value defaults to zero. The type of variant is not assured to be numeric by having set a default value. The calling routine could pass a string or some other data type. UserCount cannot be used safely in numeric operations until it is validated further. An advantage of using a default is that the value of UserCount will never be vbMissing, so the code does not need to check for it.

You should use the default assignment directly in the procedure declaration, if possible. If it is not possible to declare a default value in this way, then it is essential to validate your optional arguments, as Listing 4.22 shows:

LISTING 4.22

```
Sub ShowUsers(Optional ByVal UserCount As Variant)

    If IsMissing(UserCount) Then UserCount = nDefault

End Sub
```

In the example in Listing 4.22, the UserCount is initialized to nDefault if it is missing. This example illustrates how a default value can be set in the body of the procedure if it is not feasible to use a literal value in the procedure declaration. Note as well that the IsMissing function only works on variant data types.

Always set default values for optional arguments.

4.2.4   Validate All Arguments

Each routine should have the responsibility of validating its own arguments, whether an argument is optional or not. Valid arguments must be of the correct type. Numeric arguments must fall within the expected value range. Arguments with enumerated values must be validated as well.

Many programmers write routines and simply assume that the calling program will ensure that the arguments are valid. This assumption is not good technique. A routine cannot be reused effectively if it does not validate its own arguments. A good, reusable routine is one that can be taken from its original environment and placed safely in any new program. The programmer should not assume that the calling program will provide the correct arguments.

Consider our example in Listing 4.22 once more, this time with some additional code filling in the body of the procedure (see Listing 4.23):

LISTING 4.23

```
Sub ShowUsers(Optional ByVal UserCount As Variant)

Dim s As String

    'Validate UserCount
    If IsMissing(UserCount) Then UserCount = DEF_USERS

    'Report the percentage of users currently logged in
    s = "% LoggedIn: " & cstr(nUsersLoggedIn/UserCount * 100)
```

```
    MsgBox s

End Sub
```

In this example, the argument is given a default value if missing. However, if the argument is not missing, the code does not validate the argument. It could be zero, it could be less than the users currently logged in, or it could be nonnumeric. Each of these situations would result in an error. The example in Listing 4.24 is better:

LISTING 4.24

```
Sub ShowUsers(Optional ByVal UserCount As Variant)

  Dim s As String

  'Validate UserCount
  If IsMissing(UserCount) Then UserCount = DEF_USERS
  UserCount = Val(UserCount)
  If UserCount <= 0 Then Exit Sub
  If UserCount > nUsersLoggedIn Then Exit Sub

  'Report the percentage of users currently logged in
  s = "% LoggedIn: " & cstr(nUsersLoggedIn/UserCount * 100)
  MsgBox s

End Sub
```

Notice the care taken in this new routine to validate the argument. First, if the argument is missing, then a default value is applied. Next, the argument is explicitly typed as a numeric variant. Finally, the bounds are checked to ensure that it is within the proper range.

This is not overkill—it is good programming practice. This routine can now survive any changes or errors introduced into the world around it. It is impervious to bugs since it makes no assumptions.

Note—External Validation

Many programmers feel strongly that they should validate arguments before passing them into the calling routine. Many problems exist with this approach. First, it requires that the validation be repeated every time the routine is called. This process results in a great deal of redundant code. If the validation logic changes, it must be changed everywhere validation is performed. Even if this code can be consolidated in reusable routines, it is easy to forget to call them.

If arguments are passed from routine A to routine B and to routine C, the validation must be repeated at every level. This practice is inefficient. If validation is done only in routine A, then routines B and C are not safe. By validating only in C, every call is validated in one place with no chance of forgetting. The arguments can be passed from A to B to C without worrying about validation.

Always validate all arguments in the procedure in which they are used.

4.2.5   Use Named Arguments

When you call functions, named arguments can eliminate ambiguity and make the code more easily understandable. For example, consider the statement in Listing 4.25:

LISTING 4.25

```
If bGetUserInfo(sUserName, False) Then
```

Compare this statement to the form in Listing 4.26, which uses named arguments:

LISTING 4.26

```
If bGetUserInfo(sUserAccountName:=sUserName, _
                bShowPasswordDialog:=False) Then
```

The named arguments help to self-document the code and make the purpose of the arguments much clearer.

4.3   Arrays

Array operation is the third general area in which Visual Basic opens the door to errors by allowing implicit behaviors. This section examines a number of implicit array operations to avoid.

4.3.1   Never Assume Lower Array Bounds

Another implicit feature of Visual Basic is the default lower array bound. This feature allows you to omit the lower array bound when dimensioning arrays. The lower bound is assumed to be zero, or whatever default has been set using the Option Base statement.

However, you should always set your lower bounds explicitly for the same reasons that you should avoid other implicit practices. Failing to set them not only makes the code ambiguous, but it invites errors by forcing the programmer to look outside the routine for vital information. It breeds bugs and reduces portability for reuse.

For an example, look at the routine in Listing 4.27:

LISTING 4.27

```
Option Explicit

Sub CountDown()

Dim i As Integer
Dim sNums(10) As String

    'Create countdown strings
    sNums(10) = "Ten"
    sNums(9) = "Nine"
    sNums(8) = "Eight"
    sNums(7) = "Seven"
    sNums(6) = "Six"
    sNums(5) = "Five"
    sNums(4) = "Four"
    sNums(3) = "Three"
    sNums(2) = "Two"
    sNums(1) = "One"
    sNums(0) = "Zero"

    'Countdown from 10 to 0
    For i = UBound(sNums) To LBound(sNums) Step '1
        MsgBox str(i)
    Next

End Function
```

In this example, the code would break if it were moved into a module in which the Option Base is set to anything except the default zero. To completely prevent such problems, consistently declare both lower and upper bounds explicitly in the dimension statement, even if the lower bound is the same as the current default (see Listing 4.28):

LISTING 4.28

```
Option Explicit

Sub CountDown()

Dim i As Integer
Dim sNums(0 To 10) As String
```

```
    'Create countdown strings
    sNums(10) = "Ten"
    sNums(9) = "Nine"
    sNums(8) = "Eight"
    sNums(7) = "Seven"
    sNums(6) = "Six"
    sNums(5) = "Five"
    sNums(4) = "Four"
    sNums(3) = "Three"
    sNums(2) = "Two"
    sNums(1) = "One"
    sNums(0) = "Zero"

    'Countdown from 10 to 0
    For i = UBound(sNums) To LBound(sNums) Step -1
        MsgBox str(i)
    Next

End Function
```

The code in Listing 4.28 will not break no matter what implicit behavior Visual Basic has defined. It also self-documents the array bounds more clearly without having to depend on external information.

Always explicitly set array lower bounds.

4.3.2   Don't Hard Code Array Bounds

When array bounds are known and fixed at design time, it is not necessary to use LBound and UBound. However, it is still not considered good practice to use hard-coded literals, as Listing 4.29 shows:

LISTING 4.29

```
Option Explicit

Sub CountDown()

Dim i As Integer
Dim sNums(0 To 10) As String

    'Create countdown strings
    sNums(10) = "Ten"
    sNums(9) = "Nine"
    sNums(8) = "Eight"
    sNums(7) = "Seven"
```

```
      sNums(6) = "Six"
      sNums(5) = "Five"
      sNums(4) = "Four"
      sNums(3) = "Three"
      sNums(2) = "Two"
      sNums(1) = "One"
      sNums(0) = "Zero"

      'Countdown from 10 to 0
      For i = 10 To 0 Step -1
          MsgBox str(i)
      Next

End Function
```

In the example in Listing 4.29, the use of hard-coded numbers makes the code harder to maintain. If a future change should require that the bounds change, it would be easy to miss one of the numbers and introduce an error.

If fixed array bounds are called for, the version in Listing 4.30 would make it both simple and safe to change the limits of the array at a later date:

LISTING 4.30

```
Option Explicit
Sub CountDown()

Const COUNT_MIN = 0
Const COUNT_MAX = 10

Dim i As Integer
Dim sNums(COUNT_MIN To COUNT_MAX) As String

      'Create countdown strings
      sNums(10) = "Ten"
      sNums(9) = "Nine"
      sNums(8) = "Eight"
      sNums(7) = "Seven"
      sNums(6) = "Six"
      sNums(5) = "Five"
      sNums(4) = "Four"
      sNums(3) = "Three"
      sNums(2) = "Two"
      sNums(1) = "One"
      sNums(0) = "Zero"
```

```
'Countdown from 10 to 0
For i = COUNT_MAX To COUNT_MIN Step -1
    MsgBox str(i)
Next

End Function
```

Again, if you think in the long term, you will see the sense in anticipating errors, not only those made by the user but by future programmers who may use the code.

Use constants for array bounds.

4.3.3 *Avoid Using Option Base*

Earlier I recommended explicitly setting both the upper and lower array boundaries in array declarations. If this step is completed, the Option Base statement will have no effect. In fact, explicit dimensioning is recommended to avoid the problems introduced by using Option Base.

4.4 Coding Recommendations

This section contains some recommendations of good explicit coding practices that will improve your code.

4.4.1 *Always Include an Else*

Always try to use an Else clause in every If-Then or Select Case block. Even if you are very sure that no additional situations are possible, including an Else clause ensures future maintainability. Consider the examples in Listings 4.31 and 4.32:

LISTING 4.31

```
Option Explicit

Sub HandleMenu(mnuChoice As Integer)

    Select Case mnuChoice

        Case MNU_OPEN
            OpenFile

        Case MNU_CLOSE
```

```
            CloseFile

        Case MNU_SAVE
            SaveFile

        Case Else
            MsgBox "An unrecognized menu choice was selected"

    End Select

End Sub
```

LISTING 4.32

```
Option Explicit

Sub HandleMenu(mnuChoice As Integer)

    If mnuChoice = MNU_OPEN Then
        OpenFile
    ElseIf mnuChoice = MNU_CLOSE Then
        CloseFile
    ElseIf mnuChoice = MNU_SAVE Then
        SaveFile
    Else
        MsgBox "An unrecognized menu choice was selected"
    End If

End Sub
```

It may be true that at the time this routine was written, "mnuOpen," "mnuClose," and "mnuSave" are the only possible values for mnuChoice. However, if new menu items are added in the future, this offensive (rather than defensive) programming style will quickly reveal that this code block needs to be updated.

Always include an Else clause.

4.4.2 *Avoid Using Default Properties*

Visual Basic allows a default property for an object to be identified. This feature allows you to quickly refer to a commonly used property without having to indicate it explicitly. It eliminates typing and can make complex statements much shorter.

For example, the two lines of code in the sample in Listing 4.33 display the same information:

LISTING 4.33

```
MsgBox Err.Number
MsgBox Err
```

This code works because Number is the default property of the Err object.

Despite their benefits, default properties are to be avoided. They result in implicit coding logic that is not necessarily apparent without access to outside information. If in the future the default property should change, explicitly identified properties will not break. Additionally, by leaving off the default property name, it may not be clear immediately whether the intent is to reference the object or the default property.

Another more technical reason to avoid them is because a known memory bleed exists in some COM objects, including some RDO objects, when using default properties.

One of the most commonly used defaults is the recordset field value. Most programmers obtain the value of a field by using something like rs("FieldName"). This is a double implicit default. The full, and preferred, reference should be rs.Fields("FieldName").Value.

Avoid using default properties, other than the "item" property.

4.4.3 Avoid Mixing Data Types in Expressions

Programmers can take many shortcuts if they know the peculiarities of the language. These should be avoided.

One such shortcut is the mixing of data types in expressions. An experienced programmer may know how to exploit these. For example, the following expression in Listing 4.34 is valid:

LISTING 4.34

```
'Set the current date to tomorrow
CurDate = Now + 1
```

This example works because Visual Basic allows this mixed expression (see Listing 4.34). It is evaluated properly because of how Visual Basic stores dates. Although this technique works, I cannot recommend it. It contains implicit behavior that is not explicitly apparent in the expression. It requires knowledge of this particular behavior of Visual Basic, and the code is not necessarily portable or even guaranteed to remain true.

A much better alternative is to use date functions that are explicitly designed for this operation. The version in Listing 4.35 would never reasonably fail, no matter what changes are made to the underlying compiler:

LISTING 4.35

```
'Set the current date to tomorrow
Curdate = DateAdd("d", 1, Now)
```

Programmers can use many similar programming tricks. In fact, using these sorts of tricks often distinguishes programmers as being more knowledgeable. Their use of such tricks should be discouraged, however, if explicit alternatives are available that avoid assumptions and non-obvious logic.

Tricks should only be used to achieve specific performance optimizations. When used, they should be thoroughly documented in the code.

4.4.4   Use Constants

Never hard code items such as array bounds, control indexes, or grid column positions. If their positions change, then it can be extremely difficult for the programmer to find and edit these hard-coded values without causing errors.

Quite often these values do change. In the majority of cases when they need to be changed, the programmer could not have foreseen the reasons earlier. Coding for the short term because the programmer cannot anticipate the future is one of the classic false assumptions in coding. The examples in Listings 4.36 and 4.37 illustrate the use of constants rather than literal values in the code:

LISTING 4.36

```
'Using literals
Dim nums(0 to 10)
grid.Col(4).Text = "12345-6789"
txtInput(4).Text = "333-44-5555"
```

LISTING 4.37

```
'Using constants
Dim nums(NUMS_LOWER to NUMS_UPPER)
grid.Col(GRID_ZIP).Text = "12345-6789"
txtInput(TEXT_SSN).Text = "333-44-5555"
```

Always use constants instead of hard-coded values for indices.

4.4.5   Avoid Operator Precedence

Think of precedence in mathematical and logical statements: precedence is the order in which a sequence of operations occurs. For example, consider the statement in Listing 4.38:

LISTING 4.38

```
DblResult = dblBase + dblCost * dblUnits
```

We assume that the multiplication is performed first and the addition next because multiplication has precedence over addition. We assume as well that this will always be true, even if we export this code to another environment. Also, we assume that future programmers will be equally familiar with this convention.

The liberal use of parentheses eliminates these assumptions. The statement in Listing 4.39 will be valid no matter how the compiler handles precedence. Further, it is clear and unambiguous to any programmer:

LISTING 4.39

```
DblResult = dblBase + (dblCost * dblUnits)
```

It may seem silly to include parentheses in such a simple example. The rigor that we apply to simple situations, however, will carry through into more complex situations, as shown in Listing 4.40:

LISTING 4.40

```
DblResult = dblBase + dblCost * dblUnits + 4.6 / dblAdj
```

The previous listing, while still relatively simple, shows how quickly it can become complex. Even if you are very familiar with precedence, it would still probably take a bit of thought to understand this expression. Many actual expressions become far more complex than this example.

Notice that the version in Listing 4.41 quickly becomes understandable with the use of parentheses:

LISTING 4.41

```
DblResult = dblBase + (dblCost * dblUnits) + (4.6 / dblAdj)
```

Use parentheses liberally to avoid implicit precedence.

4.4.6   *Check String Lengths*

Another common assumption is to assume string length in string handling functions. Remember that the built-in Visual Basic library is not safe. Although the string functions in Visual Basic 6 are not as susceptible to run-time errors as earlier versions, any of the string handling functions can still generate an erroneous result. One of the most common errors is failing to verify that a string is long enough for a particular string operation.

The example in Listing 4.42 illustrates this point:

LISTING 4.42

```
Function GetZipOnly(strZip As String) As String
'Purpose: Return the zip portion of a zip+4 zip code

Const ZIP_BASELENGTH = 5

    GetZipOnly = Left$(strZip, ZIP_BASELENGTH)

Exit Function
```

This operation looks simple and innocent enough, but what happens if strZip is less than five characters long? Visual Basic 6 will return strZip. Earlier versions will generate a run-time error. It is not enough to simply blame the calling routine and place the burden of error prevention there. This routine should defend itself against bad data, as shown in the revision in Listing 4.43:

LISTING 4.43

```
Function GetZipOnly(strZip As String) As String
'Purpose: Return the zip portion of a zip+4 zip code

    If Len(strZip) < 6 Then
            GetZipOnly = strZip
    Else
            GetZipOnly = Left$(strZip, ZIP_BASELENGTH)
    Endif

Exit Function
```

String operations are especially vulnerable to length errors. Every precaution must be taken whenever a string handling function is called to verify that the string has sufficient character length for the operation to succeed.

It may be tempting to handle this situation differently, as in the alternative shown in Listing 4.44:

LISTING 4.44

```
Function GetZipOnly(strZip As String) As String
'Purpose: Return the zip portion of a zip+4 zip code

    On Error Resume Next
    GetZipOnly = Left$(strZip, ZIP_BASELENGTH)

Exit Function
```

In this example, any error that is generated is suppressed. This strategy is not recommended because it is never a good idea to substitute error trapping, error handling, or (as in this case) error suppression for error prevention. It is a misuse of error coding that has serious consequences each time the code is expanded and enhanced. It also does not explicitly document or address the specific error that has been anticipated.

Always check string lengths before using string operations.

Never use error coding as a substitute for error prevention.

4.4.7   *Close All Open Objects*

If any object has a close method, this method should be explicitly called each time the object is ready to be closed. The most common objects that must be closed are recordset objects in database applications. Consider the example in Listing 4.45:

LISTING 4.45

```
Private Sub LoadName()

Dim sName As String
Dim rs As Recordset

    'Load the name
    Set rs = OpenRecordset(db, sql)
        sName = rs.Fields("Name").Value
    rs.Close

End Sub
```

Of course this sample shows many potential errors, but consider only the closing of the recordset for now. Some programmers may argue that there is no reason to close this recordset object. After all, when the function ends, the recordset will close automatically. This assumption may be true, but it may not be. Although the object goes out of scope, some objects may not be closed until their parent objects are closed. This would cause a memory bleed. Why worry about this level of technical detail? Because there is no reason to trust or assume that objects will close properly when we can simply close them explicitly.

Also, additional code may be inserted following this particular code block but before the function ends. It would not be prudent to leave the object open during that time, and it could cause future bugs.

Closing objects also applies to file handles. Be sure to explicitly close all file handles at the end of the code block in which they are opened.

Always close open objects as soon as possible.

4.4.8 Set Objects to Nothing

In Visual Basic, objects you create, including forms, may not be completely removed from memory unless you explicitly set them to Nothing. There is a great deal of confusion about this behavior. Rather than struggle with it, it is simply wise practice to explicitly set all objects equal to Nothing when you are finished with them. This step not only ensures that all memory is released but also explicitly indicates the point at which the object is terminated.

This practice applies to form objects as well. The following line should appear in every form module, where Form1 is the name of the form being unloaded (see Listing 4.46):

LISTING 4.46

```
Private Sub Form_Unload(Cancel As Integer)

    'Completely remove the form from memory
    Set Form1 = Nothing

End Sub
```

Note that this particular example will have no effect if the form was loaded as an object variable. In that case, you should set the form object equal to Nothing. It will also have no effect if another object has a reference to the form or any object contained on it.

Always set your objects to Nothing when finished with them.

4.4.9 Always Explicitly Turn Off Error Trapping

The On Error statement is the primary error-coding mechanism provided by Visual Basic. We will learn about Visual Basic error handling in more detail in the next chapter. At this point, it is necessary only to point out that using the On Error statement puts Visual Basic in error handling mode. It is important that you explicitly turn off error handling after each logical block of code.

Listing 4.47 adds a bit of error coding to our previous example:

LISTING 4.47

```
Private Sub LoadName()

Dim sName As String
Dim rs As Recordset
```

```
    'Open the Recordset
    On Error Resume Next
    Set rs = db.OpenRecordset(db, sql)
    If Err.Number <> 0 then Exit Sub

    'Read the name field
    sName = rs.Fields("Name").Value
    rs.Close

End Sub
```

We should explicitly terminate error handling as soon as possible. The following revision of our last example shows the termination of error handling as soon as the OpenRecordset statement is completed (see Listing 4.48):

LISTING 4.48

```
Private Sub LoadName()

Dim sName As String
Dim rs As Recordset
Dim intErr as Integer

    'Open the Recordset
    On Error Resume Next
    Set rs = db.OpenRecordset(db, sql)
    intErr = Err.Number
    On Error Goto 0
    If intErr <> 0 then Exit Sub

    'Read the name field
    sName = rs.Fields("Name").Value
    rs.Close

End Sub
```

We should also explicitly terminate error handling as soon as possible when using the On Error Goto form of the On Error Statement, as in Listing 4.49:

LISTING 4.49

```
Private Sub LoadName()

Dim sName As String
Dim rs As Recordset
Dim intErr as Integer
```

```
On Error Goto ErrTrap

'Open the Recordset
Set rs = OpenRecordset(db, sql)
sName = rs.Fields("Name").Value
rs.Close

Exit Sub

ErrTrap:
    MsgBox "An error occurred."
    On Error Goto 0

End Sub
```

Always explicitly turn off error trapping with On Error Goto 0.

4.4.10   Never Assume Anything About the External World

This is a catchall assumption. You must never assume anything about the external world that you cannot control within your application. If you are reading files or databases, or interfacing with other systems, you cannot guarantee the status of these externals. If it is a file, it may be made read-only. If it is a database, it may be opened exclusively by another user. If it is an external system, it may be unavailable.

Anytime you deal with the external world, you cannot avoid the potential for errors. It is not enough to simply say that you assume these external systems will be in the state you expect. It is your responsibility to anticipate errors and write code to handle them intelligently.

This precaution also includes handling the DLL and OCX files that your program requires. Do you test your code to see how it will behave if one of these files is missing or corrupted, or do you just *assume* that they are present?

4.4.11   Don't Cut and Paste

If you have developers on your team who generate fantastic amounts of code, chances are quite high that they are cutting and pasting fantastic numbers of errors. The cut and paste syndrome is one of the most easily recognizable program diseases. When you find this disease, it usually means that the patient does not have long to live.

Cutting and pasting not only propagates existing errors throughout the application, but it also creates many new errors. When most developers find a code fragment that is close to the one they need, rather than create a new and safe, reusable function, they cut and paste the old one. To make the transplanted code work in the new routine, they usually have to make some minor changes. They re mark a line here and tweak a line there.

Very soon, there are many near copies of the same code throughout the application. Since the differences are hard to see, the cut-and-pasted code cannot easily be made into a common reusable function. If a fix is made to one code area, the same fix may have to be made in all near copies. It is not safe to do this without careful study, however, since each copy is slightly different. A fix in one may introduce a new bug into a transplanted copy.

The bottom line is that cutting and pasting is a sure formula for disaster. If you ever feel the urge to cut and paste, find a way to create a common reusable routine instead.

Cutting and pasting is the fastest and easiest way to generate errors.

4.4.12   Use + and & Properly

Although Visual Basic allows you to concatenate strings using the plus sign, always use the ampersand. This practice removes ambiguity and confusion from the code.

4.4.13   Pseudo-Code

Before you code, pseudo-code. This practice will make your programming effort far more efficient and successful. At the same time, it will ensure that you have meaningful and helpful commentary within your code.

4.4.14   Set Properties at Run Time

Although it is quick and convenient to set control properties in the Property Window and in property pages at design time, this habit should be avoided. When properties are set at design time, they tend to be poorly documented. A new programmer taking over the project has no easy way to determine which properties were modified from their defaults or why.

By setting your properties in code, you explicitly set them in a way that can be easily documented. Of course, you do not need to set simple properties such as tab indices and captions, but any less obvious properties should be set in code.

ANECDOTE: Property Pages

Another reason to avoid those convenient property pages is to prevent the loss of code. On several occasions when I was excited about configuring a complex control using property pages, I regretted it in every case.

One time, I spent an entire day configuring a grid using property pages. After it was finally working, I saved the project and reloaded. The form failed to load. The frx file had somehow become corrupted. All the saved properties were lost. It took another half a day to recreate what I had done.

The next week I received an update of the grid control. After the update, the control refused to load. All my property page configurations were lost again. Again, I had no documentation of what I had done. I had to recreate the work once more, but this time I did so in code. Many times since, my controls have failed to load for one reason for another. As long as most of my properties are set in code, this is only a minor nuisance. Setting control properties in code makes your project more maintainable.

Configure control properties in code.

4.5   Explicit Coding Is Fundamental

As has been shown in this section, explicit coding is a fundamental part of improved coding. To rely on implicit behaviors by Visual Basic opens the door for errors that arise from faulty assumptions.

It does not matter how unlikely the possibility that an error in the future could arise from implicit practices that you adopt today. You should be single-minded and consistent in your effort to eliminate implicit programming assumptions from your code.

The next chapter moves past what to avoid and into what to include in your coding practices. It discusses effective error-coding techniques to adopt in all Visual Basic code.

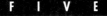

Error Coding Mechanics

The bad news is that Visual Basic, like most languages, cannot create error coding for you. If you want quality error coding in your application, you will have to do it yourself. Although there are only a few error-coding statements to learn, they can be used in a wide variety of ways. Many subtle nuances in their usage can introduce bugs into your error handling code. Developing fully error-coded Visual Basic applications can become very complicated indeed. In fact, it is so complicated that it is rarely done completely or correctly.

The good news is that Visual Basic does provide all you need to write superb error coding. Using the tools that Visual Basic gives you, it need not be difficult to bug-proof your code—if you code smarter.

This chapter reviews the different ways that these error-coding statements are normally used. Don't be frightened by it. Chapters 7 and 8 will build on this foundation by recommending much more simple and effective error coding techniques. This chapter is essential, however, to establish the background and logical derivation of the techniques presented later.

5.1   Error Coding Is Not a Given

Imagine that we asked a thousand programmers to write a Visual Basic function according to the following specification:

> *Divide two long integers and return a result with two decimal places.*

71

The majority of them would probably give us something essentially identical to the subroutine in Listing 5.1:

LISTING 5.1

```
Function sngDivide(Numer As Long, Denom As Long) As Single

    sngDivide = Numer / Denom
    sngDivide = Int(sngDivide * 100) / 100

End Sub
```

There is an obvious flaw in the previous routine. The Denominator variable might be equal to zero, causing the infamous "Divide by Zero" error. This, however, is not the only flaw; this routine has many more error-coding flaws. We look at these in detail as this chapter unfolds.

This programmer has done a poor job, right? Not necessarily. Error coding is not a given. It is possible to list many valid reasons to defend this work:

- The routine implements the requested feature.
- It was implemented very quickly.
- It doesn't deal with errors that may never occur.
- Error coding was never specified in the requirement.
- We can assume that the calling routine ensures that the denominator never equals zero.

These rationales are representative of the thought processes of many developers and their managers; they are also a reasonable result of the climate in which many programmers work. Like most workers, programmers are judged largely by their productivity. If someone has an error using a function, that person is normally blamed for introducing a bug into the calling procedure. The person who wrote the function is usually not the one held accountable. In this case, it would probably be the caller who is blamed for passing in a zero denominator. In fact, many companies might look warily on a programmer who has added a significant amount of error coding. He or she might be considered unproductive and obsessive for programming defensively. He or she might work in an atmosphere of error-coding disincentives in which directing or avoiding blame is the primary focus of attention.

A lack of error coding is not necessarily wrong, unreasonable, or irresponsible. It may be very understandable given the culture and practices within which programmers work. By implementing the Smart Coding Triangle using Visual Basic, you can create an atmosphere in which everyone takes pride in, and responsibility for, their error coding.

5.2   Visual Basic Error Handling

Visual Basic has an internal error handler that can recover from errors generated by your program. Internal error handling refers to error handling within the Visual Basic run-time libraries, as opposed to application error handling implemented within your program code. Internal and application level error handlers work hand in hand. Application level error handling activates and responds to the internal error handler.

The internal error handler has two modes of operation. At any point in program execution, it is either enabled or disabled. Unless you explicitly enable it, the internal error handler remains disabled. If not enabled by your program, errors are not trapped by Visual Basic.

If an untrapped error occurs during program operation, it is fatal, and a fatal error causes the program to crash. It is possible for the operating system or other programs to experience problems if a Visual Basic program exits abnormally after detecting an unhandled (untrapped) error.

When you enable the internal error handler, program errors are trapped. No fatal error occurs, and diagnostic error information is made available to the application. It is up to the application error coding to explicitly enable internal error handling and to explicitly check for errors after each line of code. It is then up to the developer to determine how to handle or respond to the error situation.

5.3   Without Error Handling

Listing 5.2 shows an example of code that is unprotected by an error handler. If you compile and run this code, a fatal Divide by Zero error will occur. The program will crash, probably causing you to restart your computer, and possibly resulting in the loss of data. Take my word for this, don't try it out!

LISTING 5.2

```
Sub DivideByZero()

Dim i As Integer

    i = 8 / 0 'An error will result here

End Sub
```

If you run this code in design mode, Visual Basic will trap the error and display an error message. However, you obviously cannot allow untrapped errors to occur in a compiled program. The only way to protect your program from fatal errors is to write application error coding that uses the internal error handler provided by Visual Basic.

5.4   The Error Handler

In order for the internal error handler to protect your program, you must enable the error handler using one of the On Error statements. There are two forms of the On Error statement that result in different behaviors: **On Error Resume Next** and **On Error Goto.**

5.5   On Error Resume Next

On Error Resume Next is the first way to protect your program from errors. This statement causes Visual Basic to resume execution at the line following the one that caused the error (see Listing 5.3):

LISTING 5.3

```
Sub DivideByZero ()

Dim i As Integer

    On Error Resume Next
    i = 8 / 0 'This statement will not be evaluated
    MsgBox "An error occurred."

End Sub
```

After an On Error Resume Next, any line that causes an error is essentially skipped. In the example above, the message box line is executed immediately after the error. The division statement is not evaluated.

5.6   Error Suppression

If asked to add error protection, the first thing many programmers do is add the On Error Resume Next statement, as shown in Listing 5.4:

LISTING 5.4

```
Sub DivideByZero()

Dim i As Integer
```

```
On Error Resume Next
i = 8 / 0 'This error will be supressed

End Sub
```

This is not error handling and not even error trapping. It does not prevent errors, correct errors, or report errors. It is *error suppression*. All it does is prevent an error from becoming a fatal error.

Error suppression is very dangerous. It hides errors from developers, testers, and users. Most suppressed errors eventually cause problems in either user operation, code maintainability, or both. You could argue that error suppression is itself a form of error.

HORROR STORY: On Error Resume Next

I was called in to fix a program that was long overdue. It had been under development for over a year, and the delivery had been delayed over and over again. The program was nowhere near stable enough to ship. The company was losing its credibility with its very few, very large clients.

The first thing I did was conduct a visual inspection of the code. I noticed immediately that every routine in the application began with On Error Resume Next. No other error handling was in operation.

In order to debug the first error, I had to disable the error handler at the top of this very long routine. When I did, an earlier line fired an error. I fixed that, and the next line caused an error. I fixed a half dozen errors before I was able to step into the error that I had started out to fix. The error had changed by that time. The program simply suppressed error after error until it finally crashed from the sheer weight of errors. Based on that problem, I had no choice but to recommend completely rewriting the application. The misuse of error handling suppressed so many errors that it would have been prohibitive to debug them all.

I rewrote the application and delivered a stable product in only several months, thanks largely to the proper use of error-coding techniques.

The programmer in this horror story was under the mistaken assumption that if he or she suppressed all errors and swept them under the carpet, he or she was handling them. This approach is always doomed.

The most amazing part of this horror story is that it is so common. I have been asked to work on many programs that relied on such cancerous error suppression. I do not know how or where programmers learn that this is sound coding practice; it is most definitely not good or even acceptable programming technique. In fact, it is the one unforgivable sin of programming.

In only an extremely small number of cases is it legitimate or advisable to simply ignore errors. Listing 5.5 shows one valid example:

LISTING 5.5

```
Sub InitForm()

    'Set the default name
    txtName.text = "Acme"

    'Set focus on the default name
    On Error Resume Next
    txtName.SetFocus 'Suppress error if it occurs

End Sub
```

In this example, the programmer correctly anticipated that the SetFocus method could fail for a variety of reasons. This error was not one that required action. Even if the programmer wanted to handle it, really nothing could be done. Therefore, in this case, it is reasonable to simply suppress the error. This is localized and well-considered error suppression. It does not rely on generalized, blanket error suppression.

You must explicitly check for and handle any errors after each statement while On Error Resume Next is in effect.

5.7   On Error Goto

The second way to protect your program from errors is to use the On Error Goto statement. This form of the On Error statement causes program execution to jump to a specified label after an error occurs. Presumably, application error coding is found after the label. Listing 5.6 shows an example of this error handling structure:

LISTING 5.6

```
Sub DivideByZero ()

Dim i As Integer

On Error Goto ErrTrap

    i = 8 / 0 'This statement will not be evaluated
    Exit Sub

ErrTrap:
    MsgBox "An error occurred."

End Sub
```

In this sample, the ErrTrap label is used only as an example. It could be substituted for any valid line label or number. The code that starts after the ErrTrap label is called the "error handling block." It is here that application level error coding is placed.

If an error occurs after an On Error Goto statement, then the internal error handler is said to be "active." This active state must be resolved before normal program operation continues.

5.8   Resuming Program Execution

Once the internal error handler becomes active, the program must return to its normal operation. Visual Basic provides the Resume statement for this purpose. There are three forms of the Resume statement: **Resume, Resume Next,** and **Resume line.**

The Resume statements can only be used after an On Error Goto statement has enabled the internal error handler and an error has activated it. The use of a Resume statement after an On Error Resume Next will cause an error. In effect, On Error Resume Next has already resumed operation at the next line.

5.8.1   Resume

Resume is used to return program flow to the same line that caused the error. This statement assumes that the error condition has been corrected. It is commonly used to "retry" an operation, as shown in Listing 5.7:

LISTING 5.7

```
Sub DivideByZero ()

Dim i As Integer
Dim intDenom As Integer

On Error Goto ErrHandler

    intDenom = 0
    i = 8 / intDenom

    Exit Sub

ErrHandler:
    intDenom = PromptForNewDenom()
    Resume 'Retry

End Sub
```

The example in Listing 5.7 illustrates the operation of the Resume statement. In this case, there is no way out of this retry loop. The code will continue to prompt the user for a valid denominator until the division succeeds.

5.8.2 *Resume Next*

Resume Next is similar to Resume except that execution continues at the line following the one that activated the error handler. This statement is similar to On Error Resume Next except that it allows the programmer to insert additional code prior to continuing. It is commonly used to abort an operation, as in the example in Listing 5.8:

LISTING 5.8

```
Sub DivideByZero ()

Dim i As Integer
Dim intDenom As Integer

On Error Goto ErrHandler

    intDenom = 0
    i = 8 / intDenom

    Exit Sub

ErrHandler:
    MsgBox "Division was aborted."
    Resume Next 'Skip over operation

End Sub
```

In the example in Listing 5.8, the division statement is never completed. This operation is more effective than error suppression using On Error Resume Next, since the user is at least informed of the situation. Of course, the same code could have been written using On Error Resume Next, as in the version in Listing 5.9:

LISTING 5.9

```
Sub DivideByZero ()

Dim i As Integer
Dim intDenom As Integer

    On Error Resume Next
```

```
        intDenom = 0
        i = 8 / intDenom
        If Err.Number <> 0 Then
              MsgBox "Division was skipped."
        End If

End Sub
```

The version in Listing 5.9 is an example of in-line error handling. Both these approaches have important pluses and minuses, which we discuss in greater detail a little later. You might have noticed the reference to Err.Number in this routine. If you are unfamiliar with this term, it is also discussed shortly.

5.8.3   Resume Line

The third version of the resume statement is "Resume line." In this syntax, "line" is any valid program label or number. Program execution jumps to the named line, as in the example in Listing 5.10:

LISTING 5.10

```
Sub DivideByZero ()

Dim i As Integer
Dim intDenom As Integer

On Error Goto ErrHandler

    intDenom = 0
    i = 8 / intDenom

    Exit Sub

AltCalc:
    i = ERR_VALUE
    Exit Sub

ErrHandler:
    MsgBox "Alternate calculation will be used."
    Resume AltCalc

End Sub
```

You must be very careful about the use of Resume statements. If you execute a Resume when the error handler is not active, you will generate an error. The error handler is not active if On Error Goto is not enabled, if no error has actually occurred, or if a resume has already been executed. In any of these cases, you will generate error number 20, "Resume without error."

5.9 Multiple Error Handlers

Only one error handler can be enabled in a procedure at any given time. Also, an error handler applies only within a single procedure. In order to protect each procedure in your program, it is necessary to enable a separate error handler within each procedure (see Listing 5.11).

LISTING 5.11

```
Sub DivideByZero ()

1   On Error Resume Next
2   i = 8 / 0 'This statement will not be evaluated
3   DivideByZeroAgain

7   End Sub

Sub DivideByZeroAgain ()

4   On Error Resume Next
5   i = 8 / 0 'This statement will not be evaluated

6   End Sub
```

In the example above, no fatal error will occur at run time since both errors are trapped by their respective error handlers. Although this is not a sound example of coding because it merely suppresses the error, it does illustrate the scope of error handlers.

BOOK NOTE—Line Numbers

Notice that the example in Listing 5.11 has line numbers. These are provided in order to show you the flow of code. If you were to work stepwise through this code, the line numbers would reflect the order of execution. This convention is used with certain examples in this book when it is important to show the code sequence.

5.10   Checking for Errors

If you want more than to merely suppress errors, you must determine whether an error has occurred so that you can take action to correct it. If you use the On Error Resume Next statement, then you must check to see whether an error has occurred after each line. If you don't, then you have no way of knowing which line generated the error. You also have no way of knowing how many errors were generated and whether the error information in the Err object is meaningful or merely an artifact of cascading errors.

The only time more than one statement should be executed without checking for errors is when you want to execute each line and you truly don't care if any fail. This situation is extremely rare.

One advantage of On Error Goto is that you do not need to explicitly check for errors. In the event of an error, execution automatically jumps to your error handling code.

If an error occurs while the internal error handler is enabled, the error handler becomes "active." When active, error information is contained in the Visual Basic Err object. Every Visual Basic application automatically has a reference to this object. The most commonly used properties of this object are the Number and Description properties. The Number property returns the numeric code of the last error. The Description property returns a text string describing the error.

Normally you will want to check the Err.Number property to determine if an error has occurred after each line of code when an On Error Resume Next is enabled. If Err.Number does not equal zero, then an error has occurred since the internal error handler was enabled. The code in Listing 5.12 shows an example:

LISTING 5.12

```
Sub DivideByZero ()

Dim i As Integer

    On Error Resume Next
    i = 8 / 0
    If Err.Number <> 0 Then
            MsgBox "An error occurred."
    End If

End Sub
```

In this version of the routine, the error message will be displayed since the Err.Number property equals 11, the Visual Basic code number for division by zero. The number 11 may be well-known to Visual Basic programmers, but it does not mean as much to most users. The Err.Description property can be used to display a description of the error for the user, as in the version in Listing 5.13:

LISTING 5.13

```
Sub DivideByZero ()

Dim i As Integer

    On Error Resume Next
    i = 8 / 0
    If Err.Number <> 0 Then
        MsgBox "An error occurred: " & Err.Description
    End If

End Sub
```

Visual Basic allows the description of an error in another way—through the Error function. The Error function will return the description for any Visual Basic error code, as shown in the example in Listing 5.14:

LISTING 5.14

```
Sub DivideByZero ()

Dim i As Integer
Dim lngErr As Long

    On Error Resume Next
    i = 8 / 0
    lngErr = Err.Number
    On Error Goto 0
    If lngErr <> 0 Then
        MsgBox "An error occurred: " & Error(lngErr)
    End If

End Sub
```

The last style is advantageous because it allows you to clear and disable the error handler as quickly as possible following the error without losing the error information.

5.11 Checking Err.Number

When you check whether an error has occurred, it is advisable to avoid logical functions. For example, the code fragment in Listing 5.15 works well:

LISTING 5.15

```
Sub DivideByZero ()

Dim i As Integer

    On Error Resume Next
    i = 8 / 0
    If Err.Number Then
        MsgBox "An error occurred: " & Err.Description
    End If

End Sub
```

Since Err.Number is equal to 11 after the division by zero error, the debug statement prints the error message correctly. This result would naturally lead you to assume that the logic in Listing 5.16 should work as well:

LISTING 5.16

```
Sub DivideByZero ()

Dim i As Integer

    On Error Resume Next
    i = 8 / 0
    If Not Err.Number Then
        MsgBox "No error occurred"
    End If

End Sub
```

This second version does not work, however. The "No error occurred" statement will print even though a divide by zero error has occurred. This result happens because an If statement does not follow the same logic rules. For the Not function, only 0 is False and only −1 is True. In an If statement, a 0 still evaluates as False, and any nonzero number evaluates as True. Many programmers get stung by this confusing behavior.

You can demonstrate this by executing the following tests in your debug window:

LISTING 5.17

```
?11 = True
False

if 11 Then Print "True" Else Print "False"
True
```

Notice that in the Not logic test, 11 evaluates as False. In the If logic test, 11 evaluates as True. This result may be confusing, yet it is possible to completely avoid this confusion. Simply avoid any use of logic when testing the error status. Instead, use the explicit form of this test, as shown in Listing 5.18:

LISTING 5.18

```
Sub DivideByZero ()

Dim i As Integer
Dim lngErr as Long

    On Error Resume Next
    i = 8 / 0
    lngErr = Err.Number
    On Error Goto 0
    If lngErr = 0 Then MsgBox "No error occurred"
    If lngErr <> 0 Then MsgBox "An error occurred"

End Sub
```

This code is clear and unambiguous. Logical functions such as Not aren't used; instead, the value of Err.Number is checked directly. This technique is not susceptible to errors introduced by the use of nonexplicit logic.

NOTE—Avoiding Default Properties
Notice that in the examples above, Err.Number was referenced explicitly rather than taking advantage of Number being the default property for the Err object. Good coding practice avoids the implicit, externally documented behavior of default properties.

5.12   Handling the Error

After you test for errors and find that an error has occurred, it is up to the application to handle that error, if possible. Handling may include any of the following:

- Programmatically correcting the error and resuming.
- Asking the user to correct the error and retrying.
- Aborting the operation and informing the user.

An error handler should be as specific as possible and should respond intelligently to the specific error that occurred rather than making a catchall response. For example, if a file fails to open, it might be because the file is missing, locked, invalid, or corrupted. Each of these problems would probably result in a different internal error message that should be handled uniquely at the application level of error coding. This response requires considerable experience to design and a great deal of code to implement. Both these difficulties can be mitigated only by reusing error coding.

Handling must also include resetting the error handler so that it is ready to correctly process any new error that may occur. Clearing the Err object is one necessary part of error handling. Resuming normal program execution is the other part.

5.13   Clearing the Error Object

If you encounter an error, the Err object continues to hold that error until cleared. Consider the example in Listing 5.19:

LISTING 5.19

```
Sub DivideByZero ()
Dim i As Integer

    On Error Resume Next
    i = 8 / 0
    If Err.Number <> 0 Then
        MsgBox "An error occurred: " & Err.Description
    End If

    i = 8 / 4
    If Err.Number <> 0 Then
        MsgBox "An error occurred: " & Err.Description
    End If
```

```
i = 8 / 2
If Err.Number <> 0 Then
    MsgBox "An error occurred: " & Err.Description
End If

End Sub
```

In this example, three error messages appear although only the first division statement truly has an error. It would seem that all three lines have the same division by zero error. This mistake is commonly made in error coding.

The Error object should be cleared explicitly after each error is handled. The Error Object has one method: the Clear method. This method clears the Number and Description properties of the Err object. It sets Err.Number = 0 and Err.Description = " ".

You can use the Err.Clear method to reset those properties after an error has been handled. If you fail to do this, the next line of code may appear to have the same error. The code sample in Listing 5.20 illustrates how this problem can be avoided:

LISTING 5.20

```
Sub DivideByZero ()

Dim i As Integer

    On Error Resume Next
    i = 8 / 0
    If Err.Number <> 0 Then
        MsgBox "An error occurred: " & Err.Description
        Err.Clear
    End If

    i = 8 / 4
    If Err.Number <> 0 Then
        MsgBox "An error occurred: " & Err.Description
        Err.Clear
    End If

    i = 8 / 2
    If Err.Number <> 0 Then
        MsgBox "An error occurred: " & Err.Description
        Err.Clear
    End If

End Sub
```

Note that the Err object is also cleared after the Resume statements are executed.

5.14   Disabling the Error Handler

You may wonder why you would want to disable an error handler. Why not leave it enabled all the time? It is not good technique to create a generic error handler. It is better to explicitly enable error trapping when necessary and then explicitly disable it when finished to deal intelligently with specific situations.

Regardless of how you have enabled the error handler, the **On Error Goto 0** statement is used to disable it. This statement actually accomplishes two processes. First, it disables the internal error handler so that the program is no longer protected with internal error trapping. Second, it clears the Err object so that the Err object no longer contains error information. The example in Listing 5.21 illustrates this technique:

LISTING 5.21

```
Sub DivideByZero ()

Dim i As Integer

    On Error Resume Next
    i = 8 / 0 'This error will be suppressed
    On Error Goto 0

    i = 8 / 0 'This error is unprotected!

End Sub
```

In the example in Listing 5.21, the second Divide by Zero error will cause the program to crash, since error handling was disabled in the previous statement. Error handling is automatically disabled when you exit a procedure. Nevertheless, you should always explicitly disable the error handler before exiting. This practice not only makes the code clearer, but as we will see later, this step avoids errors caused when the Err object is not cleared.

5.15   Scope of Error Handling

An error handler is also disabled on exiting a subroutine, function, or property procedure. The On Error statement is no longer in effect after returning to the calling procedure. The example in Listing 5.22 illustrates this point:

■ **LISTING 5.22** ■

```
Sub FirstSub()

Dim i As Integer

  SecondSub
  i = 8 / 0 'An unprotected error will result here!

End Sub

Sub SecondSub()

Dim i As Integer

  On Error Resume Next
  i = 8 / 4

End Sub
```

In the example in Listing 5.22, the error handler in SecondSub will not protect FirstSub. It became disabled on exiting SecondSub even though no explicit On Error Goto 0 statement was used.

Similarly, error protection in a parent procedure does not extend into any called procedures. The example in Listing 5.23 illustrates this point:

■ **LISTING 5.23** ■

```
Sub FirstSub()

  On Error Resume Next
  SecondSub

End Sub

Sub SecondSub()

Dim i as Integer

  i = 8 / 0 'An unprotected error will result here!

End Sub
```

In effect, then, each procedure can and must have its own independent error handler. The example in Listing 5.24 illustrates how this is done:

LISTING 5.24

```
Sub FirstSub()

Dim i as Integer

    SecondSub

    On Error Resume Next
    i = 8 / 0
    On Error Goto 0

End Sub

Sub SecondSub()

Dim i as Integer

    On Error Resume Next
    i = 4 / 0
    On Error Goto 0

End Sub
```

In the code in Listing 5.24, the error in SecondSub will be suppressed by its error handler. The error in FirstSub will be suppressed by its own error handler. Notice that in this example, the On Error Goto 0 statement was issued after each code block. This demonstrates good explicit coding practice. It clearly communicates that no error handler is active and avoids errors that would be caused if subsequent code had enabled an error handler when that was not the programmer's intention.

There is another reason to issue the On Error Goto 0 statement. It clears the Err object as well as disabling error handling. This point brings up a confusing behavior that is often misunderstood by programmers. Simply because the error handler is disabled automatically when you exit a procedure does not mean that the error object is cleared. You must use the On Error Goto 0 statement in order to clear the error information. The On Error Goto 0 statement not only disables the error handler, but it also clears the Err object. You could use the Err.Clear method, but it is better to accomplish both clarity and cleanup in one statement. Consider the example in Listing 5.25 that illustrates this very common programming mistake:

LISTING 5.25

```
Sub FirstSub()

Dim i as Integer

  On Error Resume Next
  SecondSub
  i = 8 / 4
  If Err.Number  0 Then Debug.Print "Error"

End Sub

Sub SecondSub()

Dim i as Integer

  On Error Resume Next
  i = 8 / 0

End Sub
```

If you run this code, the Debug.Print statement will fire even though no error is generated in the "i = 8/4" line. This happens because the programmer either forgot or thought he or she did not need an On Error Goto 0 statement at the end of SecondSub. Since the Err object was not cleared, the Divide by Zero error is still present when execution returns to FirstSub. When the value of Err.Number is checked, it looks as though an error occurred in FirstSub, even though no error actually occurred in that routine. This error is very common (partly because the Visual Basic documentation does not make this behavior clear). To further confuse the matter, this error does not occur if On Error Goto is used in SecondSub. In that case, the Err object is cleared by the End Sub.

You will improve program clarity and avoid implicit behavior by always explicitly ending each code block with an On Error Goto 0. Listing 5.26 shows a better implementation of this code:

LISTING 5.26

```
Sub FirstSub()

Dim i as Integer

  On Error Resume Next
```

```
    SecondSub
    i = 8 / 4
    If Err.Number <> 0 Then Debug.Print "Error"

End Sub

Sub SecondSub()

Dim i as Integer

    On Error Resume Next
    i = 8 / 0
    On Error Goto 0

End Sub
```

This version of the code will work properly. Better yet, you might wish to move the SecondSub call out of the first error handling block. This step will keep the code tighter and will also explicitly disable error handling in FirstSub (see Listing 5.27):

LISTING 5.27

```
Sub FirstSub()

Dim i as Integer
Dim lngErr As Long

    SecondSub

    'Divide
    On Error Resume Next
    i = 8 / 4
    lngErr = Err.Number
    On Error Goto 0
    If lngErr <> 0 Then Debug.Print "Error"

End Sub

Sub SecondSub()

Dim i as Integer

    On Error Resume Next
```

```
   i = 8 / 0
   On Error Goto 0

End Sub
```

Each procedure must have its own code handler.

5.16　Error Bubbles

It has already been pointed out that if errors are not protected by an error handler, a fatal error will result. However, that error handler does not need to be present in the routine that generated the error. To avoid subtle errors in your error coding, it is important to understand what happens when no error handling is executed in the procedure where an error occurs.

Errors bubble up the call stack until they reach the first routine with an enabled error handler. Though difficult to imagine, this result is easy to see in the simple example in Listing 5.28. Follow the numbered lines to see the sequence of execution:

LISTING 5.28

```
Sub MainSub()

1  On Error Resume Next
2  FirstSub
5  If Err.Number <> 0 Then Debug.Print "Error"
6  On Error Goto 0

End Sub

Sub FirstSub()

3  SecondSub
   i = 8 / 4

End Sub

Sub SecondSub()

4  i = 8 / 0

End Sub
```

Following the order of the numbered lines, you can see that the error at line 4 is unprotected by an error handler in that routine. Therefore, Visual

Basic will bubble up the call stack until it finds the first routine with an enabled error handler. MainSub is the first routine in the call stack with an error handler enabled. Because the error handler is On Error Resume Next, execution continues at line 5 immediately after the error in line 4. Line 5 prints the "Error" debug message.

Notice that the line "i = 8 / 4" is then not executed. Following the error at line 4, execution jumps back to line 5, skipping all remaining intermediate code at each level. This result is often a tremendous source of confusion to programmers trying to debug Visual Basic code.

What would happen if you commented out line 1 in this example? You would generate a run-time error at line 4. Visual Basic would reach the top of the call stack, and finding no enabled error handler by that point, it would generate a fatal error. The application would crash.

5.17 Errors within Errors

An error handler can only handle one error at a time. Because of that behavior, unusual and confusing execution processes happen if another error occurs while an error handler is active. Consider the example in Listing 5.29:

LISTING 5.29

```
Sub MainSub()

1  On Error Resume Next
2  FirstSub
7  If Err.Number <> 0 Then Debug.Print "Error"
8  On Error GoTo 0

End Sub

Sub FirstSub()
Dim i As Integer

3  SecondSub
   i = 8 / 4

End Sub

Sub SecondSub()
Dim i As Integer

4  On Error GoTo ErrTrap
```

```
5  i = 8 / 0
   On Error GoTo 0
   Exit Sub

ErrTrap:
6  i = 4 / 0
   On Error GoTo 0

End Sub
```

In this example, the first error occurs at line 5. While that error is still active, a second error occurs at line 6. Since the current error handler cannot handle the second error, execution bubbles up to find an error handler that can. For this reason, execution continues at line 7 after the second error is generated at line 6, even though an enabled error handler can be found in SecondSub.

If no error handler were available in MainSub, the program would crash at line 6. Therefore, it is essential that the error handler be reset immediately after each error. You might be inclined to think that you could reset the error handler within a procedure by using a sequence of code such as that shown in Listing 5.30:

LISTING 5.30

```
Sub MainSub()

1   On Error Resume Next
2   FirstSub
9   If Err.Number <> 0 Then Debug.Print "Error"
10  On Error GoTo 0

End Sub

Sub FirstSub()
Dim i As Integer

3  SecondSub
   i = 8 / 4

End Sub

Sub SecondSub()
Dim i As Integer

4  On Error GoTo ErrTrap
```

```
5  i = 8 / 0
   On Error GoTo 0
   Exit Sub

ErrTrap:
6  On Error Goto 0
7  On Error Resume Next
8  i = 4 / 0
   On Error GoTo 0

End Sub
```

As you can see from the sequence numbers, this procedure does not work. Execution still bubbles up at the point where the second error occurs. The bottom line is that you should always exit a routine as soon as possible after generating an error. You should include as little code as possible and make sure that the code you do include cannot possibly generate a new error.

Use On Error Goto 0 as soon as possible after trapping an error.

5.18   Changing Error Handlers

What happens if you switch to a different On Error statement within a procedure? It is possible, but great care must be taken. The following example illustrates how to accomplish this task:

LISTING 5.31

```
Sub FirstSub(s As String)

Dim n As Integer
Dim lngErr As Long
Dim sngResult As Single

1  On Error GoTo ErrTrap

   'Get the numeric portion of the string
2  s = Left$(s, 4)

   'Convert to a numeric
3  On Error Resume Next
4  n = CInt(s)
5  lngErr = Err.Number
```

```
6  On Error GoTo ErrTrap
   If lngErr <> 0 Then
    'An error occurred. Set a default value.
    n = 1000
   End If

  'Calculate the result
7  sngResult = 1000 / 0

  'Report the result
  MsgBox "The result is: " & sngResult

  Exit Sub

ErrTrap:
  MsgBox "Error: " & Err.Description
8  On Error GoTo 0

End Sub
```

In the example in Listing 5.31, error trapping is put in place at line 1. If an error should occur at line 2, execution will jump to line 8. At line 3, an On Error Resume Next statement changes the current error handler. If an error occurs at line 4, execution will continue to line 5. At line 6, we return to the first error handler. An error occurring at line 7 will jump to line 8.

In this way, error handling can alternate between error trapping and in-line error handling as long as the error handler does not become active. Although possible, this procedure is strongly discouraged. It is confusing and prone to error. If separate error handlers are required, it is quite preferable to create a separate routine with its own independent error handler.

5.19 The Error Trap

The Error Trap is the most commonly used error-coding method. If we were to go back to our thousand programmers and ask them to improve on their earlier error suppression techniques, they would most likely produce these steps (see Listing 5.32):

LISTING 5.32

```
Sub dblDivide(Numer As Double, Denom As Double) As Double
'Purpose: Divide two numbers

On Error Goto ErrTrap
```

```
    dblDivide = Numer / Denom

    On Error Goto 0
    Exit Sub

ErrTrap:

    MsgBox "Error in dblDivide: " & Err.Description
    On Error Goto 0

End Sub
```

The example in Listing 5.32 applies simple error trapping to the unprotected division routine. The On Error Goto ErrorTrap statement directs Visual Basic to jump to the ErrorTrap label if an error should occur.

One of the most typical mistakes in the application of error trapping is forgetting to add the Exit Sub line before the ErrorTrap label. This problem can be seen in the example in Listing 5.33; the routine will always generate an error message, even if no error exists:

LISTING 5.33

```
Sub dblDivide(Numer As Double, Denom As Double) As Double
'Purpose: Divide two numbers

On Error Goto ErrTrap

    dblDivide = Numer / Denom
    On Error Goto 0

ErrTrap:

    MsgBox "Error in dblDivide: " & Err.Description
    On Error Goto 0

End Sub
```

Always remember to exit the routine before your error trapping code.

5.20   The Error Trap Handler

One limitation of the error trap shown in Listing 5.33 is that it simply traps and reports the error. It does not handle the error. It does not diagnose the error and take any intelligent action to correct or resolve the particular error.

The natural thought progression is to add error handling to the error trap. This step results in an error trap handler, as shown in Listing 5.34:

LISTING 5.34

```
Sub dblDivide(Numer As Double, Denom As Double) As Double
'Purpose: Divide two numbers

On Error Goto ErrHandler

    'Divide the numbers
    dblDivide = Numer / Denom

    On Error Goto 0
    Exit Sub

ErrHandler:

    'Handle any errors
    Select Case Err.Number
        Case 11
            'If the denom is zero, then return 0
            dblDivide = 0
        Case Else
            MsgBox "Error in dblDivide: " & Err.Description
    End Select
    On Error Goto 0

End Sub
```

The code after the ErrHandler label is an Error Trap Handler. Notice that this label is now called ErrHandler rather than ErrTrap to indicate that it is doing more than simply trapping errors. It provides some modest error handling. If the denominator is zero, it will return a zero without any apparent error to the calling program. This response may or may not be the best in this situation. Since the Divide by Zero error can be anticipated, it should be handled and corrected. If a different, unanticipated error occurs, then the error trap practices good, offensive coding by exposing the error as soon as possible using the Else clause of the Select statement.

5.21 Handling Errors In-Line

In-line error handling is an alternative to the Error Trap Handler coding structure. In this case, On Error Resume Next is used rather than On Error Goto.

The version in Listing 5.35 demonstrates an in-line approach to the example shown in Listing 5.34:

```
Sub dblDivide(Numer As Double, Denom As Double) As Double
'Purpose: Divide two numbers

    'Divide the numbers
    On Error Resume Next
    dblDivide = Numer / Denom
    Select Case Err.Number
        Case 0 'Success. No nothing.
        Case 11 'Divide By Zero
            'If the denom is zero, then return 0
            dblDivide = 0
        Case Else
            MsgBox "Error in dblDivide: " & Err.Description
    End Select
    On Error Goto 0

End Sub
```

Notice that the error handling is now performed immediately after the statement being tested. This code accomplishes the same goal as the Error Trap Handler.

5.22   Raising Errors

The Raise method of the Err object allows you to raise your own errors from the application code. If you develop a system of managing errors, that system is unlikely to include raising errors. The goal is to identify errors as early as possible and manage them programmatically. Raising errors is, in effect, taking a step backwards.

Imagine that you receive an error message in a bottle, washed up on the shore of the great error-handling sea, telling of a breach in the defenses of your homeland. Rather than sending a series of runners off to warn the king, you throw the message back into the ocean with the wish, "I sure hope the king finds that!" That is raising errors. In upcoming chapters, you learn how to pass errors more directly to the user.

There is little need to raise errors in an intelligently error-coded application, unless writing Active X controls.

5.23   Error Trap Block versus In-Line Error Handlers

The Error Trap Block is the most common style of error handling. It integrates error trapping, error handling, and error reporting, yet it keeps the functional code clean and separates all the error coding into one block at the bottom of each routine. It allows different errors to share the same error response code. It also offers one cleanup and exit point for the function.

In-line Error Handling using On Error Resume Next is not as commonly used as other methods. Some argue that in-line error coding complicates the main body of the feature code. As another concern, it is less code efficient since the same error handling code might need to be repeated for each block.

However, strong reasons exist as well to argue against using the On Error Goto construct. The reasons stem mostly from On Error Goto being actually a glorified Goto statement. First, the Error Trap Block can quickly result in tangled, spaghetti-like error coding as execution jumps from the functional body into the error block and back again. Second, if you want to follow error coding, the spaghetti can make complete code less readable. It can force you to jump around to follow the error-coding flow. Third, spaghetti error code is difficult to reuse. If you wish to reuse a routine, you can cut an in-line block and place it within its own function. It is then self-contained. If you wish to make a function reusable in the Error Trapping style, you might have to untangle large amounts of error coding. The risk of missing codes or creating bugs in the remaining code is dramatically increased. Finally, the separation of error coding into a separate block makes it appear ancillary and not well-integrated.

The Error Trap Block works well in very small routines, such as those used for illustration purposes in this book, but it starts to become overly complicated in larger, real-world routines. You begin to see considerable jumping around and find that you need a large number of Goto statements to return to the main body. You also find that you need to use flags to indicate different error or return conditions. All this becomes very hard to understand, debug, and reuse.

We tend to look down on the use of the Goto statement in normal coding. Why, then, are we willing to tolerate it in our error coding? After all, error coding can be much more complex and abundant than feature coding. The theoretical benefits of the Error Trap Block are often lost in spaghetti when used to meet complex, real-world requirements.

5.24   When to Use the Error Trap Block

Error trapping should be used in every routine to prevent unanticipated errors. It should not be used to handle errors expected within the body of the code.

Although adding extensive error handling to Error Trap Blocks is discouraged, an Error Trap is preferable in certain situations. As an example, when you have a series of similar statements in a routine, if any of those routines should fail, the error treatment would be the same. Let's look at the example in Listing 5.36:

LISTING 5.36

```
Sub DivideByZero ()

Dim i As Integer

On Error Goto ErrHandler

    i = 8 / 0
    i = 8 / 1
    i = 8 / 2
    i = 8 / 4
    i = 8 / 8

    On Error Goto 0
    Exit Sub

ErrHandler:
    MsgBox "A division failed. Series aborted."
    On Error Goto 0

End Sub
```

In this case, error handling in the error trap is appropriate because all errors are handled identically. If any one division fails, the entire operation is aborted. It makes no difference which statement failed.

On Error Resume Next would not be efficient in this particular case. Either it would simply suppress all errors, causing repeated errors, or else the identical error handling code would need to be repeated after each division line.

When should error trapping be used in the development process? Following the Golden Rule of Error Coding, it should only be used after you have prevented all errors that can be anticipated and prevented, and you have handled all errors that can be anticipated but not prevented.

5.25 When to Use In-Line Error Handling

In-line error coding should be used to handle all errors anticipated in the body of your routines. As you saw in this chapter, this process can become complicated, especially when an error trap is used at the same time. Developing fully error-coded Visual Basic requires so much code that it is rarely implemented as completely as it should be. It clutters up the feature coding and results in too much code, which itself is a source of errors.

By reusing your error coding, you can keep your code base small, and your code clean and manageable. It is possible to do much better coding by coding smarter. You can design and implement a coding strategy that makes it possible to accomplish complete in-line error coding without complicating your code. In fact, you can accomplish complete in-line error coding within an error trap and simplify your code.

Chapters 7 and 8 present the Safe Programming Framework. This framework is built around the concept of reusable safe procedures. These safe procedures, when applied as specified in the framework, simplify your code and eliminate most of the complications identified in this chapter. As a preview, consider the pseudo-code for a safe procedure shown in Listing 5.37:

LISTING 5.37

```
Sub SafeMain ()
'Procedure header here

On Error Goto ErrTrap

'Dimension local variables here

    'SafeMain = SafeSub1()
    'If SafeMain = "" Then Exit Sub

    'SafeMain = SafeSub2()
    'If SafeMain = "" Then Exit Sub

    'Do additional code here

    Exit Sub

ErrTrap:
    'Return unanticipated errors here
    On Error Goto 0
End Sub
```

Notice that the pseudo-code above has a series of self-contained code blocks. Each block is completely self-contained using in-line error coding. Each block of code need only be two lines long: the first line calls a safe routine, and the second line handles the return error value. It has an error trap but no error handling block in the error trap. The error trap is used for unanticipated errors only. Anticipated errors are handled in-line. There is no need to raise errors in this code. You will see in Chapters 7 and 8 that this framework results in clean, reusable code that is fully error coded without the complications normally generated.

5.26 Avoiding Error Handling Completely

Before talking further about handling errors, it is important to consider prevention. Internal and application level error handling only take effect after the error has occurred. Much error handling and trapping code is unnecessary because those errors could have been anticipated and prevented.

An ounce of error prevention is worth a pound of error handling. Simple error prevention techniques can avoid the need for large amounts of error handling and trapping code. The next chapter discusses error prevention techniques before moving on to strategies for handling them.

Error
Prevention

An ounce of prevention is worth a pound of cure. That old adage has stood the test of time. No one would argue with the wisdom of it, but how many of us do everything we can to prevent illness?

In the same way, no one would disagree that preventing programming errors is preferable to fixing them. Yet how many of us do all we can to prevent errors? The word "prevention" is thrown around a great deal, but it is very difficult to learn specifically what steps to take to prevent programming errors.

Rarely do books on coding and error prevention mention prevention in the contents or index. Authors tend to talk about issues that affect prevention without addressing error prevention directly. Those other topics, however, *are* error prevention. Error prevention is not so much a method or a formulaic solution as an attitude and philosophy. Understanding prevention is not a matter of studying one example to see how it works as much as it is appreciating subtleties of design and implementation.

You must face three main challenges in preventing errors:

- Learning to anticipate errors that are preventable.
- Learning the most effective techniques to prevent them.
- Getting into the habit of anticipating and preventing errors full time.

This chapter focuses on error prevention, despite the inherent difficulty of the topic. It looks at prevention from various angles and provides concrete examples where possible.

6.1   Types of Errors

Errors can be classified into two general types: programmatic errors and logical errors. The two are quite different beasts and must be considered separately in any discussion of error prevention.

6.1.1   Programmatic Errors

Programmatic errors are those caused by mistakes in coding. This category includes errors such as the common Division by Zero error. In programmatic errors, the code either fails to work properly or it generates a programming failure.

Programmatic errors are those typically prevented or handled by most error-coding practices. You can anticipate a Division by Zero error, prevent it, handle it, report it, or suppress it. These are programmatic solutions to programmatic errors.

The number of types of programmatic errors is limited, with just a few forming the bulk of these errors. The same types of errors are well-known, yet they keep appearing over and over.

About 120 trappable errors are listed in the Visual Basic help file. This is not a complete list of possible errors, but it does include most of the common ones. In fact, many of those in the list are seldom seen. The errors seen most often are those generated by the same few typical error situations.

The following list shows the typical programmatic errors that plague most applications, organized by the type of operation to which they apply (see Table 6.1).

Most of the errors left out of this list are errors that are displayed in design mode or at compile time. Design and compile time errors are not major problems since they cannot normally enter into the compiled code.

You are left with, then, a relatively simple list of run-time errors that apply to a fairly small number of problem situations. Notice that, aside from the array and recursion errors, the rest of these run-time error situations arise only when with dealing with the outside world. Interactions with external systems such as the registry, the file system, databases, and the printer are highly susceptible to errors.

Database operations in particular require a tremendous amount of anticipatory error prevention and handling. The other external system that is normally the source of many preventable errors is the user. We talk about this particular external system in the next section.

The areas toward which you must focus your attention are very well-known and relatively isolated. It ought not be prohibitive to manage these situations effectively. Programmatic errors that can be predicted can usually be prevented by error-coding techniques.

Programmatic errors can be prevented by error-coding techniques.

TABLE 6.1	
Array Handling	Too many files
Subscript out of range	Disk not ready
Assignment Errors	Can't rename with different drive
Type mismatch	Path/file access error
Invalid use of Null	Path not found
Clipboard	Form Handling
Invalid clipboard format	A form can't be moved or sized while
Can't empty clipboard	minimized or maximized
Can't open clipboard	Invalid procedure call or argument
Database Operations	Math Operations
(Hundreds of errors in this category)	Overflow
External Objects	Division by zero
System DLL could not be loaded	OLE Automation
Component not found	Automation error
File Functions	Printing
Bad file name or number	Printer error
File not found	Printer object does not support specified
Bad file mode	property
File already open	(Miscellaneous network problems)
File already exists	Recursion
Bad record length	Out of stack space
Disk full	Registry
Input past end of file	Could not access system registry
Bad record number	Security violation (WinNT)

6.1.2   Logical Errors

Logical errors do not necessarily cause any programming problems. These are errors in which the program doesn't do what it is meant to do. Logical errors are ones such as an incorrect calculation yielding the wrong result.

There is no limit to the number of possible logical errors. Logical errors cannot be trapped or identified by the error handler. They are largely outside the scope of discussions on error coding and are more directly affected by project analysis, planning, and validation methods. However, assuming that the design of the application is correct, then that design can be implemented with fewer logical errors if the programmer follows coding standards and practices that make the code clear and maintainable. If the code is easy to understand, then it is less likely for inconsistencies with the design requirements to go unnoticed.

Logical errors can be minimized by clear coding practices.

6.2   Types of Prevention

There are two types of error prevention. It will help to separate them in your mind. The first type is coding error prevention, and the second type is user error prevention.

Coding error prevention encompasses all the techniques you can use to keep from making mistakes when writing code. These include mistakes introduced by team members, by future programmers, or even by you. Coding errors can cause programmatic or logical mistakes.

User error prevention covers strategies that prevent users from performing the wrong action. These include actions that cause bugs, but they also include actions that diminish the user experience without necessarily causing a programming error.

Effectively implementing both types of error prevention is critical to your mission.

6.3   Preventing Coding Errors

If you have any amount of programming experience, chances are very good that you will answer yes to all the following questions:

1. Have you had to fix a large number of bugs?
2. Have you often burned the midnight oil fixing those bugs?
3. Have you often thought, "This bug should never have happened if an earlier programmer had done a better job"?
4. Have there been times when you patched an error that could have been prevented earlier by adding a short-term fix but was one that failed to anticipate and prevent future errors?

If you answered yes to all four questions, don't feel bad. We are all guilty of not practicing preventative coding, even as we complain about others who did not. Even good programmers have plenty of reasons to justify cutting corners. With the right attitude and the right techniques, however, you need not skimp on error prevention again.

The following section offers some error prevention suggestions. They run the gamut from general to specific, but they all are important strategies for preventing programming errors.

Develop the habit of preventing coding errors, not responding to them.

6.3.1   Think Long Term

If you think in the short term, you cannot develop good preventative coding. There is always a tight deadline, but a time crunch cannot be an excuse to cut corners. The challenge is to find ways to think in the long term and still meet short-term deadlines.

Most of the explicit coding suggestions in Chapter 4 are examples of long-term thinking. If you think only of immediate requirements, then avoiding assumptions and implementing explicit coding may not seem as though they are necessary practices. If you think in the long term, however, then each one of those suggestions becomes very important. They prevent errors in the long term and don't cost any more in the short term.

Thinking long term means anticipating preventable errors.

6.3.2 Write for Others

When you think long term, you realize that you will probably not be the last person who needs to understand and modify your code. You appreciate that it is paramount for your inheritors to understand your work. Writing for others means following standards, making code reusable, avoiding assumptions, being explicit, and coding clearly and simply.

It is more important that code be clear and understandable than that it work correctly. This may seem irresponsible to say, but think about it: If you have code that is clear, then it can be fixed easily and maintained when necessary. If you have code that works but is not easy to maintain, then as soon as requirements change, the code may have to be disposed of. Which is more valuable in the long term? Which would you rather inherit?

Clear code makes it easier to find and repair existing errors and also helps to avoid errors in the future.

6.3.3 Code Defensively

We often hear the term "code defensively." This phrase means that we should write our routines so that we defend against errors rather than expecting the "other guy" to worry about them. To some authors, coding defensively means suppressing errors. Obviously, error suppression is not considered good practice. Good defensive practice is anticipating and accommodating to any type of situation that might break the code.

To illustrate this point, let's look at the example in Listing 6.1. This routine formats a raw nine-character social security number. If you pass it "333445555," it should return "333-44-5555."

LISTING 6.1

```
Function strFmtSSN(ByVal sNewSSN As Variant) As String

    'Format SSN
    strFmtSSN = Left$(sNewSSN, 3) & "-" _
             & Mid$(sNewSSN, 4, 2) & "-" _
```

```
              & Right$(sNewSSN, 4)

End Function
```

The example in Listing 6.1 has no error protection. Obviously, it will fail if a string with less than nine characters is passed to it. It will also fail to give the expected results if the argument is nonnumeric or has more than nine characters. It puts the responsibility on the calling routine to pass a valid nine-character string. It is not at all unusual to find routines that make these kinds of assumptions, thinking in the short term and creating disposable code that may work only in very limited situations.

At the very least, this code should be error protected. Listing 6.2 shows an example of the kind of error suppression that gave defensive programming a bad name:

LISTING 6.2

```
Function strFmtSSN(ByVal SSN As Variant) As String

    'Format SSN
    On Error Resume Next
    strFmtSSN = Left$(sNewSSN, 3) & "-" _
              & Mid$(sNewSSN, 4, 2) & "-" _
              & Right$(sNewSSN, 4)

End Function
```

The last chapter pointed out that this kind of error suppression is not effective coding practice. Listing 6.3 shows an example of better defensive coding that anticipates situations and deals intelligently with them:

LISTING 6.3

```
Function strFmtSSN(ByVal SSN As Variant) As String

Dim sNewSSN As String

    'Return empty string in case of an error
    strFmtSSN = ""

    'Validate SSN
    sNewSSN = NumbersOnly(SSN)
    If Len(sNewSSN) <> 9 Then Exit Function
    If Not AllCharsNumeric(sNewSSN) Then Exit Function

    'Format SSN
```

```
On Error Resume Next
strFmtSSN = Left$(sNewSSN, 3) & "-" _
          & Mid$(sNewSSN, 4, 2) & "-" _
          & Right$(sNewSSN, 4)

End Function
```

This version is considered better defensive programming. It takes responsibility to ensure that it can handle any legitimate variation such as "222-334444." It protects against specific predictable error situations without relying on error trapping. It may be that at the time this function was written, the programmer saw no conceivable way that an invalid raw SSN could be passed. This routine thinks long term, however, by not assuming that this condition is or will always remain true. This is good defensive programming.

Defensive programming prevents errors.

6.3.4 Code Offensively

You might think that if coding defensively is a good thing, then coding offensively must be bad. This is not the case. Coding offensively is also excellent practice.

Coding offensively means making the developer, the tester, or the user aware of errors as early as possible. Remember that the earlier an error is exposed, the more likely a preventative solution will be applied.

One example of coding offensively is using an Else clause in every If and Select block. The Else clause can be used to expose unanticipated situations as early as possible. Listing 6.4 shows another example of offensive coding, using our previous example. In this case, we are not satisfied merely to return the original string in the event of an error. We want to know about any error as soon as possible during development or program use:

LISTING 6.4

```
Function strFmtSSN(ByVal SSN As Variant) As String

    'Return empty string in case of an error
    strFmtSSN = ""

    'Validate SSN
    SSN = NumbersOnly(SSN)
    If Len(SSN) <> 9 Then
     MsgBox "Invalid SSN length in strFmtSSN: " & SSN
    Exit Function
    End If
    If Not AllCharsNumeric(SSN) Then
     MsgBox "Invalid SSN characters in strFmtSSN: " & SSN
```

```
Exit Function
 End If


 'Format SSN
 On Error Resume Next
 strFmtSSN = Left$(sNewSSN, 3) & "-" _
                 & Mid$(sNewSSN, 4, 2) & "-" _
                 & Right$(sNewSSN, 4)


End Function
```

Notice that in this offensive programming example, it is not enough merely to report that an error occurred. It is also important to provide as much detailed and accurate information as possible about it. Notice as well that this example did not go back to a simple error trap and report the error. As you can see, it is important first to program defensively and then program offensively. You need to do both, not one or the other.

Note—Stop and Assert Statements

Some authors advocate using the Visual Basic Stop statement as a good approach to exposing errors. This statement directs Visual Basic to halt at the error statement when executing in design mode. It acts as a permanent break point. In effect, you can place a Stop statement at some point in the code that you expect should never be executed, such as an Else clause of a Select or If block. Then when the Stop is encountered, you can inspect variables and continue to debug in design mode.

In compiled executables, if a Stop statement is encountered, Visual Basic will simply display a generic error message saying that a Stop was encountered, then it will end the program.

I think this approach has limited usefulness. Instead, why not place a real error message box there that will clearly inform the developer or the user of the error? The developer can still break at the following line in design mode simply by pressing Ctrl-Break.

The same idea holds true for debug.assert statements for an even stronger reason. With debug.assert statements, no protection is provided in compiled executables. These should only be used for specific tests during development and then removed.

Offensive programming prevents errors by exposing them quickly.

6.3.5 Avoid Error Suppression

Error suppression is the antithesis of offensive coding. It hides errors until they become malignant and systemic. What might have been a simple situation to prevent early in the process becomes problematic when suppressed too long. Offensive coding practices expose rather than suppress errors. The worst debugging nightmare is tracking down an error that has been suppressed until late in the development cycle.

Error suppression subverts effective error prevention.

6.3.6   *Elegance as a Prevention Technique*

Elegance—what does this word suggest to you? The dictionary defines it as "tasteful opulence." I like to use "elegant" to describe programming that is powerful and sophisticated yet unpretentious and simple. Elegance applies to both the user interface and to the underlying code.

Elegant code is efficient and understandable. It accomplishes the task without reams of code. It is simple to follow and just as simple to modify. Elegance reduces the amount of code and therefore eliminates bug opportunities.

Any programmer can write mountains of convoluted code to perform a task. Gifted programmers accomplish more with less code. The programmers who are the most talented are able to consistently add new features *and* decrease code size.

> *Elegance prevents errors by reducing code size and improving clarity.*

6.3.7   *Fool Me Twice, Shame on Me*

Running into an error may seem like a problem to avoid. Actually, the goal of good offensive coding is to make sure you are hit by errors. It is better to find out about an error and correct it than to remain unaware of it. Being hit with an error is the most effective way to learn about it.

Be happy if you encounter a new error, because from that point on you can avoid it. However, if you fail to prevent that error in the future, then shame on you. You should never have to relearn the same hard lessons.

> *Learn to anticipate errors after your first encounter.*

6.3.8   *Never Fix the Same Error Twice*

Typically, you learn the hard way about each error-prone situation. You investigate and determine the best way to prevent the error, or at least handle it. You might think that afterward, in order to practice good preventative programming, you need to remember that error. You must never forget how you handled it so that you will always remember to fix it—and how to fix it in every instance in the future.

Yet you do not have to worry about every error. You should never need to fix that same error again or to rewrite that error prevention code again. You should never have to think about it again at all. You should not even need to remember that it is a problem. Reusing error coding allows you to forget about errors.

> *Fix errors once and forever by reusing your solutions.*

6.3.9 *Reuse*

How is it possible to fix an error once and forever and then forget about it? Code reuse makes it possible. We discussed code reuse in an earlier chapter, but we did not discuss the value of reuse as an error prevention strategy. By fixing an error one time and making that code reusable, you need never worry about that error again or even remember it, as long as you reuse your code. You have effectively prevented that error from occurring again.

ANECDOTE: The Q Function

My Q function is a fine example of reuse as a prevention tool. Years ago, I was asked to change some variable types in an application. When I did, dozens of SQL statements broke because they no longer had the correct delimiters for their field types.

I waded through, fixing about half the SQL statements before it clicked that reusability was the key. I went back and changed all the SQL statements to use a Q (for Quotes) function. The Q function accepted a variable and automatically enclosed it in the correct delimiter for its data type.

That step might have seemed unnecessary at the time. Why not just fix the statements and be done with them? I was lucky to have implemented a longer-term solution, since shortly afterward I was asked to change some other variable types. It took only a few minutes because none of the SQL broke. My new Q function had handled all the changed data types automatically.

A few weeks later, I was given a bug report. It turned out, after a great deal of debugging, that apostrophe characters in user names such as O'Malley were breaking the SQL statements. I returned to my Q function and added a bit of code to preprocess the apostrophes correctly. All the code in the application was now protected from this error.

Now jump ahead six years. I was teaching my Visual Basic database course when a student asked me how to handle the apostrophes in his class project. I drew a blank. Apostrophes? That rang a distant bell, but I couldn't for the life of me remember how to handle them. I could not remember because I fixed that problem six years earlier and had never had to think about it again. By reusing my trusty Q function, that universal problem had become a nonissue for all the projects over those years.

This anecdote exemplifies nearly all the goals and techniques of error prevention presented in this section. I learned about an error the hard way and began to think in the long term. I fixed it once and was never fooled again. In fact, I had completely forgotten about the error. The solution reduced, rather than increased, the amount of code in the project and made it more elegant. Moreover, other programmers working for me since that time have not had to worry about delimiters or apostrophes. They simply know always to use the Q function in assembling SQL strings.

There is another error prevention benefit to code reuse. It reduces the amount of code in a project. The more code you write, the more errors you risk introducing. The more code you reuse, the fewer errors you are likely to introduce. You make it easier to pull out those pesky error weeds when they do surface. Code reuse allows you to write elegant code.

Code reuse is a powerful error prevention strategy.

6.3.10 Standardize

Standardization is one of the three sides of the Smart Coding Triangle. Standardization permits code reuse and error handling, but it has another major impact. It is a tremendously powerful error prevention technique in itself. Simply by following a standard, many errors are prevented that could easily slip into nonstandardized code.

Performing steps in a consistent fashion is one of the single most important habits you can form to prevent errors. No matter what your task, ask yourself what needs to be done if you have to repeat it many times without error: you need to develop a standardized system and approach.

The same holds true in writing code. By adopting and following a standard coding method, you greatly reduce the chance of introducing both random and systematic errors.

Standardizing and systematizing the coding process prevents errors.

6.3.11 Wrap System Functions

Intrinsic Visual Basic functions are not safe. Simply because they are shipped with Visual Basic does not mean they do not need error protection. On the contrary, most intrinsic functions and methods that are a part of the Visual Basic library are fragile and easily broken. They generally place the responsibility for avoiding errors on the calling routine.

Since you know that Visual Basic intrinsic functions are not safe, then why not prevent errors from occurring when you use them? To prevent intrinsic functions from failing, you should protect them with safe, reusable wrappers.

For example, the previous chapter mentioned that the SetFocus method of Visual Basic controls can fail for a variety of reasons. It showed how On Error Resume Next should be used every time this method is invoked in order to protect the application from the "Invalid procedure call or argument" error.

If you know this, why would you worry about adding error coding every time you call this method? Most likely, you or another programmer will forget sooner or later. It is much easier and more foolproof simply to wrap this method in a safe function and never call the method directly.

Listing 6.5 shows a wrapper function for the SetFocus method:

LISTING 6.5

```
Sub SetFocus(obj As Object)

    On Error Resume Next
    obj.SetFocus
    On Error Goto 0

End Sub
```

This simple wrapper has tremendous value to ensure that the unprotected SetFocus method is never used. It also reduces the total amount of code since the error coding is reused. It improves the overall clarity and maintainability of the entire project.

This example shows the simplest type of wrapper function. Other wrappers can quickly become very complex and lengthy. Think about all the error prevention, handling, and reporting code you would need in order to write a safe wrapper for coding as simple as the file system Open function. What about a file copy function? Think of the benefit of writing these codes once and having them available forever. Future programmers needing a file copy function do not need to know, relearn, or rewrite all this coding.

Use safe wrappers for your Visual Basic functions.

6.3.12   *Don't Use Error Trapping for Prevention*

Programmers have a strong tendency to use error trapping as a normal programming strategy. I do not recommend this technique. There may be times when you cannot think of another way to test a situation, but this method should be avoided if at all possible.

Consider the division routine, for example. You might think of the version in Listing 6.6 as being good error coding:

LISTING 6.6

```
Sub Divide (intDenom as Integer)

Dim i As Integer
Dim intErr As Integer

    On Error Resume Next
    i = 8 / intDenom
    intErr = Err.Number
    On Error Goto 0
    Select Case intErr
     Case 0 'Succeeded
     Case 11 'Division by Zero
    MsgBox "Enter a non-zero denominator."
     Case Else
    MsgBox "Error: " & Error$(intErr)
    End Select

End Sub
```

This is fairly good error coding. The problem is that it is unnecessary. It is preferable instead to avoid generating errors whenever they can be anticipated and prevented. Consider the alternative in Listing 6.7:

LISTING 6.7

```
Sub Divide (intDenom as Integer)

Dim i As Integer
Dim intErr As Integer

    If intDenom = 0 Then
     MsgBox "Enter a non-zero denominator."
     Exit Sub
    End If

    On Error Resume Next
    i = 8 / intDenom
    intErr = Err.Number
    On Error Goto 0
    Select Case intErr
      Case 0
      Case Else
        MsgBox "Error: " & Error$(intErr)
    End Select

End Sub
```

This approach accomplishes the same result, but the important difference is that it did not have to generate an error to diagnose the Divide by Zero problem. Whenever you can avoid error generation, you should do so.

Avoid using error trapping as a test.

6.4 Preventing User Errors

In the previous sections, we discussed the prevention of coding errors. Now, let's examine the prevention of user errors. User errors can and should be prevented with the same gusto as you approach programmatic errors.

Since user errors generally come earlier than coding errors, they almost always deserve priority, based on the goal of preventing errors as early as possible. By preventing user errors, you can prevent coding errors. If the user is not allowed to enter a bad value, the code will not need to respond to that situation. The user will have a better experience as well.

User error prevention, then, is another method for preventing programmatic errors. However, user error prevention can also be used to prevent logical, nonprogrammatic errors. It is presented in a separate section because the issues involved in its use are unique. This section examines some strategies that the programmer can use to prevent user errors.

6.4.1 The Three Cardinal Rules of Program Design

ANECDOTE: Cardinal Rules of Program Design

Early in my career, I wrote a personal information manager for the Atari ST. It was a shareware success that went on to be offered as a commercial product by a company called Gribnif Software.

Even though the shareware version was good, the owner of Gribnif requested a long list of improvements to make it even better. He gave me a little lecture in which he remarked that there were three cardinal rules of successful program design. The first rule, he said, was consistency. The second rule, he continued, was consistency. His third rule was, of course, consistency.

I have never forgotten this lesson. Even after all these years, I never fail to tell my students, "There are three cardinal rules of building a successful program . . ."

Consistency is an easy user error prevention technique. If users are presented with a consistent interface, they are less likely to experience errors. A program can be consistent, or can fail to be consistent in many ways:

CONSISTENT BEHAVIOR

Each operation should work consistently with other similar operations. The operation should not only be consistent within the application but also consistent with other applications.

CONSISTENT CAPTIONS

All text should be consistent in meaning and presentation. This includes button labels, form captions, text labels, frame names, message boxes, and any other text presented to the user.

CONSISTENT APPEARANCE

All forms should use the same color scheme, the same general layout design, and the same font style, size, and special effects, as well as the same control sizing and positioning. All controls on a form should be positioned consistently and aligned evenly from form to form and tab to tab. Colors should be used consistently throughout the application to convey meaning.

CONSISTENT MENU LAYOUT

All menus should be consistent with other Windows applications. The menu positions, menu item order, item names, and shortcut and alternate keys should be consistent. Being consistent prevents user errors because the user can easily understand where items are and how they work. It does not mean your program cannot be unique and distinctive.

6.4.2 Be Explicit

This rule is so important to bug-free coding that this book devoted an entire chapter to it. It is equally important in preventing user errors. Being explicit means removing ambiguity for the user and eliminating assumptions about how the user will or should use the application.

USE ELLIPSES

In Windows applications, the ellipses generally indicate that an action does not trigger immediately. A second opportunity will be given for the user to confirm the action. This step is important for preventing errors. Imagine a menu with a "Delete" item. If you are a user, you may be very nervous about clicking on this option. What does it mean? Will the entire file be deleted or just the current field? The action is not explicit enough. Worse yet, the user may click on the Delete item assuming it means one thing when it actually means something else.

Now imagine that the menu item says "Delete . . ." instead. You should feel quite confident to press the key knowing that you will be provided further information and prompted prior to taking any action.

AVOID HIDDEN OPTIONS

One school of thought holds that a good error prevention strategy is one that disables or hides menu items or buttons that are not applicable in a particular situation. Microsoft often takes this approach in its applications.

Dynamic menus and options may make sense from one perspective, but from another, they reduce consistency and clarity. The user interface does not remain constant; it changes dynamically. The user may not know where, when, or how a particular option might appear.

Let's consider the example of a Delete menu item again. Rather than use ellipses, you might make this menu item dynamic by disabling it when the situation is not applicable. However, users who want to delete a line may not know how to enable the delete menu item. They may become completely confused by this behavior if no feedback is given to clarify it for them.

Dynamic menus are equivalent to error suppression. It is generally better to create a more offensive user interface style and leave the Delete menu item in place consistently. If users click the Delete menu item in an ambiguous situation, then they should see a prompt for clarification. If they click it in an inappropriate situation, then take the opportunity to clarify the operation for them by providing an informative message.

6.4.3   Refine the Design

Coding an application requires diligent pre-planning to produce a functional specification. Typically, this document includes a user interface specification. Depending on the type of project, client, and staff, you might have no flexibility to modify that plan during development, or you might be given quite a bit of latitude.

If the developers do have the flexibility to tweak the user interface design, then quite often this tweaking results in superior user error prevention. Many error prevention strategies become evident during development. If in a project the developers cannot refine the user interface, then they may be forced to take less effective measures to code for user errors.

Note—Carved in Stone
In a similar vein, it is undesirable to have database designs that are carved in stone. The programmer is forced to create messy, inefficient code to accommodate a less than optimal database structure. Of course it is sometimes not possible, especially in large companies with established databases, to modify the database structure. However, in most applications it is quite possible and desirable to continue optimizing the database structure throughout the development process so that the two systems work most efficiently together.

6.4.4   Make Your User Interface Unambiguous

When you show your program to a tester or a user, he or she will often be confused or hesitant about a particular feature or situation. The natural reaction of the developer is to explain how to use that feature or how to respond in that situation.

If the user is unsure how to proceed, learning to use the feature is not a "training" issue. The programmer's response should never be to show the user what to do. The response should be to modify the user interface so that the user will have no hesitancy or confusion about how to proceed. The burden is on the programmer to make the program clear, not on the user to understand the programmer's logic in designing that feature.

Let's look at the example shown in Figure 6.1. Imagine that you are presented with that form.

This form seems clear and straightforward, right? If you want to create a new record what do you do?

1. Press the "Add" button to clear the fields, enter the new record, and press "Save."

   or

2. Enter new data and then press the "Add" button to save the new record.

Chances are probably 80 to 20 that you selected the first answer. We don't know which is correct. The operation of this form may be obvious and

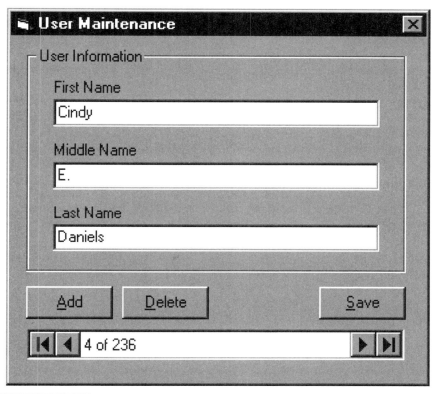

FIGURE 6.1   Ambiguous user interface

clear to the programmer, but to people who don't think the same as the programmer, this answer is totally confusing and frustrating. It demonstrates a variation of the noun/verb ambiguity that can be found in many programs. It is also unclear when the user needs to press the "Save" button. Is a new record automatically saved when the "Add" button is pressed, or does the "Save" button need to be pressed to complete the record addition?

In these situations the programmer will usually design this form one way or the other depending on whether he or she is a noun/verb or a verb/noun person. In testing, someone of the opposite persuasion will try to create a new record backwards. That person will be told the correct operation and may even be ribbed for being a stupid user. Testing may identify errors that result from the "incorrect" use of this form. Usually in these cases, the programmer will be asked to go back and add error coding to prevent the application from failing.

The better solution is to eliminate the ambiguity as soon as the first person makes a mistake. You change the application rather than changing the user. This process not only results in a more satisfying user experience, but it also reduces the need for error handling. This response is error prevention at its best.

In Figure 6.1, the best approach might be to disable the "Add" button as soon as the user edits any information. This is not a perfect solution, but at least it should prevent the user from entering too much data before discovering that he or she is using the wrong approach.

6.4.5 Make Your Messages Clear

Including clear documentation in the code will prevent future errors. Similarly, presenting clear messages to the user will prevent errors and enhance the user's experience. In every message, strive to be as helpful as possible to anticipate user questions. This technique will help reduce the number of user errors with which the program must deal.

You might consider what to use for button captions. The Windows standard is to generally to put "OK" and "Cancel" buttons in the lower right-hand corner of forms. In many cases, these generic buttons may be ambiguous or confusing. They may not clearly communicate the specific action that will be taken when they are used.

In the interest of clarity, you may be a tempted to change your button captions to ones that seems more obvious in a particular situation. I personally find even the relative positioning of these buttons counterintuitive. I would like to see the "OK" button consistently set to the right of the "Cancel" button.

However, remember the Three Cardinal Rules of Program Design? Consistency trumps everything else, including clarity. It is best to use the "OK-Cancel" standard, even if you could use clearer captions, and even if you happen to find "Cancel-OK" more logical. Most people are used to looking for "OK-Cancel," so this is the preferred design. Of course, this is not to say that you should never violate consistency if other factors benefit greatly, but consistency should never be violated lightly.

6.4.6 Filter User Input

The user is the most unpredictable of systems with which your application must interface. Your application must predict and accommodate the most unlikely user responses. It must protect itself from the most unimaginable actions.

It is not good enough simply to expect that users will respond a certain way or that every mistake they might make is a "training issue." Just as the burden is on you as the programmer to create defensive public interfaces routines, so it is your responsibility to create defensive user interfaces.

The first and easiest filtering technique is to set the MaxLength property of your text boxes to allow no more than the maximum number of allowed characters, if this number is known. If your text field displays information that is stored in a database, then this number is always known.

The next important technique is to filter user input so that users are unable to enter invalid characters. Putting code in the KeyPress event, as in the example in Listing 6.8, is the earliest intervention. Listing 6.8 illustrates how to prevent the user from entering invalid characters when a whole number is expected:

LISTING 6.8

```
Private Sub txtNumber_KeyPress(KeyAscii As Integer)

    'Limit entry to whole numbers
    If (KeyAscii <> vbKeyDelete) _
    And (KeyAscii <> vbKeyBack) _
    And (KeyAscii < KEY_0 Or KeyAscii > KEY_9) Then
       KeyAscii = 0
    End If

End Sub
```

In this validation code, only numbers, delete, and backspace are allowed. This technique shields the program from having to respond to error situations caused by nonnumeric entries. It is also the most satisfying solution from the user's perspective, since the program prevents him or her from wasting effort.

6.4.7   Validate User Input

In some cases, it is not possible to ensure correct user input by filtering. In the last example, input filtering assures that a number is entered, but what if the number is out of range? If valid numbers are 0–100, then the example in Listing 6.8 would allow numbers from 0–999, assuming the MaxLength property is set to 3. Any value over 100 could result in a coding or logical error.

It would take some complicated coding to limit entry to 100 by filtering without making the entry process cumbersome and inflexible. The next best choice is to validate the number when the LostFocus event occurs. The example in Listing 6.9 can be added to the previous one to limit entry to numbers from 0–100:

LISTING 6.9

```
Private Sub txtNumber_LostFocus()

Dim lngNumber As Long

    'Be sure the entry is in range
```

```
lngNumber = Val(txtNumber.Text)
If lngNumber < 0 Or lngNumber > 100 Then

    MsgBox "Please enter a number between 0 and 100."

    On Error Resume Next
    txtNumber.SetFocus
    On Error GoTo 0

End If

End Sub
```

This approach notifies the user as soon as possible about the invalid entry. It also provides an informative message that tells the user exactly how to proceed. Also, notice that the SetFocus method is protected against error.

Here is a pop quiz: do you need to copy and paste this code into every control in your project in order to error protect them all? Of course not. If you write this filtering and validation code once, you should never need to write it again. You should make it reusable the first time you write it and reuse it whenever needed. Here is an example of how this code should look (see Listing 6.10):

LISTING 6.10

```
Private Sub txtNumber_KeyPress(KeyAscii As Integer)

  'Limit entry to whole numbers
  KeyAscii = FilterWhole(KeyAscii)

End Sub

Private Sub txtNumber_LostFocus()

  'Be sure the entry is in range
  ValidateInteger txtNumber, 0, 100

End Sub
```

This filtering and validation code is quick, easy, and reliable to implement. It takes very little code. If the logic needs to be fixed or changed, there is one place to do it, even if these routines are applied to hundreds of controls.

HORROR STORY: LostFocus

This is a good time to make sure you are aware of some issues regarding the use of the LostFocus event. You need to be very cautious if you rely on this event.

As one problem, if the user executes a command using a "hot key," the LostFocus event fires *after* the code the "hot key" fires. If the "hot key" code uses the value entered in the text box, it may not be valid and can fail. In addition, the LostFocus event may not fire if the user Alt-Tabs to another application or window. This behavior is not consistent.

I have debugged cases in the past in which the GotFocus event of one control fired before the LostFocus event of the other. The program failed because these events fired out of the assumed logical order. In one case, simply adding a debug.print statement to another mouse event reversed the order of the GotFocus and LostFocus. Imagine trying to debug that one! The "CausesValidation" property and "Validate" event were added to Visual Basic 6 in an effort to work around some of these problems, but that property has vexing issues as well.

6.4.8 Use Control Arrays

You should use control arrays, rather than individually named controls, for data entry. This method reduces your code and code maintenance requirements. By using a control array, only one event applies to all controls. You can put all your filtering and validation code into a single common event. If additional controls are added to the array, the code is automatically applied without having to remember to do it. Similarly, if a control is removed, no orphaned code remains to clean up.

6.4.9 Select the Right Control

Another method for preventing user error is the type of control you select. For example, what if, in the previous example, the allowed entries were not 0–100, but 0–10 and 100. In this case, you could eliminate user errors completely by using a drop-down selector or up-down control rather than a text entry box. Better yet, this would require no filtering or validation code.

6.4.10 Wrap Controls

Earlier, the value of wrapping intrinsic Visual Basic functions was discussed as a coding error prevention technique. Similarly, wrapping standard controls is a great user error prevention technique.

You know that text entry is almost a universal requirement in every Visual Basic program. You also know that for good preventative programming, each control should be protected by input filtering and validation.

Knowing this, why would you repeat this code over again in each application, even if localized in reusable functions? It makes much more sense to create a wrapper for the text box that does all this for you. I use a custom control called FlexInput, which is a wrapper for the standard text box. FlexInput has a Style property that allows you to select Text, Numeric, Date, Phone Number, SSN, Zip Code, and other commonly used data entry types. Properties are used to configure each of these for the type of filtering and validation desired. It even formats all entries in standard display styles automatically. I never have to recreate these code-wheels. Better yet, I have full control over the source code.

Remember at the start of the book when I promised that it is possible to do more with less code? FlexInput and control wrappers like it are powerful examples of how to accomplish that goal!

6.5   Form Preventative Habits

It is not hard to adopt a preventative mode of programming. Think of it as lazy programming. By preventing coding and user errors, you save yourself a great deal of tedious error coding. You might think of error prevention as the best way to allow you to move onto new, exciting projects rather than being stuck debugging and maintaining a fragile application until retirement.

The next chapter shows you a coding standard that facilitates error prevention and makes it easy to write defensive programming.

Safe Coding
Framework

Early in this book I challenged you to adopt a higher coding standard in order to improve quality and productivity. Up to this point, the book has presented both general approaches and specific techniques that should be a part of your new standard of excellence. These include the Golden Rule, the Smart Triangle, implicit coding, and error prevention, among others.

General objectives and miscellaneous recommendations are not enough, however. To be successful, you need to adopt a cohesive plan of action that, when implemented, is measurable and reproducible. This chapter provides a specific plan of action for you. It is called the **Safe Programming Framework (SPF).** The SPF pulls together all the concepts we have discussed into a systematic coding architecture and specification. It provides a concrete plan that you can implement to accomplish your new mission.

The SPF provides a specification for developing routines that are fully error coded, reusable, and standardized in accordance with the Smart Coding Triangle. It will enhance both the quality and productivity of your development effort. It will not create impractical obstacles or overhead costs that developers must first overcome to do their job.

7.1   Reuse-Quality Routines

When you think of your routines as disposable, short-term components, their quality and value are diminished. The SPF forces you to treat each routine you write as a long-term, reusable investment of time and effort. Each routine must achieve *reuse quality*. It does not matter if you believe that no one else will look at the routine again—that is a self-defeating assumption. A routine that is ready for reuse must meet the following criteria:

- It must have a clear and well-articulated purpose.
- It must perform its function accurately and efficiently.
- It must be robust enough to survive abuse, misuse, or a hostile environment.
- It must be understandable enough for others to use and adapt easily.

The SPF is based on the concept of the Safe Procedure. A Safe Procedure is a routine that meets all SPF standards and achieves reuse quality based on the criteria mentioned.

7.2   Safe Procedures

Safe Procedures are the skeleton of the SPF. They are certified to be safe for use in any situation. Any user of a Safe Procedure can quickly understand its operation and can feel assured that it meets minimal standards and levels of quality.

All routines do have users, whether they be programmers, end users, or both. Therefore, all routines have an interface of some sort. It may be a graphical interface or simply the calling signature of a routine. The interface of each SPF routine should meet the following standards of quality by being:

- *Clear:* The interface must be unambiguous and intuitive to the user.
- *Consistent:* The interface must be internally consistent and consistent with other components.
- *Robust:* The interface must be robust enough to handle any input appropriately.
- *Flexible:* The interface must be flexible enough to handle a variety of input.

All Safe Procedures must meet the previous general objectives by:

- *Following the Golden Rule of Error Coding.* This means that they must be fully error coded. They must prevent all errors that can be both anticipated and prevented; they must handle all errors that can be anticipated but not prevented; and they must trap all errors that cannot be anticipated.
- *Behaving defensively.* They must take responsibility for validating all arguments.

- *Behaving offensively.* They must expose errors early—not suppress them—and they must report errors effectively.

- *Being elegant.* They must be simple, not complex in design and must effectively reuse other Safe Procedures.

In addition, Safe Procedures must adhere to the following specific rules:

Procedures

- Use sf, df, and ds only (Section 7.7).
- Return an SEM from an sf or df (Sections 7.3, 7.5).

Variables

- Always use Option Explicit (Section 4.1.1).
- Explicitly type variables (Section 4.1.2).
- Avoid DefType statements (Section 4.1.3).
- Use specific data types (Section 4.1.4).
- Initialize all variables (Section 4.1.5).
- Use one variable per line (Section 4.1.6).
- Use TypeName, VarType, and TypeOf (Section 4.1.7).
- Use Enumerations (Section 4.1.8).

Arguments

- Always use ByVal or ByRef (Section 4.2.1).
- Pass all arguments ByVal unless there is a specific reason to pass ByRef (Section 4.2.1).
- Explicitly type arguments (Section 4.2.2).
- Set explicit default values for optional arguments (Section 4.2.3).
- Validate all arguments (Section 4.2.4).
- Avoid using Variant data types except as arguments (Section 4.2.4).

Arrays

- Never assume lower array bounds (Section 4.3.1).
- Don't hard code array bounds (Section 4.3.2).
- Avoid using Option Base (Section 4.3.3).

Coding

- Always include an Else (Heading 4.4.1).
- Avoid using default properties (Heading 4.4.2).
- Avoid mixing data types in expressions (Heading 4.4.3).

- Use constants (Heading 4.4.4).
- Avoid operator precedence (Heading 4.4.5).
- Use parentheses liberally to communicate clearly to others (Heading 4.4.5).
- Check string lengths (Heading 4.4.6).
- Close all open objects (Heading 4.4.7).
- Set Objects to Nothing (Heading 4.4.8).
- Always explicitly turn off error trapping (Heading 4.4.9).
- Never assume anything about the external world (Heading 4.4.10).
- Don't cut and paste (Heading 4.4.11).
- Use + and & properly (Heading 4.4.12).
- Pseudo-code (Heading 4.4.13).
- Avoid using class properties. Use methods to set properties or arguments passed to methods as alternatives (Heading 7.7).
- Make sure each code block is like a little routine, having only one clear, complete function (Heading 7.10).
- Don't use clever tricks. Use slower, simpler code if it is clearer (Section 7.16).
- Use Public and Private instead of Dim and Global (Heading 7.13).
- Avoid the use of static routines.
- Always put your On Error Goto before local dimension statements (these can fail also) (Heading 5.15).
- Declare local variables as Static in recursive routines to avoid stack overflow. (Static variables are stored in the memory heap, not the stack.)

Error Handling

- Use in-line error handlers (Heading 5.25).
- Disable error handling after each block (Heading 5.14).

Documentation

- Provide a standard procedure header (Heading 7.16.1).
- Name variables and procedures consistently (Heading 7.16).
- Use standard prefixes for every name.
- Document any tricks you do include very well (Section 7.16).
- Comment each code block with a clear statement of purpose (Heading 7.16).
- Indent consistently. To limit horizontal line widths, use the minimum tab width that forms easily recognizable blocks. Remember you are

writing for others. Two to four spaces are usually enough for most monitors and font combinations.

There are three types of Safe Procedures:

- Safe functions
- Defensive functions
- Defensive subroutines

The following sections present these three types of Safe Procedures in detail. Each of these types must meet all of the requirements just specified. In addition, each type of Safe Procedure has some additional specifications.

Programmers know exactly what to expect from a Safe Procedure by its prefix. They know that it is error protected, and they know how it returns error information. They know the calling conventions of the routine. If they need to inspect or maintain it, they should feel immediately comfortable with how it is written.

7.3 Safe Functions

Safe Functions are the backbone of the SPF. Your application could consist entirely of Safe Functions. Name your Safe Functions just as you would any other function, but start it with the "sf" prefix to identify it as a Safe Function.

A Safe Function returns a string. The returned string is a formatted **Safe Error Message (SEM).** This response provides a consistent error messaging mechanism. The SPF is built around a standard error messaging system. If the return value of a Safe Function is an empty string, then that function succeeded. If the return string is not empty, then the calling routine will be able to handle the returned error.

Calling routines should check the SEM returned by an sf after every call, unless there is truly no need to take action in the event of an error. If the return value is not empty, the calling function can take a number of actions, depending on the program logic.

7.3.1 Ignore the Error

Situations arise in which you legitimately don't mind if an error occurs. In this case you can continue on, effectively suppressing or ignoring the error. The example in Listing 7.1 illustrates this:

LISTING 7.1

```
Private Sub txtNumber_LostFocus()

  If Not IsNumeric(txtNumber.Text) Then
    MsgBox "You must enter a number.", vbCritical
```

```
      sfFocus txtNumber
   End If

End Sub
```

Notice that although the sfFocus Safe Function returns an error message according to the standard specification, this return value is ignored by the calling routine.

The example in Listing 7.1 illustrates other elements of good preventative programming. The LostFocus event of the text entry box validates a user entry as numeric. If it is not numeric, the code alerts the user and returns focus to the text box.

As mentioned earlier in the book, the SetFocus is fragile. This code protects itself by using a safe wrapper. Since failing to set focus is not a critical error, the application does not respond if an error is returned. It simply continues on after the statement.

Why return an error message if the calling routine doesn't respond to it? It would be an assumption that no one will care about it in the future. Long-term programs don't make assumption such as this.

7.3.2 Report the Error

Reporting the error condition to the user is another option. Listing 7.2 demonstrates a variation of the example shown in Listing 7.1. In this example, a Safe Function named sfValidateNumber is used to perform more detailed tests on the user entry. If an error occurs, then the calling function reports the error to the user.

LISTING 7.2

```
Private Sub txtNumber_LostFocus()

Dim strSEM As String

   strSEM = sfValidateNumber(txtNumber.Text)
   If strSEM <> "" Then
     MsgBox strSEM
     sfFocus txtNumber
   End If

End Sub
```

7.3.3 Pass Back the Error

A third option is to pass the SEM back to the calling procedure. The purpose of the following example is to validate a number as a percentage. To do this, one safe procedure calls an sfValidateNumber() routine. If the second safe procedure returns an error, the first one passes it back to the calling function (see Listing 7.3).

LISTING 7.3

```
Function sfValidatePercent(ByVal Percent As Variant) As
    String

    'Verify that the value is numeric
    sfValidatePercent = sfValidateNumber(Percent)
    If sfValidatePercent <> "" Then Exit Function

    'Verify that the number is between 0 and 100
    If Val(Percent) < 0 Or Val(Percent) > 100 Then
        'Return SEM
        sfValidatePercent = "sfValidatePercent, _
            0, Percentage not between 0 and 100."
    Else
        'Return success
        sfValidatePercent = ""
    End IF

End Sub
```

7.3.4 *Return a New Error*

Instead of passing back the SEM, another option is to create a new SEM that is more specific or informative. Listing 7.4 illustrates this principle with an adaptation of the example in Listing 7.3:

LISTING 7.4

```
Function sfValidatePercent(ByVal Percent As Variant) As
    String

    'Verify that the value is numeric
    sfValidatePercent = sfValidateNumber(Percent)
    If sfValidatePercent <> "" Then
        sfValidatePercent = "sfValidatePercent, _
            0, Percentage not numeric."
        Exit Function
    End If

    'Verify that the number is between 0 and 100
    If Val(Percent) < 0 Or Val(Percent) > 100 Then
```

```
    'Return SEM
    sfValidatePercent = "sfValidatePercent, _
       0, Percentage not between 0 and 100."
  Else
    'Return success
    sfValidatePercent = ""
  End IF

End Sub
```

7.3.5 Add to Audit Trail

In some cases, you may want to maintain an audit trail of all errors that occurred. In this case you can append a new SEM to the one that was returned by a Safe Function (see Listing 7.5):

LISTING 7.5

```
Function sfValidatePercent(ByVal Percent As Variant) As
    String

Dim strSEM As String

  'Verify that the value is numeric
  strSEM = sfValidateNumber(Percent)
  'If strSEM <> "" Then
    strSEM = strSEM & "|" & "sfValidatePercent, _
       0, Percentage not numeric."
    sfValidatePercent = strSEM
    Exit Function
  End If

  'Verify that the number is between 0 and 100
  'If Val(Percent) < 0 Or Val(Percent) > 100 Then
    'Return SEM
    sfValidatePercent = "sfValidatePercent, _
       0, Percentage not between 0 and 100."
  Else
    'Return success
    sfValidatePercent = ""
  End IF

End Sub
```

When adding error messages together in a Safe Error Message, by convention the most recent error messages come first. The next section looks at the structure of the Safe Error Message in greater detail.

7.3.6 *Handle the Error*

The final option is to handle the error. Handling the error means determining which specific error occurred and taking appropriate corrective action. The next chapter provides some simple utility routines you can use to determine the error codes returned in a Safe Error Message.

7.4 Safe Error Messages

All Safe Functions return a Safe Error Message (SEM). The SEM includes all error information so that the Err object does not need to be referenced.

A SEM can contain one or more separate error messages delimited by vertical bars:

StrSEM = "Error Message A | Error Message B | Error Message C"

This example might be the structure of an error message created if Routine A calls Routine B, which calls Routine C. Routine C would create "Error Message C." Routine B would add "Error Message B," and Routine A could add "Error Message A."

Each error message (A, B, and C) in the complete SEM consists of three fields delimited by commas. The first field is the name of the routine in which the error occurred. The second field is the number of the error. This could be Err.Number or any application-defined error number. The third field is a description of the error. The description could be Err.Description or any error message fabricated by the application.

The following are examples of the hypothetical error messages included above:

Error Message A = "Routine A, 1, Divide by Zero"
Error Message B = "Routine B, 2, Invalid entry"
Error Message C = "Routine C, 3, Your entry was invalid."

The complete error message for our example would then be:

"Routine A, 1, Divide by Zero | Routine B, 2, Invalid entry | Routine C, 3, Your entry was invalid."

This SEM tells us not that three errors occurred, but that one error occurred which was passed back through two safe routines. It provides an audit trail that allows us to accurately debug this error. Of course, each routine can add its own detailed information to the description to assist with debugging. For example, each routine could include the values of any relevant variables.

It is not advised to present this entire error message to the user. Usually you will only wish to display the most recent error message in a SEM and write the full error message to an error log for debugging purposes. The next chapter demonstrates some simple functions that you can use to manage these Safe Error Messages.

> *You must handle the returned SEM immediately after returning from every Safe Procedure you call.*

7.5 Defensive Functions

Defensive Functions are an alternative to the Safe Function. They return a value rather than a SEM. This type of function begins with the "df" prefix. Use a df *only:*

- When it *greatly* benefits in-line functions with no assignment.
- When no errors can be generated or all errors can be suppressed.
- When there is no need to return error information.

Listing 7.6 shows an example of a Defensive Function designed to safely assign a variant to a string variable:

LISTING 7.6

```
Function dfVntToTrimStr(ByVal StringVar As Variant) As
    String

On Error Goto ErrTrap

    dfVntToTrimStr = ""
    If IsNull(StringVar) Then Exit Function
    dfVntToTrimStr = Trim$(StringVar)

    On Error GoTo 0
    Exit Function

ErrTrap:
    On Error GoTo 0

End Function
```

This df is a particularly useful one and one of the routines I use often in my own applications. I use it when assigning a value to a string variable. It protects against Null assignment errors and also ensures that any padded string, such as a database text field, is trimmed.

Notice that it returns a string, but it is not an SEM string. This routine could have been written as a Safe Function, returning the new string by reference. However, this function is used so frequently that it has great value by requiring no more than one line of code to make an assignment. Also, there is no need to return error information from this function. It is purely a protective function, and it is capable of handling any error that might occur.

Listing 7.7 shows an example of how it is used:

LISTING 7.7

```
Function sfDisplayRecord (rs As Variant) As String

On Error Goto ErrTrap

    sfDisplayRecord = ""

    'Validate the recordset argument has a current record
    If Not dfIsRecord(rs) Then
        sfDisplayRecord = "sfDisplayRecordset, 0, _
                        Invalid Record"
        Exit Function
    End If

    txtName.Text = dfVntToTrimStr(rs.Fields("Name").Value)
    txtSSN.Text = dfVntToTrimStr(rs.Fields("SSN").Value)
    txtZip.Text = dfVntToTrimStr(rs.Fields("ZipCode").Value)

    On Error GoTo 0
    Exit Function

ErrTrap:
    sfDisplayRecord = "sfDisplayRecord, Err.Number, _
                    Err.Description
    On Error GoTo 0

End Function
```

Notice that in this example, another Defensive Function, dfIsRecordset, is used to validate the single argument. Notice also how the sample Safe Function returns an SEM in the event of an error.

7.6 Defensive Subroutines

Defensive Subroutines must meet all the requirements of Safe Procedures. They are given names beginning with the "ds" prefix. This naming convention explicitly identifies a Safe Procedure as a Defensive Subroutine.

As in all Safe Procedures, a Defensive Subroutine must be completely protected by error prevention, error handling, and error trapping. The main difference is that it does not return any error information. It is expected to appropriately handle all errors that occur.

Although a ds has no return value, you can still pass back values by reference. Note, however, that you should never pass back error information by reference. If error information is needed, the sf must be used.

The Defensive Subroutine should be used only in very limited situations:

- When all possible errors can be handled or suppressed.
- When there is no need to return error information.

Since most coding operations can produce errors, a legitimate example of a Defensive Subroutine is a rarity. Even if you aren't worried about any potential error when you write the subroutine, reuse-quality demands that you return the information to meet unanticipated future needs. When in doubt, you should use a Safe Function. You can ignore the error information if you wish, but future situations might benefit from the error information.

Despite its limited usefulness, the Defensive Subroutine is still provided for cases in which truly no meaningful error information will be returned. In these cases, it is better to use a ds than a typical subroutine, since the ds tells the user that all SPF conventions have been followed.

7.7 Safe Classes

When you develop class modules, these segments can fit into the Safe Programming Framework very easily. Any class methods can be made safe procedures. Starting a method name with the sf, df, or ds prefix clearly communicates to the user that it is a safe procedure.

Properties have one problem: when you try to set or retrieve a property, this process can fail. In the event of an error, the typical action performed is to raise an error. As mentioned earlier, raising errors is not the most effective error-coding technique. It adds no further diagnostic information and simply tosses the error back into the run-time system.

There are alternatives to properties that offer benefits and fit more consistently within the SPF strategy. One beneficial alternative is using safe methods to set values rather than using properties. See Listing 7.8, for example:

LISTING 7.8

```
'Setting a variable through a property
On Error Resume Next
cls.Caption = "Hello"
If Err.Number <> 0 then Exit Sub

'Setting a variable in a class through a method
If cls.sfSetCaption("Hello") <> "" Then Exit Sub
```

The latter approach in Listing 7.8 is recommended because, being more consistent with the SPF, it can provide more precise error information. A second approach is using arguments to class methods rather than setting properties, and then calling a method. See Listing 7.9, for example:

LISTING 7.9

```
'Display a hello world message using properties
On Error Resume Next
clsMessage.Caption = "Hello"
If Err.Number <> 0 then Exit Sub
ClsMessage.ShowMessage
If Err.Number <> 0 then Exit Sub

'Display a hello world message using method arguments
If clsMessage.sfShowMessage("Hello") <> "" Then Exit Sub
```

Again, the latter approach is preferred. It is not only more code-efficient, but it also provides a closer integration of property and method. It allows more localized and efficient error coding and response coding as well. For cases in which you need to set a variable number of properties, named arguments can give you maximum flexibility. See Listing 7.10, for example:

LISTING 7.10

```
'Display a hello world message using properties
On Error Resume Next
clsMessage.Caption = "Hello"
If Err.Number <> 0 then Exit Sub
clsMessage.Icon = vbInformation
If Err.Number <> 0 then Exit Sub
ClsMessage.ShowMessage
If Err.Number <> 0 then Exit Sub

'Display a hello world message using named arguments
```

```
If clsMessage.sfShowMessage(Icon:=vbInformation, _
            Caption:="Hello") <> "" Then Exit Sub
```

By using named arguments, you can set any number of "properties" in the same call as the method that will use them. This approach is commonly used in many large and complex object models, such as the Word object model. There is no reason not to use the same powerful approach in your classes—and still retain complete compatibility with the Safe Programming Framework.

The only real loss when not using properties is in the design-time access of ActiveX control properties through the Property Window. You can still provide both, offering properties for design-time settings and methods, and arguments for run-time properties. In any event, it is beneficial to minimize design-time settings, since these should be avoided where possible.

Avoid using class properties.

7.8   Reuse of SPF Procedures

Since no code should be written twice, SPF routines should use other SPF routines wherever those functions are required. Routines should not contain code blocks that reinvent functionality when it is already available in other SPF routines or can be copied from other routines.

Whenever you start to cut and paste a block of code, it should trigger the question, "Shouldn't I make this a reusable function?"

7.9   Self-Contained Procedures

Each function should be self-contained. It should not rely on globals or other sources for state information that could be communicated through arguments or properties. Remember that at any point in the future, a routine not currently being reused should be ready for reuse.

7.10   Code Blocks

Not only should routines be reused and reusable, but each block of code in a routine should be easily reusable. Each block should have a single, clear purpose. If at any point in the future you would like to reuse that block of code, you should be able to adapt that functionality to a new, reusable routine with little effort.

Although the standard does not require dimensioning local variables at the point of use, many other strategies will ensure that code blocks are self-contained:

- Open and close files in the same block.
- Enable and disable error handling in the same block.
- Perform all error handling in-line within the same block.
- Initialize all variables at the start of the block.
- Open and close recordsets in same block.

7.11 Naming Conventions

All Safe Procedures should follow the sf, df, and ds name prefix convention. This practice clearly tells the user that the routine follows standard conventions and assures him or her that it meets quality error-coding standards. Prefixes other than sf, df, and ds should not be used for functions, methods, properties, or arguments. Prefixes should be used consistently for variables and objects to indicate type and scope. (See Appendix A, "Variable Naming Conventions," for a recommended listing of specific prefixes.)

The main part of function names should be clear and unambiguous. The same holds true for arguments, properties, and methods. If their purpose is truly atomic, naming should not be difficult. If you find it difficult to name a procedure, ask yourself whether it should really be two separate procedures.

Use a name just long enough to communicate the purpose clearly. Typically you will use either a noun-verb or verb-noun combination, depending on which form results in a more consistent series of functions.

For example, let's imagine you could name a function either ShowPlot or PlotShow. The deciding factor should be the other functions. If you are showing many different plots, then a Show__ series would result in all Show functions appearing together. On the other hand, if you are not showing many plots, but are performing a large number of different operations with the plot, then a Plot__ series would be better. Avoid using superfluous words, such as in the name ShowThePlot.

Collections should be plural, and member objects should be singular. For example, Buttons is expected to be a collection of Button objects.

7.12 Arguments

The SPF specifies accepting all arguments as variants. This is perhaps the most controversial element of the standard. It does make sense from the perspective of unambiguous programming to explicitly type all arguments as string, long, and so on. However in practice, you may need to pass some variables as variant, such as properties intrinsic to Visual Basic and related objects. To impose a more tightly specified calling signature goes against the grain. If you attempt this, you will find that you have one calling scheme for your custom routines and another for built-in routines. You have then created an internal inconsistently in your application.

Also, the standard aims to make our routines highly reusable. Variant arguments assure the greatest flexibility and ease of reuse. For example, the use of variant arguments assures the greatest portability to and from VBScript. In VBScript, variants are the only type of argument supported.

A good defensive routine takes on the burden of validating all arguments in any case. Validation must be completed for all arguments, regardless of type. It only takes a bit more code to ensure that the variant is a valid type.

From the perspectives of consistency, reuse, and defensive programming, it makes sense to use variant arguments. I suggest, therefore, to pass all arguments as variant. This habit makes your routine flexible enough to handle any situation and forces you to validate arguments completely. Remember that you want your arguments to be flexible. Why force an argument to be an integer when a valid value of a long would be acceptable as well?

ANECDOTE: Variant Arguments

Because I was weaned on other languages, it was not easy for me personally to accept variant arguments. In previous versions of a personal programming standard, I specified the rigid typing of arguments.

It simply did not work. I found myself fighting against Visual Basic commands constantly. Too often I found myself frustrated and limited by argument typing. I ended up repeating code on the calling side to ensure that the correct argument type was passed. This was not effective reuse, compared to conversion and validation completed in one place within the routine.

Visual Basic finally forced me to accept that variants were the way to manage this difficulty. This is a perfect example of customizing your approach to make the most effective use of the language, rather than trying to impose general programming wisdom.

The biggest compromise that you must make in order to gain the benefits of using variants is the loss of the IntelliSense feature to view argument information. This Visual Basic feature displays the argument list as a ToolTip when you type it in. If the argument type is Variant, then you do not see specific type information, as you would in Figure 7.1.

You can compensate for loss of the argument list ToolTips in a number of ways. You can name your arguments to give a good sense of what type of argument is expected.

Look, for example, at the following safe procedure:

```
dfValidateRecordset(rs As Variant)
```

Even though the argument is a variant, the expectation is clear. IntelliSense is a useful feature, but it is not critical to your goals. It is a shame to lose that feature, but the value of using variants is greater.

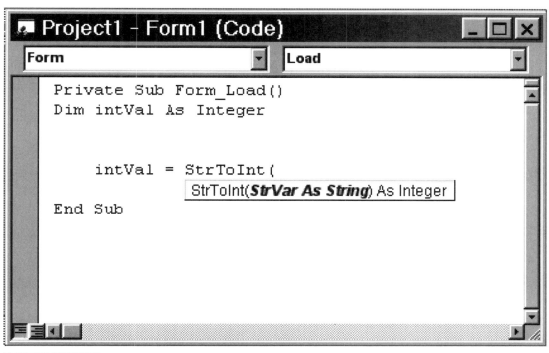

FIGURE 7.1   Using IntelliSense to view the argument list

Standard prefixes should be used to name your arguments, just as you name variables, so that they communicate the expected variable type clearly. Note that if your routine accepts variants, you can pass in any type of variable that can be converted to the expected type. For example, consider the following routine:

sfFindUserByID(intID As Variant)

This routine expects an integer, but since it accepts a variant, you can pass it along in the correct range, a variant, or even a string that can be converted to an integer. It should be the responsibility of sfFindUserByID to perform the appropriate conversions. This method gives the calling routine the greatest flexibility and minimizes coding.

7.13   Limited Scope

In order to ensure that your code is reusable, you should minimize the scope of all objects. This step is important to assure that code is self-contained and does not require external support in order to do its job.

- Use local variables before modular variables.
- Use modular level variables before global variables.
- Use static locals as an alternative to modular variables.

In order to explicitly and clearly define scope, use the keywords Private and Public rather than the older Dim and Global.

7.14   Counter Variables

Although the SPF calls for adherence to naming conventions for variables, an exception is made for the standard loop counters, i, j, and k. It is permissible to use them as local counters only. Although it violates the naming conventions, programmers are so familiar and comfortable with these terms that using them actually improves the readability and maintainability of the code.

You may use i, j, and k for naming your local loop counters.

7.15   Revision Numbering

It is important that all compiled executable code follow a consistent revision numbering scheme. Visual Basic supports a revision numbering scheme with three parts: Major, Minor, and Revision. In the version number "1.2.3" for example, 1 is the Major version number, 2 is the Minor version number, and 3 is the Revision number. The following are SPF criteria for revision numbering:

- Increment the Revision number as each build is released during development.
- Increment the Minor number at key milestones, such as when a new project phase is initiated. Set the Revision number to zero when the Minor number is incremented.
- Increment the Major revision number when you start a new generational version of the project. Set the Minor and Revision numbers to zero.

7.16   Reuse-Quality Documentation

Possibly the one task that developers dislike more than any other is documentation. After all, if you are documenting, then you are not developing. Documenting is a part of coding, however, and a very important one. Earlier it was pointed out that even broken code that is clearly written and maintainable is superior to working code that can't be maintained. By extension, it could be argued that a program consisting of good pseudo-code with no working code is more valuable in the long term than working code with poor comments.

It is essential to add the optimum amount of internal documentation so that others can understand what the code is doing. You need to include enough to describe, clarify, and expand on the code. However, if you add too much verbiage, the comments interfere with the code and reduce readability. Some comments are essential, but too many are counterproductive.

The optimal amount of commenting is not the same for all code. If code is written unsystematically with many cute tricks, then a considerable amount of commenting may be required to clarify it. However, code written for others that follows the SPF guidelines needs very little commenting to augment the code.

The following are some general guidelines for commenting with your Safe Procedures:

- Add a comment in the declarations section of a module or form to explain its purpose and to document any copyright information and usage notes.

- Include a header at the top of each Safe Procedure, as described below.

- Include short procedure descriptions to appear in the Object browser.

- Add one comment line at the top of each code block to explain its purpose.

- Stating the obvious is not commenting. The trick to commenting is anticipating user questions and adding value with your comments.

- In most cases, if you cannot comment a code block in one line, either your comments are too verbose or your code block should be broken up.

- Include additional comments when necessary to explain nonobvious code.

- Avoid banner comment lines, such as a row of asterisks or dashes designed to draw attention without communicating any useful information. They reduce the amount of useful content visible on screen without significantly benefiting the user. Use them only for very important comment blocks, such as the block at the procedure head.

- Add revision comments when modifying existing code, and clean these up periodically. See 7.16.3 for additional suggestions.

- Include a Readme file, manual, or a Help File for external documentation.

7.16.1 *Procedure Headers*

At the head of each procedure, include the following information:

Purpose: A short description of what this function will do.

Inputs: A list of all input arguments that the function is not changing with short descriptions. Typically, these should be passed ByVal.

Passed: A list of all input arguments that the function may change, with short descriptions. These are values passed ByRef that you will be passing back to the calling routine.

Returns: A Safe Error Message in the case of a Safe Function, or an actual value in the case of a Defensive Function.

Outputs: Any code that may be output from the function. Outputs differ from return values in that these are not returned to the calling routine but ones written to a device. For example, if the function writes to a disk or printer, that would be an output.

Notes: Any information about your routine that is not really covered by the above categories but is pertinent to the use of the function.

Usage: How the function is expected to be used. This statement can be an example that demonstrates calling your function.

Revisions: Use them sparingly. Only include revisions that change the expected functionality of the procedure. For example:

Author: mm/dd/yyyy—Original

Revisionist Initials: mm/dd/yyyy—Brief description of revision

This may seem like an awfully large header, but the descriptions above are generally much longer than the actual information. It helps to create a standard header template that you can cut and paste quickly into every new procedure.

7.16.2 *A Sample Header*

None of the example procedures up to this point have displayed an SPF header. The following is a sample header for a simple procedure. You will see many more examples in the next chapter, which presents actual SPF routines.

The header may seem large, but it is important. All lines should be included, even if they say "None" or "Nothing." This practice ensures that all lines are explicitly documented and also provides a structure if header information should ever change.

LISTING 7.11

```
Sub dsShowMsg(ByVal Message As Variant)
'------------------------------
'Purpose:    Display an informational message box
'Inputs:     Message is the string to display
'Passed:     None
'Returns:    Nothing
'Outputs:    None
```

```
'Notes:     If Message is invalid,
'           no message will be displayed
'Usage:     dsShowMsg "New High Score"
'Revisions: 6/23/99 Tyson Gill - Original
'--------------------------

   On Error Resume Next
   MsgBox Message, vbInformation
   On Error GoTo 0

End Sub
```

7.16.3 *Revision History Comments*

One practice that many programmers consider valuable is to add revision comments in the code. Whenever a change is made, the programmer enters his or her name, the date, and a description of the change.

The benefit of revision notes is their ability to inform team members or remind the primary programmer exactly what was changed and why. With this information available, if the changes should cause unanticipated problems, it is much easier to identify and diagnose the source of these problems.

The disadvantage of revision notes is that they quickly pile up. A simple routine can become very long very quickly with line after line of revision notes. An overload of comments can have an adverse impact on the readability of the code. Moreover, the lifetime of revision notes is relatively short. No one generally cares about the content of any revision notes prior to the last one or two. All the earlier revision notes are obsolete baggage.

To achieve the benefit of revision notes without cluttering up the code, you can purge revision notes periodically. The SPF calls for this to be done each time the Minor revision number is changed. Presumably at this point, testing has been completed and the changed functionality has passed.

The revision comments can be cleaned up easily if a standard identification is used that makes search and replace easy. Alternatively, a product like VB Compress Pro can be used to automatically clean up revision comments at the same time as the cleanup of unreferenced variables is performed.

Remember that if you are using revision control software such as Microsoft SourceSafe, then you always have access to the revision comments for previous revisions without having to keep them in the current working version.

7.17 Cleanup

Before finishing your SPF routine, you must make sure you have cleaned up any unused variables, constants, or procedures. This useless material detracts from the long-term maintainability of the code.

NOTE: Cleanup

I always clean up my code with a product called VB Compress Pro available from Whippleware. This program analyzes the source code and reports any unused objects. The best time to clean up is just prior to a major version upgrade or just prior to shipping. Doing so ensures that your code is clean and tidy for the next person to move in. VB Compress Pro will optionally clean these up for you automatically or simply create a report, and you can clean up the unused variables yourself.

7.18   Using the SPF

At first glance, it might seem as though adhering to the SPF requires a great deal of work. But you will almost certainly find that once you get used to using it, your programming work will be much easier. You won't need to redesign each routine or study routines that other programmers have written to understand their operation.

You might be concerned that following a standard will inhibit the creative process, producing lower quality cookie-cutter results. This universal sort of fear often appears whenever any standard is adopted. You will find that this is not true. If anything, adopting a standard will make it easier for you to move past the tedious part of programming and spend more time on the creative aspects.

We cannot say that the standard has no drawbacks. Compromises must be made any time a standard is adopted. You can feel free to adapt this standard to best meet your needs. But if you do, make sure your changes contribute to a cohesive, synergistic standard. Do not make changes merely to cater to individual preferences.

The details of the standard are important. Certainly, adopting a bad standard serves no purpose. However, at some point further refinement becomes a matter of trade-offs. At that point it becomes preferable to adopt what you have, rather than continue to debate the trade-offs of particular options.

The Safe Programming Framework is not the only approach that will work, but it is a good one. As you follow it, you will find that any concessions you must make to conform to the framework will be far outweighed by the benefits it will bring.

7.19   Implementing the Standard

This chapter has presented a description of the Safe Programming Framework. Chapter 8 provides sample SPF code to give you a much more concrete idea of how it works.

In order for a coding standard to be effective in a team environment, it must be adopted consistently by all team members. Chapter 9 offers suggestions and strategies for deploying the SPF in a corporate environment.

SPF Sampler

In the last chapter, the Safe Programming Framework (SPF) was introduced to provide a concrete plan for implementing the Smart Coding Triangle. This chapter provides a sampler of Safe Procedures to give you intimate familiarity with the SPF.

8.1   General Structure

Most Safe Procedures should follow the same basic structure. This is, in fact, one of the strengths of the framework. No matter what you write, you can approach it in the same way. Notice that the structure in Listing 8.1 accepts a wide range of argument types, converts and validates them, calls other Safe Procedures, traps unanticipated errors, and returns a Safe Error Message.

LISTING 8.1   The general Safe Procedure structure

```
Function sfProcedure(ByVal strName As Variant, ByRef _
                 lngNumber As Variant, Optional ByVal _
                 intOption As Variant = 1) As String
'------------------------------
'Purpose:   Do an operation and return a SEM
'Inputs:    strName should convert to a string and is
'           passed ByVal
```

```
'            intOption is optional and should convert to
'            an integer
'Passed:     lngNumber should convert to a long and is
'            passed ByVal
'Returns:    Safe Error Message
'Outputs:    None
'Notes:      Notice that the Optional value has a default value
'Usage:      strSEM = sfProcedure(vntString, "5", lngOption)
'----------------------------

On Error Goto ErrTrap

'Dimension locals. Errors could occur here!

    'Convert and validate all arguments
    strName = dfVntToTrimStr(strName)
    lngNumber = dfVntToLng(lngNumber)
    intOption = dfVntToInt(intOption)
    If intOption < OPT_MIN Or intOption > OPT_MAX Then
       sfProcedure = sfSEMCreate("sfProcedure", 0, _
                "Invalid intOption: " & cstr(intOption))
    End If

    'Do procedure step one
    sfProcedure = sfProc1(strName)
    If sfProcedure <> "" Then Exit Function

    'Do procedure step two
    Select Case intOption
       Case OPT1
          sfProcedure = sfProc1(strName, lngNumber)
          If sfProcedure <> "" Then Exit Function
       Case OPT2
          sfProcedure = sfProc2(strName, lngNumber)
          If sfProcedure <> "" Then Exit Function
       Case Else
          'Code offensively
          sfProcedure = sfSEMCreate("sfProcedure", 0, _
                     "Invalid Else: " & intOption)
    End Select

    'Be sure to exit function prior to error trap
    Exit Function

ErrTrap:
```

```
'Return error to calling procedure
'The topmost procedure can decide whether to log or _
    report the error
sfProcedure = sfSEMCreate("sfProcedure", Err.Number, _
    Err.Desciption)

'Clear and explicitly disable error handler
On Error Goto 0
```

```
End Function
```

Notice that no error handling is performed in the error handling block of this procedure skeleton. The error trap is used for just that, simple error trapping. Although there appears to be little error handling code, this structure should yield a fully error-coded function. It achieves the benefits of in-line error handling, without cluttering the code, by means of Safe Procedures.

In the sections that follow, examples of routines are provided that follow the same general framework. These sample routines are broken down into six sections:

- Safe Error Utilities
- Array Handling
- Type Conversion and Data Validation
- String Handling
- Forms and Controls
- Database Routines

The routines presented here are not intended to provide a comprehensive library. It is up to you to create your own. They are presented only to illustrate the SPF and to offer a representative sampling of the range and type of Safe Procedures that you may wish to build on and leverage.

8.2 Safe Error Utilities

Effective error messaging must become a key part of any programming standard. It is so important, in fact, that the Safe Programming Framework was essentially built around the Safe Error Message. Many other approaches, such as using error DLLs or error classes, have been tried over the years, but they lacked the simplicity and directness of the SEM.

As described in the last chapter, the Safe Error Message (SEM) can contain one or more error messages, forming an error trail. Each error message consists of three pieces of information: the procedure name, the error number, and the description of that particular error. You could easily expand the SEM to include additional information, such as version numbers and date/time of the error. The content was kept to the minimum for this sample set. The following reusable Safe Procedures allow you to work with Safe Error Messages efficiently.

8.2.1 Create a Safe Error Message

The first routine makes it easy to create a new Safe Error Message. You simply pass the routine the name of the routine that generated the error, the error code number, and the error description. Of course, the error number of the message can identify any of the standard Visual Basic errors or your own application-defined errors. You can also optionally pass it the previous SEM in order to create an audit trail (see Listing 8.2).

LISTING 8.2   Creating a Safe Error Message (SEM)

```
Function dfSemCreate(ByVal strCallingRoutine As Variant, _
                     ByVal lngErrorCode As Variant, _
                     ByVal strErrorDetails As Variant, _
                     Optional ByVal strPrevSEM As Variant _
                     = "") As String
'------------------------------
'Purpose:    Create a Safe Error Message (SEM)
'Inputs:     strCallingRoutine is the name of the calling
'            routine
'            lngErrorCode is the VB or application-specific
'            error number
'            strPrevSEM is the optional value of the
'            previous SEM
'Passed:     None
'Returns:    Safe Error Message
'Outputs:    None
'Notes:      The returned SEM could be an error generated
'            in this routine
'Usage:      strSEM = dfSemCreate("RoutineName", _
'                       Err.Number, Err.Description, strSEM)
'            strSEM = dfSemCreate("RoutineName", -45, _
'                       "Application defined error")
'------------------------------

On Error Goto ErrTrap

    'Convert and validate all arguments
    strCallingRoutine = dfVntToTrimStr(strCallingRoutine)
```

```
    lngErrorCode = dfVntToLng(lngErrorCode)
    strErrorDetails = dfVntToTrimStr(strErrorDetails)
    strPrevSEM = dfVntToTrimStr(strPrevSEM)

    'Create the SEM
    dfSemCreate = strPrevSEM & strCallingRoutine & vbTab & _
          CStr(lngErrorCode) & vbTab & strErrorDetails & vbLf

    Exit Function

ErrTrap:
    'If there is an error in this routine, return that error.
    dfSemCreate = "dfSemCreate" & vbTab & _
                  CStr(Err.Number) & vbTab & _
                  "Could not create Safe Error Message." & vbLf
    On Error GoTo 0
End Function
```

8.2.2   Count Errors in a Safe Error Message

Since a Safe Error Message can contain any number of separate error messages, the routine in Listing 8.3 returns a count of these messages. Notice that this routine has no apparent error handling. Since it uses only Safe Functions, this is theoretically unnecessary. However, you may still wish to protect this code with an error trap rather than trust even Safe Functions. This precaution is especially important if this code is going to be executed within MTS.

LISTING 8.3   Counting errors in a Safe Error Message (SEM)

```
Function sfSemCount(ByVal strSEM As String, _
                 ByRef intSemCount As Variant) As String
'-----------------------------
'Purpose:    Count the number of messages in a Safe Error
'            Message (SEM)
'Inputs:     strSEM is the error message to count
'Passed:     intSemCount is the number of error messages
'Returns:    Safe Error Message
'Outputs:    None
'Notes:      None
'Usage:      sfSemCount strSem, lngErrCount
'-----------------------------

On Error Goto ErrTrap

    'Validate all arguments
```

```
        strSEM = dfVntToTrimStr(strSEM)
        intSemCount = dfVntToInt(intSemCount)

        'Get the error count
        sfSemCount = sfDelimitedCount(strSEM, intSemCount, vbLf)
        If sfSemCount <> "" Then
            'An error occurred. Pass back zero.
            intSemCount = 0
            Exit Function
        End If

        'Success. Pass back number of errors in SEM.
        'Error count will be one less since SEM ends with a vbLf
        intSemCount = intSemCount - 1

        Exit Function

ErrTrap:
    sfSemCount = "sfSemCount" & vbTab & _
                 Err.Number & vbTab & _
                 Err.Description & vbLf
    On Error GoTo 0
End Function
```

8.2.3 Parse a Safe Error Message

Once you create a SEM and you know how many error messages it contains, the next step might be to retrieve the information from a particular error message. The routine in Listing 8.4 can be used to parse a Safe Error Message. It returns the name of the calling routine, the error code, and the error details for any particular message. The message number is passed as an optional argument that defaults to one.

LISTING 8.4   Parsing a Safe Error Message (SEM)

```
Function sfSemParse(ByVal strSEM As Variant, _
            ByRef strCallingRoutine As Variant, _
            ByRef lngErrorCode As Variant, _
            ByRef strErrorDetails As Variant, _
            Optional intSemNumber As Variant = 1) As String
'-------------------------------
'Purpose:  Parse safe error message (SEM)
'Inputs:   strSEM is the error message to parse
'          intSemNumber is the optional error number to parse
'Passed:   strCallingRoutine is the name of the calling
'          routine
```

```
'            lngErrorCode is the VB or Application-Specific
'            error number
'            strErrorDetails is the SEM details
'Returns:   Safe Error Message
'Outputs:   None
'Notes:     Error number 1, the most recent error number,
'           is the default
'Usage:     sfSemParse strSEM, strCaller, strErrNum,
'           strErrDetails
'-----------------------------


On Error Goto ErrTrap

Dim strFields() As String 'Array to hold error information
Dim intFields As Integer  'The number of fields in the
'                          message

   'Validate all arguments
   strSEM = dfVntToTrimStr(strSEM)
   strCallingRoutine = dfVntToTrimStr(strCallingRoutine)
   strErrorDetails = dfVntToTrimStr(strErrorDetails)
   lngErrorCode = dfVntToLng(lngErrorCode)
   intSemNumber = dfVntToInt(intSemNumber)

   'Get error message segment requested
   sfSemParse = sfDelimitedField(strSEM, intSemNumber, _
                                 strSEM, vbLf)
   If sfSemParse <> "" Then
      sfSemParse = dfSemCreate("sfSemParse", 0, "Could not _
                     get SEM in: " & strSEM, sfSemParse)
      Exit Function
   End If

   'Verify that there is information in that segment
   If strSEM = "" Then
      sfSemParse = dfSemCreate("sfSemParse", 0, "No SEM in: " _
                            & strSEM, "")
      Exit Function
   End If

   'Parse the error information in that segment
   strFields = Split(strSEM, vbTab, 3, vbBinaryCompare)

   'Make sure 3 fields were returned
   sfSemParse = sfArrayCount(strFields, intFields)
```

```
      If sfSemParse <> "" Or intFields <> 3 Then
        sfSemParse = dfSemCreate("sfSemParse", 0, "Not enough _
                           fields in: " & strSEM, sfSemParse)
        Exit Function
      End If

      'Assign values returned by reference
      strCallingRoutine = strFields(0)
      lngErrorCode = strFields(1)
      strErrorDetails = strFields(2)

      Exit Function

ErrTrap:
   sfSemParse = "sfSemParse" & vbTab & _
                CStr(Err.Number) & vbTab & _
                "Could not parse Safe Error Message." & vbLf
   On Error GoTo 0
End Function
```

8.2.4 *Reporting a Safe Error Message*

Once you parse a Safe Error Message, you may want to display it for the user. The details should be user-friendly. The technical description can be obtained from the error number; the code number will probably be meaningful to developers only. The routine in Listing 8.5 simply displays a SEM in a message box. If you are developing a layered application, this function should be called only in the User Layer.

LISTING 8.5   Reporting a Safe Error Message (SEM)

```
Function dsSemReport(ByVal strSEM As Variant)
'------------------------------
'Purpose:   Report a SEM
'Inputs:    SEM is the Safe Error Message to report
'Passed:    None
'Returns:   Nothing
'Outputs:   None
'Notes:     None
'Usage:     dsSemReport strSEM
'------------------------------

On Error Goto ErrTrap
```

```
Dim lngErr As Long        'Parsed error code
Dim strRoutine As String  'Parsed routine name
Dim strDetails As String  'Parsed error details

    'Validate the argument
    strSEM = dfVntToTrimStr(strSEM)

        'Display first error in SEM
    If dsSemParse(strSEM, strRoutine, lngErr, strDetails) _
        <> "" Then
            'Could not parse. May not be an SEM. Simply _
            display string.
            MsgBox strSEM
    Else
            'Display SEM
            MsgBox "Function: " & strRoutine & vbCrLf & _
                "Error Code: " & lngErr & vbCrLf & _
                Error$(lngErr) & vbCrLf & strDetails, _
                vbOKOnly, "Error Report"
    End If
    Exit Function

ErrTrap:
    'If an error occurs in this routine, report it.
    MsgBox "Function: dsSemReport" & vbCrLf & _
        "Error Code: " & Err.Number & vbCrLf & _
        Err.Description, vbOKOnly, "Error Report"
    On Error GoTo 0
End Function
```

In the function in Listing 8.5, a good enhancement would be to add error logging. You could provide an optional parameter that would also cause the error to be logged to the Event Viewer on Windows NT systems or to a log file for other versions of Windows. If running in MTS or some other unattended environment, you will want to disable the message box notification. This single function can be expanded to give you the flexibility you need for any environment.

8.3   Array Handling

The following set of routines accomplishes two goals. First, both demonstrate the safe handling of arrays. Second, together they show how Safe Procedures call each other to build on reusable functionality and provide entry points at many levels.

8.3.1 Getting the Lower Array Bound

This Safe Procedure is a safe wrapper for the Visual Basic LBound function. This routine is designed to return the lower bound. You could create a nearly identical function to return the upper array bound (see Listing 8.6).

LISTING 8.6   Getting the lower array bound

```
Function sfArrayLB(ByRef BoundedArray As Variant, ByRef _
    LowerBound As Variant) As String
'-----------------------------
'Purpose:    Pass back the lower bound of an array
'Inputs:     BoundedArray is the array to be tested
'Passed:     LowerBound is the lower bound of BoundedArray
'Returns:    Safe Error Message
'Outputs:    None
'Notes:      None
'Usage:      strSEM = sfArrayLB(intArray, intLower)
'-----------------------------

On Error Goto ErrTrap

    'Get lower array bound
    'Note an error can occur if BoundedArray has not been
    'instantiated
    LowerBound = LBound(BoundedArray)
    sfArrayLB = "" 'Success

    Exit Function

ErrTrap:
    sfArrayLB = "sfArrayLB" & vbTab & _
                CStr(Err.Number) & vbTab & _
                Err.Description & vbLf
    On Error GoTo 0
End Function
```

8.3.2 Getting Both Array Bounds

The routine in Listing 8.7 builds on the one in Listing 8.6 and its sfArrayUB counterpart. It demonstrates how to use Safe Procedures to call each other, creating a hyper-library of safe routines.

LISTING 8.7   Getting both array bounds

```
Function sfArrayBounds(ByRef BoundedArray As Variant, _
    ByRef LowerBound As Variant, ByRef UpperBound As _
    Variant) As String
'-----------------------------
'Purpose:    Pass back the bounds of an array
'Inputs:     BoundedArray is the array to be tested
'Passed:     LowerBound is the array lower bound
'            UpperBound is the array upper bound
'Returns:    Safe Error Message
'Outputs:    None
'Notes:      None
'Usage:      strSEM = sfArrayBounds(intArray, intLower, intUpper)
'-----------------------------

On Error Goto ErrTrap

    'Get lower bound
    sfArrayBounds = sfArrayLB(BoundedArray, LowerBound)
    If sfArrayBounds <> "" Then Exit Function

    'Get upper bound
    sfArrayBounds = sfArrayUB(BoundedArray, UpperBound)
    If sfArrayBounds <> "" Then Exit Function

    Exit Function

ErrTrap:
    sfArrayBounds = "sfArrayBounds" & vbTab & _
                    CStr(Err.Number) & vbTab & _
                    Err.Description & vbLf
    On Error GoTo 0
End Function
```

Note—Typical Safe Functions

Many of the Safe Procedures presented in this chapter are Defensive Functions (df prefix) as opposed to Safe Functions (sf prefix). These examples should not be representative of your applications.

   This chapter demonstrates so many df functions because the samples shown are mostly low-level building blocks and preventative wrappers. The vast majority of your routines in a full application should be sf procedures that use the relatively few lower-level functions. Most of your routines will be more like sfArrayBounds. They will consist mostly of only two line blocks of Safe Function calls. Although rather boring to show as a sample, sfArrayBounds is most representative of the typical Safe Function.

8.3.3 Getting an Array Count

The Safe Function in Listing 8.8 moves a little farther up this tree of array functions. It uses the sfArrayBounds routine in the previous section to safely determine the count of members in an array.

LISTING 8.8   Getting an array count

```
Function sfArrayCount(ByRef BoundedArray As Variant, _
                      ByRef lngArrayCount As Variant) _
                      As String
'-----------------------------
'Purpose:   Pass back the member count of an array
'Inputs:    BoundedArray is the array to be tested
'Passed:    lngArrayCount is the number of members in
'           BoundedArray
'Returns:   Safe Error Message
'Outputs:   None
'Notes:     None
'Usage:     strSEM = sfArrayCount(intArray, intCount)
'-----------------------------

On Error Goto ErrTrap

Dim lngLower As Long
Dim lngUpper As Long

    'Get array bounds
    sfArrayCount = sfArrayBounds(BoundedArray, lngLower, _
                              lngUpper)
    If sfArrayCount <> "" Then Exit Function

    'Calculate count
    lngArrayCount = lngUpper - lngLower + 1
    sfArrayCount = "" 'Success

    Exit Function

ErrTrap:
    sfArrayCount = "sfArrayCount" & vbTab & _
              CStr(Err.Number) & vbTab & _
              Err.Description & vbLf
    On Error GoTo 0
End Function
```

8.4 Type Conversion and Data Validation

The SPF requires that every routine be responsible for validating its own arguments. It also requires that each routine accept variants and convert them to the required data type. This process requires a great deal of conversion and validation code. It need not translate into a large amount of conversion and validation code, however, if you reuse Safe Procedures for this purpose. In any event, including this code once in your Safe Procedure is far more code efficient and reliable than performing this routine in every calling function.

This section presents some routines to give you a flavor of the kinds of procedures that you should find useful if you are practicing efficient and safe programming. Validation should occur when the variable is converted. For example, when a variant parameter is converted to an integer, validation code may be required to ensure that it falls within an expected range. Such validation should take place in reusable Safe Procedures.

8.4.1 Converting a String

The routine in Listing 8.9 is used to convert a variant to a valid string. This technique is useful not only in converting arguments but also in database operations to safely assign a string field to a string variable. To make the routine more useful for database assignments, the function also trims the resulting string. This process eliminates the padding that some databases perform on strings.

These conversion routines are Defensive Functions. This method is warranted because they always return a valid value, and there is considerable advantage in being able to assign the return value in a single line of code.

LISTING 8.9   Converting a variant to a string

```
Function dfVntToTrimStr(ByVal StringVar As Variant) As
     String
    '-----------------------------
    'Purpose:    Return a trimmed string from a variant that
    '            may be Null
    'Inputs:     StringVar is the variant to convert
    'Passed:     None
    'Returns:    A valid string
    'Outputs:    None
    'Notes:      Useful in database operations or validating
    '            arguments
    'Usage:      strArgument = dfVntToTrimStr(strArgument)
    '            txtName.Text = dfVntToTrimStr(rs("Name"))
    '-----------------------------
```

```
On Error Resume Next

'Initialize return value
dfVntToTrimStr = ""

'Create string
If Not IsNull(StringVar) Then
   dfVntToTrimStr = Trim$(StringVar)
End If

On Error Goto 0

End Function
```

Notice in the routine in Listing 8.9, an On Error Resume Next is used to suppress errors. In this case, this method is legitimate since any subsequent error would result in an empty string being returned. Using this defensive function, we can expect any variant string that cannot be converted successfully to result in an empty string.

8.4.2   Converting a Date

The routine in Listing 8.10 takes a variant and converts it to a valid date string. It accepts an optional format argument.

LISTING 8.10   Converting a variant to a date string

```
Function dfVntToDateStr(ByVal DateVar As Variant,
        Optional ByVal FormatString As Variant =
        "mm/dd/yyyy") As String
'---------------------------
'Purpose:  Return a date string from a variant that may
'          be Null
'Inputs:   DateVar is the variant date such as a recordset
'          datetime field
'          FormatString is an optional VB format
'Passed:   None
'Returns:  Valid date string
'Outputs:  None
'Notes:    If an error occurs, an empty string is returned
'Usage:    strArgument = dfVntToDateStr(strArgument,
'          "mmm dd, yyyy")
'          txtDate.Text = dfVntToDateStr(rs("BirthDate"))
'---------------------------

On Error Goto ErrTrap
```

```
   'Initialize return value
   dfVntToDateStr = ""

   'Create formatted date string
   If Not IsNull(DateVar) Then
      If IsDate(DateVar) Then
         dfVntToDateStr = Format$(DateVar, FormatString)
      End If
   End If

   Exit Function

ErrTrap:
   On Error GoTo 0
End Function
```

8.4.3   Converting a Number

Listing 8.11 shows an example of a Safe Procedure to validate a whole number.

LISTING 8.11   Converting a variant to a long

```
Function dfVntToLng(ByVal lngVar As Variant) As Long
'_____
'Purpose:    Return a long from a variant
'Inputs:     lngVar is the variant to be converted
'Passed:     None
'Returns:    A valid long
'Outputs:    None
'Notes:      Returns zero if the variant is invalid
'            This may not be acceptable in all situations
'Usage:      intID = dfVntToLng(vntID)
'            intID = dfVntToLng(rs("ID"))
'_____


On Error Goto ErrTrap

   'Initialize return value
   dfVntToLng = 0

   'Create long
   If Not IsNull(lngVar) Then
      If IsNumeric(lngVar) Then
         dfVntToLng = CLng(lngVar)
      End If
```

```
      End If

      Exit Function

ErrTrap:
   On Error GoTo 0
End Function
```

8.4.4   *Validating a Number*

After conversion, you may need to validate your argument to ensure that it is not only the right type but also has an acceptable value. Wherever possible, this validation should be performed in reusable procedures. Listing 8.12 shows one such procedure, used to check that a numeric value falls within limits.

LISTING 8.12   Validating the range of a number

```
Function dfIsInRange(ByVal vntNum As Variant, _
                     ByVal vntMin As Variant, _
                     ByVal vntMax As Variant) As Boolean
'------------------------------
'Purpose:    Return an integer from a variant
'Inputs:     vntNum is the variant to be validated
'            vntMin is the minimum value
'            vntMax is the maximum value
'Passed:     None
'Returns:    True if in range, otherwise False
'Outputs:    None
'Notes:      The range is inclusive of the limits
'Usage:      If Not dfIsInRange(vntNum, 1, 10) Then Exit Sub
'------------------------------

On Error Goto ErrTrap

   'Initialize return value
   dfIsInRange = False

   'Validate all arguments
   If Not IsNumeric(vntMin) Then Exit Function
   If Not IsNumeric(vntMax) Then Exit Function

   'Validate the range
   If IsNumeric(vntNum) Then
```

```
        If Val(vntNum) >= Val(vntMin) And Val(vntNum) <= _
        Val(vntMax) Then
            dfIsInRange = True
        End If
    End If

    Exit Function

ErrTrap:
    On Error Goto 0
End Function
```

Notice that the routine in Listing 8.12 does not assume that the input arguments are numeric.

8.5 String Handling

String handling is a problematic area of coding. String processing is very common in any application, and many errors are introduced as a result. This section provides a sampling of some Safe Procedures to ensure that your string operations are safe.

Note—Visual Basic Library

In my old library, I had a large number of Safe Functions to prevent string handling errors. As I updated these to write this book, I realized that the string library in Visual Basic 6 had changed substantially from earlier versions.

Earlier versions had a tremendous number of ways to break the Visual Basic string functions. Many of these have been corrected in Visual Basic 6. The new functions accept a variant and convert that variant to the expected data type. For example, the earlier Left$ function raised an error if an invalid string was passed to it. In Visual Basic 6, it accepts a "string expression" instead. Here is the Visual Basic Help definition of a "string expression":

> Any expression that evaluates to a sequence of contiguous characters. Elements of a string expression can include a function that returns a string, a string literal, a string constant, a string variable, a string **Variant,** or a function that returns a string **Variant (VarType** 8).

This means that you can pass any value to this function that can be converted to a string. Consider, for example, Left$(123, 2). The Left$ function will not accept the numeric "string expression" 123 and convert it to "123" internally. It will return "12" as the result. If you say Left$("123", 5), this operation will not fail as in previous versions. It will now return "123" as the result.

This strategy is almost identical to the approach advocated in this book. The Safe Programming Framework requires that each procedure behave in exactly this way. This should offer some assurance that the Safe Programming Framework is on the right track. The Framework goes much further, however, by extending these practices to user-defined routines.

8.5.1 Safe Len Wrapper

It may seem trivial to provide a safe wrapper for routines as simple as the
Len function. These simple ones, however, are the most ubiquitous source of
errors. For example, in Visual Basic 6, the Len function will no longer raise
an error if a Null value is passed to it. Instead, it will simply return the Null
value. This result could cause the calling routine to fail unless it specifically
checks for a Null return value. Rather than assume, and require, that the calling routine prevent errors, why not use the function shown in Listing 8.13
wherever Len is needed, to ensure that errors are avoided?

LISTING 8.13   Safe len wrapper

```
Function dfLen(ByVal strText As Variant) As Long
'_____

'Purpose:    Safely return the length of a string
'Inputs:     strText is the string to be tested
'Passed:     None
'Returns:    Long string length
'Outputs:    None
'Notes:      None
'Usage:      For i = 1 to dfLen(strName)
'_____


On Error GoTo ErrTrap

    'Return string length
    If IsNull(strText) Then
       dfLen = 0
    Else
       dfLen = Len(strText)
    End If

    Exit Function

ErrTrap:
    dfLen = 0
    On Error GoTo 0

End Function
```

Similar safe wrappers should be created to protect the other intrinsic
string functions. Listing 8.14 shows one more example of a safe wrapper of
the Mid$ function. This routine will be used in the example in Section 8.5.2.

LISTING 8.14   Mid$ safe wrapper

```
Function dfMid(ByVal strText As Variant,
               ByVal lngStart As Variant,
               Optional lngLength As Variant) As String
'----------------------------
'Purpose:    Safely return the length of a string
'Inputs:     strText is the string to be tested
'            lngStart is the start of the substring
'            lngLength is the optional substring length
'Passed:     None
'Returns:    Specified substring
'Outputs:    None
'Notes:      No optional default is used
'            Input string is trimmed
'Usage:      For strInitial = dfMid(strName, 1, 1)
'----------------------------

On Error GoTo ErrTrap

    'Initialize return value
    dfMid = ""

    'Convert and validate string to parse
    strText = dfVntToTrimStr(strText)
    If strText = "" Then Exit Function

    'Convert and validate start position
    lngStart = dfVntToLng(lngStart)
    If lngStart <= 0 Or lngStart > dfLen(strText) Then Exit _
                Function
    'Determine substring
    If IsMissing(lngLength) Then
       dfMid = Mid$(strText, lngStart)
    Else
       lngLength = dfVntToLng(lngLength)
       If lngLength <= 0 then Exit Function
       dfMid = Mid$(strText, lngStart, lngLength)
    End If

    Exit Function

ErrTrap:
    dfMid = ""
```

```
    On Error GoTo 0

End Function
```

8.5.2   SSN Format

The Safe Functions in Listings 8.15 and 8.16 demonstrate how to accomplish string processing. The first function strips nonnumeric characters from a string. The second function uses the first to format a social security number.

LISTING 8.15   Stripping nonnumeric characters from a string

```
Function dfStripNonNumeric(ByVal strText As Variant)
        As String
'-----------------------------
'Purpose:    Remove nonnumeric characters from string
'Inputs:     strText is the string to strip
'Passed:     None
'Returns:    Stripped string
'Outputs:    None
'Notes:      An empty string is returned if an error occurs
'Usage:      strStrippedSSN = dfStripNonNumeric(strSSN)
'-----------------------------

On Error GoTo ErrTrap

Dim i As Integer
Dim intChar As Integer
Dim strNew As String

Const intMIN_CHAR = 48
Const intMAX_CHAR = 57

    'Initialize return value
    dfStripNonNumeric = ""

    'Convert and validate argument
    strText = dfVntToTrimStr(strText)
    If strText = "" Then Exit Function

    'Strip nonnumeric characters
    strNew = ""
    For i = 1 To dfLen(strText)
       intChar = Asc(dfMid(strText, i, 1))
```

```
      If intChar >= intMIN_CHAR _
      And intChar <= intMAX_CHAR Then
         strNew = strNew & Chr$(intChar)
      End IF
   Next
   dfStripNonNumeric = strNew

   Exit Function

ErrTrap:
   On Error GoTo 0

End Function
```

LISTING 8.16   Formatting a string as a social security number (SSN)

```
Function dfSSNFormat(ByVal strText As Variant) As String
'-----------------------------
'Purpose:   Format a string as a SSN
'Inputs:    strText is the string to format
'Passed:    None
'Returns:   Formatted string
'Outputs:   None
'Notes:     An empty string is returned if an error occurs
'Usage:     strFormattedSSN = dfSSNFormat(strSSN)
'-----------------------------

On Error GoTo ErrTrap

   'Initialize return value
   dfSSNFormat = ""

   'Convert and validate argument
   strText = dfVntToTrimStr(strText)
   If strText = "" Then Exit Function

   'Strip nonnumerics to start at a known condition
   strText = dfStripNonNumeric(strText)
   If dfLen(strText) <> 9 Then Exit Function

   'Format
   dfSSNFormat = dfLeft(strText, 3) & "-" & _
                 dfMid(strText, 4, 2) & "-" & _
                 dfRight(strText, 4)
```

```
        Exit Function

ErrTrap:
        On Error GoTo 0

End Function
```

8.6   Forms and Controls

Almost every Visual Basic project displays forms and controls. A number of "gotchas" can sneak into almost every project, due to common errors in form and control operation.

The philosophy of the SPF is that if you know about a common problem, it should be fixed once and forever. The following Safe Routines give you some examples of reusable code that can prevent these common form and control handling errors.

8.6.1   Determining If a Form Is Loaded

The function in Listing 8.17 can be used to safely determine whether a form has previously been loaded. This task is a bit tricky: you can't check any form properties without inadvertently loading the form. This routine avoids the problem by looking for the form name in the Forms collection.

LISTING 8.17   Determining if a form is loaded

```
Function dfIsFormLoaded(ByVal strFormName As Variant)
        As Boolean
'------------------------------
'Purpose:    Determine if a form is loaded
'Inputs:     strFormName is the form name to be verified
'Passed:     None
'Returns:    True if form is loaded
'Outputs:    None
'Notes:      Used to see if a particular form is loaded
'Usage:      If Not dfIsFormLoaded(frmInp) Then frmInp.Show
'------------------------------

On Error Goto ErrTrap

Dim i As Integer

    'Initialize return value
    dfIsFormLoaded = False
```

```
    'Convert and validate argument
    strFormName = dfVntToTrimStr(strFormName)
    If strFormName = "" Then Exit Function

    'Look for strFormName in Forms collection
    For i = 0 To Forms.Count - 1
        If UCase$(Forms(i).Name) = UCase$(strFormName) Then
            dfIsFormLoaded = True
            Exit Function
        End If
    Next

    Exit Function

ErrTrap:
    On Error GoTo 0
End Function
```

8.6.2   *Unloading All Forms*

The routine in Listing 8.18 can be called to clean up all forms in your application except one. This technique is most useful when your application is shutting down. At that time, you should shut down and clean up all forms except the main form, just before the main form unloads. The routine in Listing 8.18 also demonstrates the use of the TypeOf keyword.

LISTING 8.18   Unloading all forms

```
Function sfFormsUnload(ByRef frm As Variant) As String
'----------------------------
'Purpose:    Unloads all forms other that one
'Inputs:     Form to leave loaded, typically the main form
'Passed:     None
'Returns:    Safe Error Message
'Outputs:    All other forms are affected
'Notes:      Used in the main form unload to
'            ensure all other forms are unloaded
'Usage:      sfFormsUnload frmMain
'----------------------------

On Error Goto ErrTrap

Dim i As Integer

    'Validate argument
```

```
    'If Not TypeOf frm Is Form Then
          sfFormsUnload = dfSemCreate("sfFormsUnload", -1, _
          "Invalid argument")

    End If
    'Unload all forms except frm
    For i = Forms.Count - 1 To 0 Step -1
      If UCase$(Forms(i).Name) <> UCase$(frm.Name) Then
        Unload Forms(i)
      End If
    Next

    'Exit with success
    sfFormsUnload = ""
    Exit Function

ErrTrap:
      sfFormsUnload = dfSemCreate("sfFormsUnload",  _
                                  Err.Number,Err.Description)

      On Error Goto 0
End Function
```

8.6.3   *Setting Focus*

LISTING 8.19   Setting focus

```
Function sfFocus(ByRef ctrl As Variant) As String
'-------------------------------
'Purpose:   Set focus on a control
'Inputs:    ctrl is the control to receive focus
'Passed:    None
'Returns:   Safe Error Message
'Outputs:   None
'Notes:     None
'Usage:     sfFocus txtUserName
'-------------------------------

On Error Goto ErrTrap

    'Initialize the return value
    sfFocus = ""

    'Validate argument
    If Not TypeOf ctrl Is Control Then
    sfFocus = dfSemCreate("sfFocus", -1, "Invalid control")
    Exit Function
```

```
End If

    'Set focus
    ctrl.SetFocus
    DoEvents 'To allow operation to complete

    Exit Function

ErrTrap:
    sfFocus = dfSemCreate("sfFocus", Err.Number, Err.Description)
    On Error Goto 0
End Function
```

Notice that in the function in Listing 8.19, a Safe Error Message is returned, even though this message will normally be ignored. It is there if someone has need to handle it.

8.6.4 *Making Sure It Is Safe to Resize*

The function in Listing 8.19 was a safe wrapper to prevent errors in an intrinsic function. The function in Listing 8.20 demonstrates a preventative routine used to avoid known error situations. In this case, most programmers know that you cannot attempt to resize a form if the window is minimized. Forgetting to check for a minimized form is a common source of error. The Safe Procedure in Listing 8.20 can be called at the start of a Form_Resize event to ensure that it is safe to proceed. Note that preventative programming practice demands that such a call be performed, even if a form is not resizable. At some point in the future the form may be made resizable. Preventive practices must encompass not only current situations but also potential situations in the future.

LISTING 8.20   Determining if it is safe to resize a form

```
Function dfSafeToResize(ByRef frm As Variant) As Boolean
'----------------------------
'Purpose:   Determine if it is safe to resize a form
'Inputs:    frm is the Form to Test
'Passed:    None
'Returns:   True if Safe, otherwise False
'Outputs:   None
'Notes:     None
'Usage:     sfFocus txtUserName
'----------------------------

On Error Goto ErrTrap

    'Initialize the return value
    dfSafeToResize = False
```

```
    'Validate argument
    If Not TypeOf frm Is Form Then
     dfSafeToResize = dfSemCreate("dfSafeToResize", -1, _
                      "Invalid form")
    Exit Function
    End If


    'Check if form is currently minimized
    if frm.Windowstate <> vbMinimized Then dfSafeToResize = True

    Exit Function

ErrTrap:
    dfSafeToResize = dfSemCreate("dfSafeToResize", _
                     Err.Number, Err.Description)
    On Error Goto 0
End Function
```

8.6.5 Copying a List Control

Utilities make up another class of safe functions designed to safely perform a common operation. The code-wheel in Listing 8.21 is a utility function to safely copy the contents of one ListBox control or ComboBox control to another.

LISTING 8.21   Copying one ListBox or ComboBox to another

```
Function sfListCopy(ByRef ListFrom As Variant,
                    ByRef ListTo As Variant) As String
'------------------------------
'Purpose:    Duplicate a ListBox or ComboBox
'Inputs:     ListFrom is the source list control
'Passed:     ListTo is the destination list control
'Returns:    Safe Error Message
'Outputs:    None
'Notes:      None
'Usage:      strSEM = sfListCopy(cboBoxFrom, lstBoxTo)
'------------------------------

On Error GoTo ErrTrap

Dim i As Integer

    'Initialize return value
    sfListCopy = ""
```

```
     'Validate arguments
     If Not (TypeOf ListFrom Is ComboBox Or TypeOf ListFrom _
             Is TextBox) Then sfListCopy = dfSemCreate_
             ("sfListCopy", -1, "Invalid ListFrom")
        Exit Function
     End If
     If Not (TypeOf ListTo Is ComboBox Or TypeOf ListTo Is _
             TextBox) Then sfListCopy = dfSemCreate_
             ("sfListCopy", -1, "Invalid ListTo")
        Exit Function
     End If

      'Clear target list then copy all items and ItemData values
      ListTo.Clear
      For i = 0 To ListFrom.ListCount - 1
        ListTo.AddItem ListFrom.List(i)
        ListTo.ItemData(ListTo.NewIndex) = ListFrom.ItemData(i)
      Next

     Exit Function

ErrTrap:
    sfListCopy = dfSemCreate("sfListCopy", Err.Number, _
                 Err.Description)
    On Error GoTo 0
End Function
```

Notice again in this routine the TypeOf keyword is used to help validate object arguments.

8.7 Database Routines

Earlier it was pointed out that the vast majority of error-prone situations stem from dealing with the unpredictable outside world. Anticipating and handling errors caused by file operations, printers, or even users is difficult. However, these errors are trivial in comparison to the nasty situations that arise when working with a database.

Of all the external systems with which a Visual Basic program may interact, databases are both the most common and the most error-prone. The state of a database, particularly a multi-user database, can be highly unpredictable. Further, the range and complexity of database operations are extremely broad and deep. The object models for DAO and ADO are complex. Any of the database properties and methods is susceptible to a wide range of errors.

One key point to remember is that prevention is just as important in database coding as in other types of coding. You should never rely on errors returned by the database to test, diagnose, or detect error situations. Preventative programming is always preferable to reactive programming.

It is possible to prevent most database errors, to handle those that cannot be prevented, and to expose those that are unanticipated, but it requires a great deal of experience. If that experience can be captured by creating reusable functions, then it is possible to achieve efficient, robust database programming. The following Safe Procedures illustrate the sorts of routines that should be available in your safe database library.

8.7.1 *Formatting SQL Strings*

This is the Q function mentioned in the anecdote in Chapter 6, renamed here to conform to the SPF. This function can be used to prevent errors when creating SQL query statements. This version formats variables for Access; modifications may be required to support other databases.

Note that this routine also demonstrates the use of the VarType function to determine the data type stored in a variant (see Listing 8.22).

LISTING 8.22   Formatting a Variant for including in SQL

```
Function dfToSQL(ByVal SqlVariable As Variant) As String
'------------------------------
'Purpose:    Format a variable for inclusion in an SQL statement
'Inputs:     SqlVariable is the variant to format
'Passed:     None
'Returns:    The formatted form of SqlVariable
'Outputs:    None
'Notes:      Useful in creating properly formatted SQL
'            statements
'Usage:      sql = "SELECT * FROM Table WHERE Name = " & _
'            dfToSQL(vntName)
'------------------------------

On Error Goto ErrTrap

    'Initialize return value
    'Return passed value in case of error
    dfToSQL = SqlVariable

    'Format the string
    Select Case VarType(SqlVariable)

        'Null or empty variable
        Case vbNull, vbEmpty
```

```
                    'Return NULL
                    dfToSQL = "NULL"

            'String variable
            Case vbString
                'Replace any single quotes with two single quotes
                'and enclose entire string in single quotes
                dfToSQL = "'" & Replace(SqlVariable, "'", "''") & "'"

            'Date variable
            Case vbDate
                'Format and enclose in pounds signs for Access
                dfToSQL = "#" & _
                        Format$(SqlVariable, "General Date") & _
                        "#"

            'Otherwise treat as numeric
            Case Else
                On Error Resume Next
                dfToSQL = CStr(SqlVariable)
                If Err.Number <> 0 Then dfToSQL = SqlVariable

    End Select

    Exit Function

ErrTrap:
    On Error GoTo 0
End Function
```

8.7.2   *Checking the Cursor Position*

Of the many important protections that you must put in place for complete database error coding, the most crucial is to never neglect the cursor position rather than to trust that the cursor is placed at a valid record. When you simplify this task with reusable Safe Procedures, then you are more likely to do it. Also, you are less likely to make a mistake in this tricky logic.

The routines in Listings 8.23 and 8.24 determine the ADO cursor location.

LISTING 8.23   Determining if the cursor is at a record

```
Function dfIsAdoCursorCurrent(ByRef rs As Variant) As Boolean
'------------------------------
'Purpose:   Determine if the cursor is at a current record
'Inputs:    rs is the ADO recordset
```

```
'Passed:    None
'Returns:   Safe Error Message
'Outputs:   None
'Notes:     None
'Usage:     If dfIsAdoCursorCurrent(rs) Then rs.Edit
'----------------------------


On Error Goto ErrTrap

    'Initialize return value
    dfIsAdoCursorCurrent = False

    'Check recordset
    If Not rs.EOF And Not rs.BOF Then dfIsAdoCursorCurrent = _
        True
    End If

    Exit Function

ErrTrap:
    dfIsAdoCursorCurrent = dfSemCreate("dfIsAdoCursorCurrent ", _
                        Err.Number, Err.Description)
    On Error GoTo 0
End Function
```

LISTING 8.24   Determining if a recordset is empty

```
Function dfIsAdoRecordsetEmpty(ByRef rs As Variant) As Boolean
'----------------------------
'Purpose:   Determine if an ADO recordset is empty
'Inputs:    rs is the ADO recordset
'Passed:    None
'Returns:   Safe Error Message
'Outputs:   None
'Notes:     None
'Usage:     If Not dfIsAdoRecordsetEmpty(rs) Then rs.MoveFirst
'----------------------------


On Error Goto ErrTrap

    'Initialize return value
    dfIsAdoRecordsetEmpty = True

    'Check recordset
```

```
    If Not rs.EOF Or Not rs.BOF Then dfIsAdoRecordsetEmpty _
        = False
    End If

    Exit Function

ErrTrap:
    dfIsAdoRecordsetEmpty = dfSemCreate("dfIsAdoRecordsetEmpty ", _
                            Err.Number, Err.Description)
    On Error GoTo 0
End Function
```

8.7.3 *Editing a Field*

When you need to edit a field in an updatable ADO recordset, many potential errors can arise. Since you can anticipate many of these errors, they should be prevented. Not only should they be prevented, but they should be prevented with reusable coding so that you need never think about them again.

The function in Listing 8.25 illustrates this design philosophy. It provides a Safe Function to edit a field safely, without prohibitive amounts of code and the associated maintenance that excessive coding requires.

LISTING 8.25   Editing a recordset field

```
Function sfAdoEditField(ByRef rs As Variant,
                        ByVal strField As Variant,
                        ByVal vntNew As Variant) As String
'-----------------------------
'Purpose:    Edit a field in an RDO recordset
'Inputs:     rs is an RDO recordset
'            strField is the field name or index number
'            vntNew is the new field value to assign
'Passed:     None
'Returns:    Safe Error Message
'Outputs:    None
'Notes:      None
'Usage:      If sfAdoEditField(rs, "FName", "Tom") <> "" Then
'-----------------------------

On Error Goto ErrTrap

    'Initialize return value
    sfAdoEditField = ""

    'Validate the recordset has been instantiated
```

```
If rs Is Nothing Then
   sfAdoEditField = dfSemCreate("sfAdoEditField", -1, _
                             "Recordset is Nothing")
Exit Function
End If

'Validate that rs is really a recordset
If Not TypeOf rs Is ADODB.Recordset Then
   sfAdoEditField = dfSemCreate("sfAdoEditField", -2, _
                    "Not a Recordset")
 Exit Function
End If

'Validate that the rs is updatable
If Not rs.LockType = asLockReadOnly Then
   sfAdoEditField = dfSemCreate("sfAdoEditField", -3, _
                    "Recordset not Updatable")
   Exit Function
End If

'Validate that the rs cursor is positioned at a valid record
If Not dfIsAdoCursorCurrent(rs) Then
   sfAdoEditField = dfSemCreate("sfAdoEditField", -4, _
                    "No current record")
    Exit Function
End If

'Validate that the field is updatable
If Not rs.Fields(strField).Attributes And adfldUpdatable Then
   sfAdoEditField = dfSemCreate("sfAdoEditField", -5, _
                    "Field not Updatable")
   Exit Function
End If

'Update field
rs.Fields(strField).Value = vntNew

Exit Function

ErrTrap:
  sfAdoEditField = dfSemCreate("sfAdoEditField ", _
                     Err.Number, Err.Description)
  On Error GoTo 0
End Function
```

Why all the fuss in this routine? It would be possible to simply attempt the field update and trap any error. However, this practice is not in keeping with the philosophy of preventative, rather than reactive, programming and the need to avoid generating errors as a diagnostic. This routine returns very specific and friendly messages about the exact nature of the problem. And why not? This code is maintained in one place and does not need to complicate every field assignment. If anything, the routine in Listing 8.25 should be expanded to provide even more diagnostic preventative programming.

8.8   Putting Safe Procedures to Work

You can see that these sample routines are quite simple. They accept Variant arguments, convert and validate them, perform in-line error handling through other Safe Procedures, and protect themselves with simple error trapping. The procedures are very easy to read and maintain. They are clean and uncluttered because they leverage reusable error coding. Even though they are fully error coded, they are prone to few of the typical complications demonstrated in Chapter 5. They are easy to understand because they follow a standard, predictable pattern. They use the good preventative coding practices identified in Chapter 6. They implement all the standards set forth in Chapter 7. In effect, they are the culmination of coding practices in the book to this point.

Once you have the sense of how to develop these Safe Procedures, they come automatically and easily. Early in this book, you were promised that complete error coding need be no more difficult and time-consuming than coding unprotected features only. These Safe Procedures are the best teachers to show you how to accomplish that goal.

It is up to you to take it from here. By following the higher standard, and the examples presented in this chapter, you can put Safe Procedures to work in your projects. The next chapter offers some suggestions for implementing the Safe Programming Framework for your own work or within a company.

Corporate Strategies

It should be an easy matter for you to implement the software development principles described in this book in your own work. What if you are a part of a team, however? What if you are part of a large software development firm?

Clearly, the more fully that standard coding practices are adopted across a project team and throughout a company, the greater the benefits. The rewards reaped from the retention of corporate knowledge through code reuse are directly proportional to the number of developers who contribute to the standard. Anyone in a company who is producing standardized, long-term code enhances the productivity of the team, now and in the future.

Knowing that, how do you promote smart coding practices across a team? This chapter looks at some issues and offers recommendations to help you meet this challenge.

9.1 Smart Coding Teams

If you are an independent consultant or an individual programmer, it is easy to implement the SPF to your work. You simply do it. As an individual, you can follow the standard and set about building a personal library. You might wish to document your library, but you probably know what is in it and where to find it. Even if you have only a few employees, you can communicate this information easily to your staff.

If you are a part of a larger organization, however, your job is much more complicated. Programs that are easy for the individual or small group to implement can be immensely more difficult for a larger organization. The negotiation and communication overhead becomes daunting.

Many mom-and-pop shops can develop small to mid-size products for a fraction of the cost of equivalent products produced by a larger firm. They do not have to underwrite the overhead and inefficiency inherent in coordinating a larger team. Also, very small groups can adopt new standards much more quickly and efficiently than can a larger organization.

If you are a part of a company with more than just a few developers, you must find ways to minimize the costs of implementing a standard across your enterprise.

9.2   Cooperative Competition

When discussing information as technical as programming standards, why digress into a discussion of competition? It is extremely relevant: without a healthy atmosphere of cooperative competition, your organization cannot succeed in its mission. It takes a great deal of cooperation and teamwork to write routines that may benefit others in the future. It takes some healthy competition to stimulate the best quality work.

What is healthy competition? With too little competition, work stagnates. With too much, plans self-destruct. The right dose can best be described as cooperative competition.

How do we cooperate and compete at the same time? Perhaps we can learn some hints from the Japanese; they practice a much more cooperative form of competition than in the West.

ANECDOTE: Japanese Exchange Students

My most powerful lesson in cooperative competition came from a Japanese exchange student who stayed at our house. One day, we hosted a beach party with all the Japanese students in the exchange program and their host families.

I was intrigued watching the Japanese students improvising games on the beach. While the American kids ran around pushing each other over, the Japanese students formed a spontaneous circle and started playing a mound-building game. They placed a flag on top of a small mound of sand and took turns pushing more sand onto the mound. The object was to work together to make the mound as tall as possible before the flag fell over. The Japanese students shouted encouragement to each other and cheered their collective effort, even after the flag finally tipped over.

Although they tried to involve some American kids, the locals showed little interest. The Japanese students then located a beach ball that the American kids had tired of throwing at each other. They formed a circle again, and this time volleyed the ball around the circle. The object was to keep the ball in the air as long as possible. They cheered each other every time someone made a heroic save. They cheered even more warmly after a failed attempt.

> This game interested some of the host family kids. The Japanese students encouraged them to join in. What happened next was startling. As the ball bounced around the circle, it came near one of the American boys. He quickly jumped up and smashed the ball into the ground, grinning from ear to ear at his accomplishment. The Japanese students looked confused but cheered politely.
>
> Each time the ball reached an American child, the result was the same. Smash! Each time, the Japanese students tried to be polite. I finally tired of this and angrily told the American kids that the object of the game was to keep the ball in the air as long as possible. They looked at me as if I were from another planet. Next time the ball came around to them . . . smash!

We in the West, and particularly Americans, do not normally practice cooperative competition. We practice individualistic competition or antagonistic competition. The Japanese students were no less competitive. They had a strong competitive urge to build the highest mound or to keep the beach ball bouncing the longest. Their competition was very different, however—it was cooperative. The American students saw competition individualistically, smashing the ball down so no one else could stop it.

I would not prefer to work in Japan than in the U.S. Their cultural view creates a different set of disadvantages and limitations. However, we can still learn something new from the contrast. The Western type of competition makes it very difficult to create an atmosphere in which the experiences of one and all are respected, captured, and shared. Another anecdote further illustrates the American penchant for individualistic competition:

ANECDOTE: Do You Have a Routine to . . .

> Very early in my career, I went to work as a temporary programmer for a very well-respected company. The project I stepped into was quite far along. It had a huge number of routines available in the project, but no effort had been made to document these or make them easily available for reuse.
>
> As I started working, I quickly found that I had need of a simple function. I would have bet my mouse that such a routine had been written before! Not wanting to reinvent the wheel, I found the regular staff together and inquired whether any of them could locate such a routine. One of the senior developers leaned back and announced that what I had asked for was trivial to write. He offered to show me how. I assumed that they must have misunderstood my question. I could have written the routine easily myself; I simply didn't want to place redundant code into the project.
>
> I tried several more times to ask the regular staff about existing routines, and each time I found myself put down for it. One time, I asked while the company president was near, thinking that the staff would certainly want to be more helpful with him there. One of the developers said something that once again elevated himself at my expense. This time I felt humiliated in front of the company president. After that, I quit asking. If I needed a new function, even if I was reasonably sure that someone else must have already written it, I simply created a new one.

The staff programmers in the previous anecdote knocked that reuse beach ball back at me every time I tossed it up–and the company president apparently saw nothing counter-productive in the attitude of his staff. These attitudes are ingrained in our culture, but they also come from the top down.

My wife and I used to frequent a restaurant with an extremely rude and discourteous staff. It was convenient for us, and it was also somewhat of a joke to see just how rude the staff could be. Finally we tired of the poor treatment and stopped going. A year later we returned, only because we were starving. The same staff were there, but they were different. This time they were kind, courteous, and attentive. We asked one of the employees—the one we remembered as being the rudest—what had happened since our last visit. "We have a new manager," she replied warmly.

This story illustrates how incredibly powerful the influence of the leader is. The leader cannot avoid setting a tone and atmosphere that permeates the entire enterprise. Leaders' values and expectations are conveyed in such subtle ways that they are often genuinely unaware of how their influence is being felt. It is not uncommon for managers to blame their staff for behavior that is a normal response to the atmosphere they have created.

It is possible for managers to make a difference. It requires a plan, but it also requires creating a special atmosphere in the organization—one of cooperative competition in which every team member works together to keep that beach ball bouncing. The management team must provide the system to accomplish this—they must set the clear expectation that their objectives will be met, that they will reward and recognize contributions, and that they intend to create an atmosphere that nurtures these efforts. If they fail in any of these areas, the effort will fail.

In a company that pits one team against another too strongly, it is natural for teams to be reluctant to share code. Why should one team work hard to produce good, reusable code, when it will benefit their internal competition?

In the West, our thinking is shaped by a deeply ingrained notion of "checks-and-balances." In government contexts, this can certainly be a strength, but it can also be a danger. We have seen cases in which checks-and-balances between political parties have turned into counterproductive or paralyzing attacks. This same notion of checks-and-balances as both a strength and a danger is apparent in Microsoft's team model as it is often implemented. There you are likely to find team members who think in terms of "watching" their peers rather than "watching out for" them. Team members will be disinclined to simply say to each other, "How can I help you?"

Encouraging your team members to ask that simple question will ensure that your teams stay positive, productive, and mutually supportive. Microsoft's team model can be implemented in a highly cooperative and supportive manner. It merely requires that the subtle attitude shift that encourages cooperative competition start at the top.

9.3   Developing Your Standard

If the Safe Programming Framework meets your needs, you can adopt it in its entirety, adapt and modify it to suit your company, or develop your own standard from scratch.

Beware of the natural tendency to turn whatever work you completed in the past into your standard. Certainly, you will want to keep practices that have worked for you, but don't hold onto them simply because this strategy is easy or because old practices validate previous decisions or long-held beliefs. Be sure that your standard is cohesive and synergetic, not just a hodgepodge of conventions.

If you do create or modify your own standard, be cautious of becoming bogged down in the drafting and approval process. Every programmer holds onto conventions that he or she has followed for years. He or she will be most vocal in defending those practices and insisting that these appear in the standard.

It is important to listen to all perspectives, but it is also critical at some point for a strong leader to take charge and simply say, "This is the way it will be." If that does not happen, endless debates will ensue until the enthusiasm inherent in adopting a standard withers and dies. The whole team must acknowledge that when any standard is adopted, it will have flaws and they will need to make compromises. For example, if you do open your standard to discussion, the specification for the number of tab spaces required is guaranteed to be one of the most heated topics of debate and one almost certainly never to be resolved by consensus. If everyone understands that no perfect standard will result, then an agreement can be reached much more easily.

Once you adopt your standard, it is important to prepare it in clear written form and make it readily available to current, future, and temporary employees, as well as to your consultants and clients.

9.4   Creating Safe Procedures

It should not be difficult to create Safe Procedures. At first, your staff might worry that it will mean a great deal more work for them, though this should not be the case. Implemented correctly, the SPF should not require much more effort than they are currently expending. It should definitely require much less time with continued use.

Primarily, you will went to learn to write procedures that follow all the standard conventions. That done, the rest will come automatically. You will no longer have to think about how to structure a new procedure. Until it does become second nature, you can use the checklist provided in Appendix B to verify that all standards have been met.

As suggested earlier, it helps to create a standard procedure header that can be pasted into any new procedure. Better yet, you might create a Visual Basic Add-In that will create the skeleton of a Safe Procedure for you. At WinResources, we have developed an Add-In for this purpose. It appears under the "Add Procedure . . ." item in the Tools menu. When you click on "Add Safe Procedure . . ." and it displays a wizard that allows you to select the type of Safe Procedure needed, what arguments will be passed, whether arguments should be validated, and whether error trapping should be added automatically.

The Add-In is a powerful tool, making it easy for you to follow the standard consistently and with minimal effort. It is an excellent example of what I call **Motivational Catalysis.**

9.5   Motivational Catalysis

How does a company motivate its staff to follow the Safe Programming Framework in its coding practice? More importantly, how does it motivate its staff to contribute enduring code-wheels so that the wealth of corporate knowledge is reusable?

Compliance can be gained by dictum. Second, compliance can be made voluntary but strongly encouraged. Third, it can be gained by adding incentives, such as bonuses and raises for meeting certain measurable objectives.

Since my background is actually in chemistry, not in computer science, I still think like a chemist at times: when I think about how to motivate people, I find myself falling back on my fundamental chemistry training. Out of this cross-fertilization, my theory of motivational catalysis was born.

In chemistry, you start with a pot of chemicals. You want those chemicals to engage in some reaction to form your desired product. Instead, they just sit there, vibrating at their own pace, because a certain level of activation energy is required for the reaction to occur. At room temperature, they do not produce enough energy to overcome the activation energy barrier. To force a reaction, you can heat the pot. Alternatively, you can add an electrical spark or another source of energy that will force the reactants to overcome their activation energy barrier.

This process reflects the typical motivational strategy. By adding bonuses, raises, threats, or cajoling to the system, you cause those "molecules" to do what you want. Whether they be chemicals or people, this is an expensive and volatile approach.

In chemistry, however, there is an alternative strategy. It is called catalysis. Simply by finding the right catalyst and dropping it in the pot of chemicals, you can cause many reactions to occur without adding energy. Suddenly, almost magically, your stubborn reaction begins on its own, without having to light a fire under it. Figure 9.1 illustrates this concept.

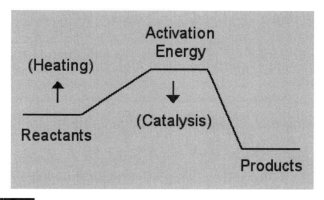

FIGURE 9.1   Catalysis

Catalysis works for chemical reactions, not by increasing the energy until the reactants become unstable, but by removing the activation energy barrier. In motivating people, removing barriers can be much more gentle and effective than forcing people to overcome them. If you remove the barriers to your goal, making it incredibly easy and natural for people to produce, then you don't have to worry about motivating them.

The goal of the Safe Programming Framework is to act as one catalyst for producing a superior product. The corporate strategies that support that framework should also catalyze, rather than force, the desired reaction.

9.6   Certifying for Reuse

It is not enough to publish a standard, encourage compliance, and make the resulting procedures available for reuse. If segments of your shared library fail to perform properly or to meet the standards, then they undermine confidence in the entire library. Your staff won't use code they can't trust; they will write new routines instead. If they don't use procedures, they tend not to contribute. The effort will stall and decay.

The quality of all routines in the shared library must be ensured. The only way to accomplish this is to run each routine through a quality control process. The quality assurance process must include both an inspection to verify that the candidate code follows all SPF requirements and guidelines, and a process to verify that it performs its function accurately and reliably.

Certification can be performed by a single person who is the gatekeeper of the library, or by a certification panel that meets periodically to review certification candidates. Only after passing this quality control test should a candidate be certified and included in the safe library. Appendix C is a Certification Rating Sheet you can use to evaluate certification candidates.

9.7 Sharing Certified Procedures

Once code is certified, you can move it into your **Safe Library.** Your library can be maintained in SourceSafe or another version control system. Anyone should have rights to the source code, but only the certification gatekeeper should have permission to update the files. It is your choice whether to allow developers to cut and paste routines from source modules, or whether you want them to use executable versions in a DLL that is periodically compiled.

Filling a Safe Library is one thing; making the contents known and available is another altogether. The simplest solution to accessibility is maintaining a searchable text document or help file that allows developers to search by key word. Another alternative is adding a searchable library listing to your corporate Intranet.

The best strategy would be to develop a system that would search a directory tree of source files directly, recommending routines based upon key word matches with the name and contents. Such a search engine would be self-maintaining.

9.8 Using Hyper-Libraries

One of the first tasks you might dream of as you start to develop reuse-quality procedures is creating a substantial library of Safe Procedures to call on. You might hope that your library will grow rapidly, becoming too large for one library. Perhaps you should begin by creating several separate libraries, perhaps one for string functions, one for form functions, one for math functions and so on. Perhaps you could create a separate DLL for each library so that development teams could choose among those they need for a particular project.

Since the routines are highly interdependent, envisioning a one-dimensional list with routines that do not rely on each other is too simplistic. If your reusable code reuses other code as it should, then you end up with more of a code network than a code library. In the hyper-library, safe procedures are interdependent.

It may not be feasible to break up your hyper-library as much as you might with a standard, linear function library. It might make the most sense to include all your Safe Procedures in one general purpose DLL so they leverage each other. Certainly, larger, reusable components can have their own OCX or DLL, even if they still use your general purpose DLL.

As a user of the library, it is important not to think of it as linear. Think of it not as a list of discrete functions but as interdependent code with multiple entry points. You can call a high-level procedure, or you can call any of the lower-level procedures, as the situation demands.

9.9   Rewarding Lasting Contributions

When employees write new routines that become certified, they have made a lasting contribution to the company. Their contributions should be acknowledged and rewarded and additional contributions encouraged.

Acknowledgement and rewards need not be expensive. With a little imagination, you can find many ways to show the appreciation of the company without spending a lot of money. Instead of one big reward, many small rewards are often as effective.

These small rewards can be as simple as listing the author's name in the library directory, for example. Even speaking highly of the employee's contribution in informal conversation around the office can be a huge motivator. Recognition can also include merit points when employee evaluation time comes around.

As an organization, you might consider a more formal process of recognition to augment, not replace, other informal strategies. The Certification Rating Sheet provided in Appendix C asks the reviewers to award points for seven measures of quality:

- How large is the **size and scope?**
- How **innovative** is it?
- How **useful** is it?
- How **reusable** is it?
- How **standardized** is it?
- How **elegant** is it?
- How **bug-proof** is it?

You could devise a recognition scheme based on the total number of points awarded. After milestones of so many points, you could recognize the contributor in different ways. One idea might be to simply generate a nice looking "Certificate of Rank" as a developer reaches total point milestones. (Use your imagination to come up with a few creative awards.)

9.10   Code Review through Certification

Code review is a very important process. It not only helps to ensure quality code, but it also helps to train, to communicate, and to generate new ideas and approaches. Despite its well-known benefits, code review is seldom practiced. When it is practiced, it is often unsystematic, irregular, or viewed with suspicion.

The Safe Certification Process offers the added benefit of built-in code review. It has none of the negativity sometimes associated with code review, and it can offer all the benefits.

Review code through the Safe Certification Process.

9.11 Adaptive Development

No such thing exists as a perfect project plan. That fact may seem like blasphemy. In this current era of emphasis on project planning and management, the common business ideal today is that better planning and tighter management are the answers to every problem.

In the software business, the vast majority of software development projects run into problems. Unanticipated questions and difficulties are extremely common. Ask yourself what you typically hear when problems occur:

- "We should have planned better."
- "We need to adhere to the plan more carefully next time."
- "We have to do more planning up front next time."

Make no mistake about it. We can and should make every effort to create the "perfect" project plan. As with any ideal, however, you should also acknowledge that you will seldom, if ever, achieve it. It is unhealthy to expect perfection and to berate yourself when you fail to achieve it.

Companies that do expect the perfect project plan are likely to fail to achieve one. To avoid finger-pointing, they end up rigidly adhering to the plan, even after imperfections are uncovered during development. This response results in a far from satisfactory product. They develop a product that may adhere to the plan but fails to meet the customer's needs.

Personal motivations are at stake here, also. The project planner is normally the same person who decides whether that plan should be revised, so he or she has a strong emotional stake in the plan. Even if it proves to be highly flawed, the project planner will often rigidly refuse to revise it. To do so would be an admission that he or she did a less than perfect job.

Whenever a project has problems, the natural response is to implement more planning and tighter control. Even if that additional planning has an extremely unfavorable cost/benefit ratio, or if rigid management is the source of many of the problems, more of the same is always considered the solution.

If more project planning and tighter management control are not always the solution, what are? The answer may include adaptive development. Adaptive development means that your development process is flexible and malleable. It means that if changes are required, these are not a problem and do not disrupt the timeline. It means that you think of the development process as an optimization, rather than building from a blueprint.

What is the biggest fear? It is that an unanticipated situation will arise, causing a problem in the development plan. If development is forced to make a change, then this might cause widespread fallout, which severely undermines the profitability of the project.

Again, the usual response to this situation is that better planning should have been done. Maybe, but I contend that there may be another problem.

The development effort should not be thrown off course if there is a change in the specifications. It should be able to adapt and accommodate to changes easily. If it cannot, this is a serious flaw in development. The best solution to that flaw is not to simply do more planning. By following the Smart Coding Triangle, a project should always be maintainable and adaptable without difficulty and without breaking other areas of the program. If it is so fragile that it cannot quickly and easily respond to changing design specifications, then it will be difficult to maintain as needs change after release.

Even though every possible strategy must be undertaken to create a complete and accurate project plan, the expectation must also be that the project will be adaptable to any changes that arise during or after development.

9.12   Eliminating Nontechnical Barriers

It is crucial to the success of your mission to eliminate all nontechnical barriers. What are these nontechnical barriers? They can be extremely difficult to diagnose. Sometimes an outsider can see them more clearly than can those who are intimately involved.

As a consultant, I was called on quite often to cure ailing projects. In these cases, one of the key questions I always asked was whether it was acceptable to the client if I worked off-site.

In some cases, good reasons were given why this was not feasible. If the project had specialized hardware requirements, for example, that answer was understandable. Another valid reason was when the client needed someone to mentor a staff member.

In other cases, the client simply objected to my working off-site. It was obvious that the client wanted to ensure that they maintained control over the consultant. In these cases I declined the job. I didn't actually mind working at the client site, but I knew that their reluctance was a red flag. There was a strong possibility that in their environment programmers had been prevented from succeeding in the past. I did not want to put myself in a situation in which I was prevented from succeeding as well. The clients who finally gave up, those who said, "We've failed—you tell us what to do," were those for whom I was able to provide the greatest benefit.

Even if you do adopt a sound coding standard, add motivational catalysts, and set an atmosphere of clear expectations and cooperative competition, your efforts may still flounder.

The problem could be your people. Certainly, it takes talented, experienced, and trained developers to implement standards accurately yet creatively. If you suspect that is the case, you can try replacing some of your staff. If that doesn't improve the situation, however, then perhaps you should look elsewhere. Your organization could be creating other technical or nontechnical barriers to success.

The nontechnical barriers may be hard to recognize and deal with even though every programmer might know what they are. Code development is also a creative process, and there is an elusive magic associated with every creative endeavor.

If you are having problems with your project, try taking it outside for some fresh air. Ask for the input of an independent consultant who has no political baggage to inhibit an honest assessment. This person may be able to identify your technical or your nontechnical barriers to success.

9.13   You're Not There Yet!

At this point, it may seem that we have covered all the important issues that you need to consider in order to accomplish your mission. Not yet. Even if you achieve all of the recommendations presented in this book so far, you may still fail to produce an application that is scalable and maintainable.

The underlying reason might be a limited amount of layering. Inadequate layering will often undermine the success of an otherwise well-conceived and implemented project. The next chapter discusses layering as a high-level architectural structure within which the Safe Programming Framework can flourish.

Program Architecture

This book has discussed error coding, reuse, and standardization, and has provided the Safe Programming Framework as a means to accomplish your mission of improved quality and productivity. That is still not enough, however. Even if you do apply the principles presented to this point, you can still end up with a program that fails to meet expectations. Even if your program succeeds in meeting its immediate objectives, it may fail to survive when required to adapt to changing requirements. This chapter takes a truly long-term perspective, one that extends beyond the current project phase.

10.1 Modes of Program Failure

Projects fail for various reasons, but only a few typical failure modes are directly related to programming technique.

10.1.1 Failure to Complete

Have you ever been involved in a project that simply couldn't seem to reach completion? The main cause of failure to complete is a moving target. This situation happens when the project specifications keep changing. The protection against this type of failure is a clear, well-considered project plan.

Even if the timeline is realistic, the project may be late. In this case, the ability to reuse standardized routines may speed up the development process so that the timeline can still be met.

195

10.1.2   Failure to Perform

Sometimes a project fails to pass testing after it has reached feature completion. It may have bugs that refuse to come under control. The most common cause of failure to perform is a lack of proper error coding and preventative practices.

Using the SPF will help to protect against this mode of failure by avoiding assumptions and imposing programming discipline.

10.1.3   Failure to Maintain

The third mode of program failure is an inability to maintain the program. In this case, it has reached completion and passed testing, but failure occurs when requirements change or enhancements are requested. At that point, the program proves to be too fragile to accommodate change. The programmers become afraid to touch the program for fear of breaking it. It may be easier to scrap the code and start over than to modify the existing code.

This mode of failure can usually be traced to the high-level architecture of the application, or the lack of it. Even a program that is based on a sound project plan and adheres to the SPF can fail if the architectural framework is flawed.

10.2   Beadwork Programs

Did you ever do any beadwork as a child? You lay out parallel lines of thread on a form, and then you thread through each multi-colored bead, weaving them across the parallel threads to form an exact pattern. It is painstaking craft work, but in the end you produce the beaded pattern you designed.

Remember what happened if your threads got tangled? The whole piece was ruined if you were not able to untangle those threads. Most of us write programs so that they end up like bead work with tangled threads. You couldn't make a usable bead belt that way, yet we frequently write far more complex computer programs without a well-organized, high-level architecture.

Programming is much like beadwork. So far, the book has discussed how to create standardized, high-quality routines; the beads are like the routines in your program. But having a string of beads or a module full of safe routines is only the start. You must thread them together. In a program, these threads are the operational and business logic that tie the routines together. The finished beaded belt is like your finished program.

The desired bead pattern is like your functional specification. It is entirely possible to achieve that pattern with any random threading route, as shown in Figure 10.1. The thread need not be parallel or at right angles. You could send your thread through any path and still achieve the specified pat-

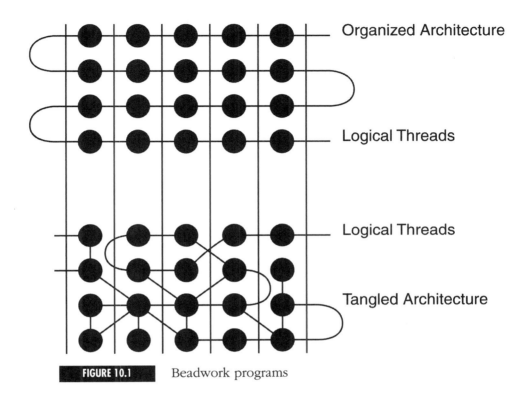

| FIGURE 10.1 | Beadwork programs

tern, but that would be an inefficient use of time and materials. Such unsystematic threading is far more prone to error. If an error were to occur, it would be extremely difficult, or even impossible, to correct the flaw without starting over.

You need to have well-made functions to make a quality product, but well-made functions alone don't ensure a quality product.

10.3   Maintainability

In this discussion, the term "maintainability" encompasses the ability of the program to adapt to changing specifications, planned additions, and evolving optimization during development. It also includes the ability to tolerate bug fixes and tweaking during testing without breaking, as well as adapt to changing needs after release, whether these be enhancements or modifications. Enhancements and modifications can include new features, new versions of third-party components, and changes required to accommodate industry or business changes.

The better the maintainability of a program, the longer its product life cycle. Programs with poor maintainability must sometimes be scrapped as soon as the changing world in which they exist forces them into early retirement.

Evolutionary versions of a program are, in essence, modifications of the current code. Generational versions are generally those requiring a complete rewrite. The more maintainable programs can accommodate more extensive evolutionary revisions without requiring the investment in a completely new generational version.

Even well-written programs, ones that meet all accepted standards of programming quality, often become difficult or impossible to maintain as they grow in complexity. Most commonly, the typical techniques used to structure programs are sometimes not entirely adequate. The threads of business logic become entangled with those of the user interface. It becomes extremely difficult to follow any particular thread for debugging or enhancement. Eventually, it becomes nearly impossible to make any modifications.

In effect, these programs have a steep maintenance curve. As the program grows in size and complexity, the maintenance difficulty rises exponentially. At some point on the curve, it becomes so difficult to make changes that the program must be replaced. Most often, one unmaintainable version is replaced by another program with the same architecture and the same steep maintenance curve. In effect, the existing curve is replaced by a new one, just offset to the right a bit on the diagram, as shown in Figure 10.2.

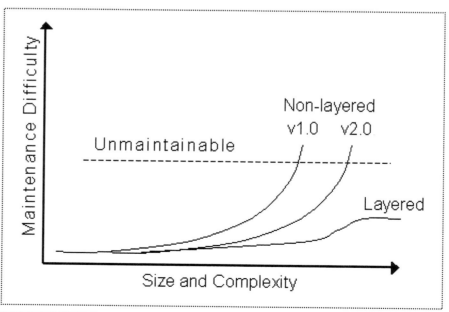

FIGURE 10.2   Program maintenance curve

The curve labeled v2.0 is a new version of v1.0. The flat curve is much more desirable than successive versions that will become unmaintainable.

Programs can become unmaintainable when needs are clarified, when the target moves, when users ask for new features, or when external changes force program changes. They can also become unmaintainable when members of the development team change or when the underlying technology changes. It is virtually impossible for a successful program *not* to require maintenance changes. So how can you ensure the longevity of your programs?

It is possible to design the architecture of your programs in such a way that they do not become tangled knots. When you do this, you achieve the nearly flat maintainability curve shown in the graph in Figure 10.2. If your maintenance curve is flat, you can develop programs that are easily scaled, modified, and debugged without causing unanticipated fallout elsewhere in the code.

Maintainability is largely an architectural issue.

10.4   Maintenance Nightmares

Like cars, all programs require maintenance eventually. In programs, as with cars, maintainability is not achieved by workmanship, but by design. Some programs, because of their complex requirements, can easily become maintenance nightmares. The programs that are the most difficult to maintain are those in which there are numerous derived calculations and dynamic field updates, causing logical tangles.

Consider the simplified business application shown in Figure 10.3. It is a database front-end program that allows the user to enter two sets of values. The application computes the subtotal for each set and the grand total for both sets. In the business module, there are three routines. CalcA calculates and displays the total of the two A fields. CalcB does the same thing for the two B fields. The third routine, called CalcGrand, computes the grand total. With these three routines in their own module, you might think that you have done everything possible to make this simple application maintainable.

Consider some minor enhancement requests to this simple form. Suppose that, for whatever reason, you are asked to remove Value 2B. If you remove this control from the form, both the code and the calculations will break. In order for the totals to be displayed correctly, you would probably save Value 2B as a separate variable and correct the calculations. Alternatively, you may simply make the Value 2B field invisible and leave it on the form to avoid the code changes, but that would not be very clean.

What if you were next asked to add a tab control to the form and repeat SubTotal B control on two different tabs? In order to keep them synchronized, you would have to update one when the other changes. In this situation, the Grand Total calculation would be triggered twice, once as each SubTotal is

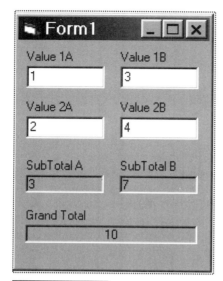

FIGURE 10.3 A simplified business application

updated. In this case, the double calculation may be acceptable, but what if the calculation were lengthy? What if it had to go out to the database as part of its computation? Then you would certainly attempt to inhibit multiple calculations using flags of some sort. That is not a trivial exercise. The resulting code would be neither very easy to follow nor to maintain.

You can see by now how a few very simple changes can cause both the business logic and the interface logic to become very messy. Imagine a real application with dozens of special requirements like these. Changes to one control can have extensive repercussions in other areas—and the maintenance curve starts turning skyward.

This problem need not happen if you use a layered design. If this were a layered application, deleting or copying a control would make no difference. The calculations would be unaffected since they occur entirely in a separate layer.

In a layered application, most enhancements should be neither difficult nor dangerous.

10.5   Implicit Business Logic

In the previous example, the events that controlled the user interface quickly and insidiously became an implicit part of the business logic. Implicit logic is logic necessary for one layer but which is an artifact of the operation of another layer.

Many programmers imagine that if they create a separate module for all their business calculations, they have segregated their business logic. This belief is only partially true. Their business routines are called in response to events in the user interface. The timing and sequence of the calls become important parts of the implicit business logic, which is buried in the user interface logic and driven by events and flags.

Any implicit business logic makes the program fragile because changes to one area break other areas. The program becomes difficult to document, trace, and debug. As the program becomes more complex, this buried logic creates hidden tangles.

10.6 Architectural Dimensions

If program architecture is the solution to program maintenance, then what architecture is the most maintainable? There are a number of very different architectural dimensions to program design. If you are primarily a project planner, you might think first of the logical architecture of the program. This architecture would be expressed, perhaps, as a flow chart of the business operations that the program must perform.

If you are a lead developer, to you architecture might mean the component architecture. This would include the commercial or custom OCX and DLL components that the application uses. If you are a programmer, to you architecture might mean the forms, classes, and code modules that form the structural architecture of the application. To a systems engineer, the architecture might mean the deployment strategy that organizes where and how various components are installed on various server and client-side systems.

All of these architectural dimensions interrelate, but none of them really tackles the fundamental structural issues that govern maintainability. There are two more types of architectural organization to consider. These are dimensions I call *lobes* and *layers*.

10.7 Lobes and Layers

If you have an interest in anatomy, the phrase "lobes and layers" probably brings to mind images of brain structure. The human brain is highly structured: it is divided into lobes, which are different areas of the brain that are responsible for different functions. The frontal lobe handles higher reasoning, the occipital lobe is responsible for vision, and the brain stem takes care of autonomic body functions.

Lobes are the topological layout of the brain. You can map brain function by labeling the various sections that handle different types of activities. Within the brain is another architectural dimension called layers. As you go deeper within each lobe, you enter layers with different responsibilities. They are like the layers of an onion. In the auditory lobe, one layer may take care of processing raw sounds, another layer may process musical notes, and a third layer may handle word recognition.

A well-structured program has lobes and layers, just as the brain does. Lobes are relatively easy to achieve. To create lobes, you simply segregate different functional areas into discrete program areas. Organizing a program into components or modules is not the same as organizing it into functional lobes. Different lobes may use the same components or may reside in the same module. It is not the physical location of the lobe that is critical; it is the logical isolation of its functionality that is key. Figure 10.4 illustrates the concept of lobes.

Lobes are application-specific. For the typical business database application, sample lobes might include client maintenance, inventory tracking,

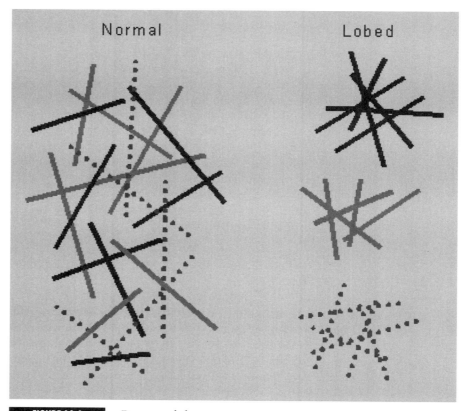

FIGURE 10.4   Program lobes

accounts receivable, payroll, employee information, and so on. Each lobe is independent and isolated from changes made to other lobes, and this independence is a key factor affecting program maintainability.

Even if you do a fine job creating independent program lobes, each of them can become unmaintainable. After all, each is like a separate little program; therefore, each of them can become a tangled knot. Lobes alone cannot eliminate tangles; they only reduce the size of each knot. To completely prevent tangles, layering is required.

Layers are much harder to create than lobes. Figure 10.5 illustrates how layers differ from lobes. The process of layering separates and orders the random program threads into much cleaner and maintainable code. Layers provide independent, and sometimes reusable, planes of code that can be easily maintained. Each layer can extend across multiple lobes to provide common functionality.

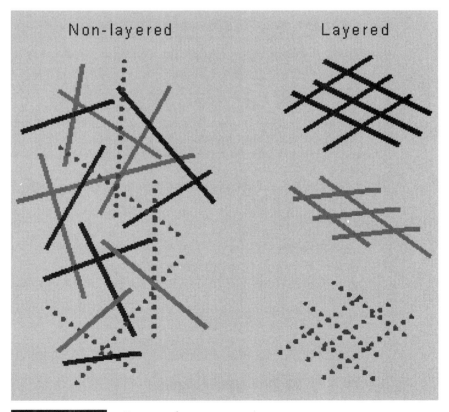

FIGURE 10.5 Program layers

10.8   Universal Layered Architecture

Abstract analogies are helpful to communicate the essence of layering, but a concrete example is necessary to give you a practical understanding. Consider what I call the **Universal Layered Architecture (ULA).** Since most Visual Basic applications are database applications, the ULA is designed to provide a layered infrastructure for database applications. The ULA organizes a database application conceptually into the following layers:

- User Layer
- Business Layer
- Data Layer
- User Connection Layer
- Database Layer
- Data Connection Layer

In a typical application, these layers are intertwined within a single layer, even if the application is organized into modules, components, objects, or lobes. Each of these is a separate, but intimately connected, layer of the ULA onion. Whereas other architectural entities are commonly connected through narrow lines of communication, layers are exposed along their entire surface.

10.8.1   The User Layer

The User Layer is that portion of the application that is exposed to the user. It contains all forms and controls as well as all logical threads required for their operation. Event-driven control procedures are threads that permeate this layer.

The following are characteristics and requirements of the User Layer:

- Contains only forms and controls, and the minimum code required for their operation.
- Contains no specific business knowledge, either explicit or implicit.
- Is the only layer to interact with the user.
- Is not aware of any layer except the adjacent Business Layer.

A good User Layer should contain the minimum amount of code necessary to allow your forms and controls to behave the way you wish them to. It should not include any database operations, nor should it contain any persistent data or any business rules, including input validation rules.

10.8.2   The Business Layer

The Business Layer contains all business rules and logic, including calculations and validation. No other layer should have any knowledge of the business rules specific to the application. This layer receives and processes requests from the User Layer, but it has no knowledge of the User Layer. It does not recognize whether the user layer is a Visual Basic form or an HTML document, nor does it recognize what specific information is displayed in it.

The calculations performed in the Business Layer are requested by the User Layer, but they are not affected by User Layer logic. Since it contains all business logic, the Business Layer touches most of the other layers in the following ways:

- It performs calculations and places results in the Data Layer.
- It performs data validation based on business rules.
- It determines how data will be formatted when displayed.
- It requests data from the database through the Data Connection Layer.

10.8.3   The Data Layer

In most applications, the User Layer both displays and contains the working data values. When a value is read from the database, it is often stored locally in the same control that displays it. This kind of program architecture is messy and will cause tangles.

In the ULA, all data is stored and maintained in the Data Layer and displayed in the User Layer. The Data Layer has no specific knowledge of any other layer. The Data Layer is a local data store that contains the information read from the database. It can also store other information that is not queried from the database, such as calculated fields.

The Data Layer also stores database table and field specifications so that it can validate changes against database specifications and constraints. It stores original values of each data element so that it can easily determine whether data has changed, and so that changes can be discarded without having to reload data from the database. While DAO does not store previous values, ADO stores both an underlying and a changed value.

10.8.4   The User Connection Layer

The User Connection Layer ties the User and Business Layers to the Data Layer. Its responsibilities are to update the User Layer with data and to provide data required by the Business Layer. This is the only layer that recognizes the User Layer. It knows about VB or HTML controls, forms, and documents, but it does not know about the specific information displayed there.

Information is "broadcast" from the User Connection Layer and received by any control in the user interface that is tuned in. User Layer controls are "bound" to data fields through property tags. The User Connection Layer loops through the controls on the form or document, looking for tags. If it finds a tag, it updates that control with the appropriate information from the Data Layer.

This makes for a very robust display mechanism. If fields in the Data Layer have no controls mapped to them in the User Layer, then that information is simply not displayed. It is still present in the Data Layer for internal operations. If User Layer controls are mapped to fields that have not been loaded into the Data Layer, then those are simply not displayed. These situations may need to be fixed so that all information is displayed properly, but in the meantime the application is in no danger of breaking.

Similarly, if a field is displayed on several controls, perhaps on different forms simultaneously, all controls are updated correctly from one underlying data value.

10.8.5   The Database Layer

The Database Layer is simply the physical database. It can be a standard database, a data warehouse, an OLAP cube, or any other type of information store that can be accessed by the Data Connection Layer. If the database has stored procedures and triggers that contain business logic, these items are actually part of the Business Layer, even though they are not located together.

10.8.6   The Data Connection Layer

This Data Connection Layer is the only layer that communicates with the Database Layer. It is completely generic and does not recognize or evaluate what specific information is in the database. This layer reads data, writes data, and submits stored procedures. The Data Connection Layer does not store information in this layer but uses the data stored within the Data Layer. It is the only layer to know about DAO or ADO.

10.9   Reusable Layers

Each layer of the ULA is relatively independent and insulated from the other layers. This makes them reusable, replaceable, and maintainable. Three of the layers in the ULA are completely generic and reusable in any application; the other three are application-specific.

Generic, Reusable Layers

- Data Layer
- Data Connection Layer
- User Connection Layer

Application-Specific Layers

- User Layer
- Business Layer
- Database Layer

Once you create your reusable layers, they should not need to be recreated for subsequent projects. Of the application-specific layers, the User Layer contains mostly forms layouts. If you create a well-designed prototype, your User Layer should be almost complete. You would have to create a database no matter what kind of architecture you adopted, layered or not. The Business Layer must be created for each project, but implementing nicely segregated business logic is far easier than implementing and debugging logic that is superimposed on other layers.

10.10 Layered Flow

Let's reconsider our simplified business application when implemented with a layered architecture. It is shown again in Figure 10.6. It looks no different on the surface.

In the layered version, the controls are not referenced anywhere in code in the User Layer. Instead, they are tagged with the field names to which they are mapped. The labels containing the totals are mapped as well. Since the total values are not stored in the database, they are mapped to calculated field names. Remember, the Data Layer is not limited to the storage of fields retrieved from the database.

To initially display the form, the User Layer calls an Initialize method in the Business Layer. That method creates an SQL statement, asks the Data Connection Layer to load the values into the Data Layer, and asks the User

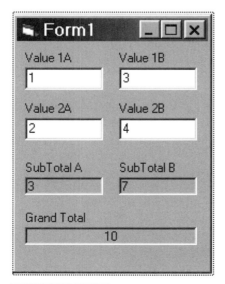

FIGURE 10.6 A simplified business application

Connection Layer to display the values in the User Layer. The Data Connection broadcasts all values, and they are displayed in any controls mapped to them.

When the user edits a field, a number of things happen:

1. In KeyPress event, a method is invoked in the Business Layer to validate the proposed new value.

2. The Business Layer validates the proposed value according to business constraints. If the value violates business rules, a zero key is returned to filter out the key press.

3. If the proposed new value meets business constraints, then it is passed to the Data Layer for validation according to database constraints. Again, if it fails to meet database constraints, then a zero is returned and the key press is not allowed.

4. If the value is validated, the result is formatted, if necessary, by the Business Layer.

5. The Business Layer updates the Data Layer with the new value.

6. After updating the Data Layer, the Business Layer recalculates any dependent data fields in the Data Layer. Any recalculated data is broadcast to the User Layer.

This is a very efficient process. As a result of one method called by the User Layer, much is accomplished. The proposed value is validated according to both business and database rules, it is formatted for display, and any dependent calculations are performed. All dependent variables are displayed as well, and any cascading calculations they trigger are handled correctly.

The three business routines, CalcA, CalcB, and CalcGrand are now located in the Business layer. They can reside in a code module, just as before, or they can be packaged in a replaceable DLL. The major difference is that now these calculations are not called implicitly as a part of User Layer events but explicitly within the Business Layer, where they are well-documented and clearly organized.

How would layering affect the minor enhancements that were made earlier? Remember that one request was to remove Value 2B? If you remove this control from the form, nothing will break. The field is still loaded from the database and exists independently from the control. The subtotal and grand total are still calculated correctly. The fact that it is not displayed does not matter.

The other enhancement was to put a tab control on the form and repeat the SubTotal B control on two different tabs. In our layered version, this works without modification to the code. When a value changes, SubTotal B is calculated in the Business Layer. When displayed, it appears on both tabs. No duplicate calculations are triggered, since the calculations in the Business Layer are independent of the User Layer.

You could make many other changes to this application without ramifications. If you change the business requirements, these changes to the Business Layer result in correct validation without changes to the User Layer, even if there are many duplicate fields. If you change the database schema, for example changing a long field to an integer, the correct input validation is automatically applied by the Data Layer.

If you added a "Save" button to this form, then clicking it would fire a Save method in the Business Layer. That method would request the Data Connection Layer to update the database.

10.11   Layering versus Binding

Bound controls, while attractive at first, almost by definition undermine the goal of good layered design. They exacerbate the fundamental problems that layering attempts to correct. Bound controls jump directly from the User Layer to the Database Layer, circumventing all intervening layers. They may be easy to use for simple applications, but they complicate both program development and maintenance in even moderately complex programs.

Even though controls in a ULA application are tagged with a field name, this is not just another form of binding. The data in the User Layer is mapped to a field in the Data Layer, not the Database Layer. The programmer has full control over all aspects of the display and modification of the field.

Field mapping in a layered application is not the same as binding.

10.12   Layering versus Classes

A layer can be composed of one or more class objects. However, it does not need to contain any class objects at all. A nicely layered application can be created using old-fashioned, non-class-oriented programming techniques.

Simply using classes does not assure a logical layering of your application; a class-oriented program can be just as logically tangled as any other program. A program that is not class-oriented, but is well-layered, is likely to be much more maintainable than a non-layered, class-oriented program.

While the use of class-oriented programming methods does not assure layering, it can greatly increase the power, flexibility, and clarity of your layered code. Class-oriented designs can accomplish superior layering with greater elegance.

Classes can improve layering, but they do not assure it.

10.13   Layering versus Tiers

You have probably heard much about tiers. It is hard to pick up a programming magazine without a cover story about a new 3-tier or n-tier technology or solution. Tiered applications accomplish some layering, but nowhere near as much as the ULA.

In many tiered applications, the business tier is the middle tier, residing wholly or in part within the database in the form of stored procedures and triggers. In a layered application, stored procedures and triggers can still be used to whatever extent the particular situation warrants. In this case, the stored procedures and triggers are still a logical part of the Business Layer. The main difference in the ULA is that stored procedures and triggers cannot comprise the entire Business Layer in themselves.

Layered applications can also be multi-tiered.

10.14   Layer Packaging

Component architectures can improve the usability of your layers. Since several of the layers can be made reusable, these can be shared effectively as DLL or OCX components.

In particular, since the Data Connection Layer requires no display forms, it is a good candidate for a DLL. In fact, you may wish to have several interchangeable versions of your Data Connection Layer. One might be a DAO version, another an ADO version. In the future new database integration strategies could stimulate the creation of new Data Connection Layer components.

The Data Layer and the User Connection Layers are two more layers that can be easily packaged as reusable DLLs. In fact, unless you have some special deployment needs, it might make the most sense to bundle these together into a single DLL. If packaged as DLLs, it means that your applications can easily reuse three major layers simply by referencing two DLLs.

The Business Layer can be included in your main program as a code module, but you may wish to package this as a DLL as well. The advantage of this practice is that you can replace the Business Layer with a different version just by referencing an alternate DLL.

There is no one best way to package layers. Use the best strategy to meet your needs.

10.15   Deploying Layers

Another advantage of packaging your Business Layer as a DLL is that it gives you tremendous flexibility to deploy your layers in various configurations. For a single user application, you can package all your layers in one executable. To improve maintainability, you can separate your layers into components. Again, layering is not the same as creating components.

For client/server applications, you can deploy your Business and Data Connection components on the database server side. For an Internet database application, you can deploy your Business and Data Connection layers within MTS.

> *Layer packages can be deployed in a wide variety of configurations to achieve the best performance.*

10.16   Benefits of Layering

There are many advantages to applications developed around layered architecture. They:

- *Have a flat maintenance curve.* Controls and business rules can be added without making the application significantly more difficult to maintain.
- *Are robust.* Any control can be removed or added without breaking anything, even if the value is used in intermediate computations.
- *Are synchronized.* The same field can be displayed and edited in different controls without User Interface logic. Changes to any one of them are automatically synchronized.
- *Are data-driven.* Fields can be modified, removed from, or added to the database without breaking any code.
- *Are preventative.* All validation and filtering is automatically applied at the earliest point after user input.
- *Are replaceable.* The layers are replaceable. The Business Layer can be replaced with any business model variation. The Data Connection Layer can be replaced with a version for DAO, ADO, or other interface library.
- *Need no binding.* No data binding or bound controls are used.
- *Have built-in Undo.* The local Data Layer allows automatic Undo capability without requerying the database. It also allows true dirty checking, which is not fooled if a field is changed and then changed back to the original value by the user.
- *Are flexible.* The Data Layer can contain data that is not displayed directly in the User Layer or saved in the database. The Data Layer can be technology independent.

10.17   Layering Case Study

The ULA is a conceptual design strategy. LADS is one implementation of this architecture. LADS stands for **Layered Architecture Development System.** It is composed of two application independent DLLs:

- *lads.dll:* The Data and User Connection Layers
- *ladsADO.dll:* The Data Connection Layer

The chart in Figure 10.7 shows the six layers of organization of the LADS ULA architecture. The User Layer can be either a VB form or a DHTML document. Other User Layers could be supported; they would simply require code to support them in the User Connection Layer. Three boxes are shown in the Business Layer to illustrate that this can be a replaceable layer support-

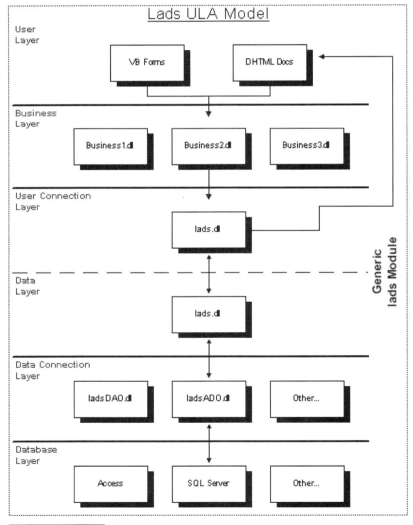

FIGURE 10.7 The LADS architecture

ing different business models. The User Connection Layer and the Data Layer are both provided in lads.dll. The Data Connection Layer is also replaceable to support any data interface library, current or future. The Database Layer can, of course, be any database supported by the Data Connection Layer.

In one medium-sized application that used LADS, substantial benefits were realized. The program included about fifty Visual Basic forms that managed about forty database tables. Following is a breakdown of the distribution of lines of code in the application:

Application Code Distribution

Layer	Code Lines
User Layer	24,000
Business Layer	6,200
Data Layer and User Connection Layer	3,200
Data Connection Layer	1,400

Of the 24,000 lines of code in the User Layer, 95 percent are pure user interface code, such as resizing windows, positioning forms, updating user information and so forth. Although 24,000 may seem like a large amount of code, the total amount in an unlayered application would be much greater. The code in the User Layer that deals with data is simply a series of high-level calls to the Business Layer. Although only 6,200 lines of code appear in the Business Layer, the amount of code would be much higher if integrated into the User Layer, and that code would be tangled extensively with the User Layer logic.

If this were not a layered application, the code in the Data Connection Layer would also be interspersed throughout the User and Business Layers. It is safe to say that the application would be much larger, even if the same degree of reuse were achieved, since additional code would need to be added to mitigate tangles. Further, the code would be much more difficult to maintain.

10.18 Datasets

In LADS, the Data Layer maintains a Datasets collection of Dataset objects. These objects are used in the Data Layer to store information locally. Each Dataset can have any number of fields and records. The Data Layer creates and maintains the Datasets so that the programmer does not need to be concerned with how data is managed or stored. The Data Layer stores the original and current values of each field. The original values allow Undo operations without having to return to the database. This process also allows the application to determine at any time if changes have actually been made to the Dataset.

Each Dataset has several properties, including the Name and RecordCount. Another property is the SQL statement or stored procedure name that is used to load or save it. Datasets have several methods, including Load, Save, and Undo.

Data is stored in each Dataset in a Data Dictionary. The Data Dictionary provides a high degree of flexibility and good performance. In a Data Dictionary, values are stored by key word.

TABLE 10.1	Dataset keywords
Keyword	**Description**
FieldCount	Field Count
Field.n.Name	Name of field n
fldname.Type	Type of field fldname
fldname.Length	Length of field fldname
fldname.n.Value	Current value of fldname in record n
fldname.n.Original	Original value of fldname in record n

The conceptual leap in using Datasets is to disassociate them from recordsets and forms. Once you do that, you will realize their true flexibility and power. A one-to-one relationship does not exist between Datasets and forms. Each Dataset can update the same or different parts of different forms. Many Datasets can be used to update a single form. No necessary correlation exists between the contents of a Dataset and the forms that display the data in it.

Similarly, they have no one-to-one relationship with recordsets. Datasets can contain raw database values, derived values, or data generated completely within the application. One SQL query can be used to load a Dataset, and another can be used to save a portion of it. Datasets are not simply repackaged recordsets.

This flexibility makes it preferable to base the application on Datasets rather than on disconnected ADO recordsets. It also insulates the application from technology changes.

10.19   Insulation from Technology Changes

LADS was originally designed with desktop applications in mind, before Web applications began to appear. When it became obvious that Web applications were gradually replacing a large number of traditional applications, my first reaction was that LADS was obsolete. I eventually realized that Web applications suffer from the same design flaws and limitations as traditional desktop applications. They can become just as tangled unless the basic architecture is layered.

An HTML page is simply another User Layer. With only a few small enhancements to the User Connection layer, LADS now supports both HTML documents and VB forms. Voila! You are able to export VB applications to the Web virtually without modification. All that is necessary is to lay out the forms in HTML documents.

Clearly, there is a need for layering in Web applications as well as in desktop applications. This fact in itself demonstrates and validates the power of the ULA approach. LADS integrates desktop and Web designs so completely that any layered desktop application can easily migrate to a Web application and vice versa, and both applications can look and behave identically since they share 90 percent of their code.

Put another way, LADS made it possible to move applications from the desktop to the Web without throwing away any code. If another User Layer technology appears, all that is required to support it are some enhancements to the User Connection Layer. The new User Layer could be a new computer interface or it could be completely unrelated, such as an ATM machine, a cell phone, or a neural implant.

Another example is the Data Connection Layer. When LADS was first written, I developed a DAO Data Connection Layer. When ADO came on the scene, I was able to move applications to ADO simply by replacing the Data Connection component. No other layers were affected. In most typical programs, this method would have required a major generational revision.

When I talk to people about LADS, the first question they often ask is, why use Datasets to store your data locally? Why not use ADO recordsets? They can be disconnected, and they offer tremendous flexibility and functionality.

That may be true, but by using Datasets, an application can easily support any changes to ADO or any successors to ADO. It is not limited to the functionality that technology has to offer. It also makes your application independent of database technology. It is a dangerous assumption, especially in database technologies, to assume that ADO is the last word. When the next acronym appears, a layered application will be able to adapt quickly and easily to take advantage of it.

10.20   Implementing a Layered Application

This chapter has introduced you to the theory and practical considerations that underpin the layered architecture. Implementing a layered application using LADS is fairly easy using the following steps:

1. Design your database.
2. Lay out your forms.

3. Tag each control.

4. Add a few method calls to load, validate, and save Datasets.

5. Add custom computations and business logic to your Business Layer.

The next chapter helps you to gain a more concrete understanding of this process by walking through the design of a layered application.

Designing a Layered Application

You may have a good idea by now of what layering is on a conceptual level. A more intimate working knowledge of layering can only come by actually creating one. This chapter will walk you through the design of a simple layered application. After studying this chapter, you should have enough concrete understanding to begin to develop your own layered applications.

The layering sample presented here is a simple database application designed to keep track of candy sales for a school fund-raiser. It has most of the elements that are commonly found in database applications. Let's assume that the functional specification is complete and we have a nonfunctional prototype. As shown in Figure 11.1, the prototype displays a combo box that allows the user to select a student. For each student, the prototype displays a list of customers. For each customer selected, it displays detailed information about that customer, items sold to that customer, and sales summary information. In the summary section, it displays the sales total for that customer as well as a grand total for all customers for that student. You can't modify the student list in this application, but you can add, edit, or delete customers and customer sales information.

Starting with the Visual Basic form shown in Figure 11.1 as your approved prototype, the following is an overview of the steps required to turn it into a working layered application:

1. Remove all temporary code from your prototype.
2. Implement a database to support your application.

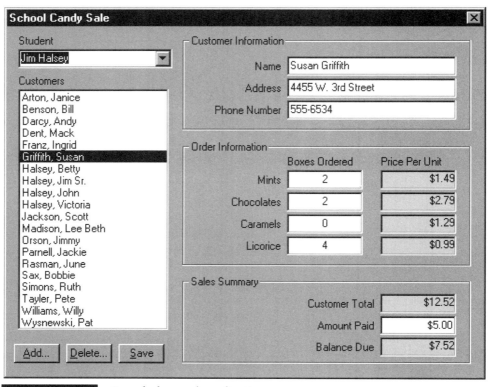

FIGURE 11.1   Sample layered application

3. Map all controls on your forms to database fields.
4. Pseudo-code your application.
5. Code and test each feature.
6. Test the overall application.

After clearing all temporary code from the prototype, you need to design your database and populate it with some representative sample data. This step assumes, of course, that you do not have a preexisting database.

11.1   The Database

To support this application, we create three tables. The first, tblStudents, contains a list of all student names. The second table, tblOrders, has a one-to-many relationship with tblStudents, with one student having many customers.

This table contains both the customer and order information. The third table, tblPrices has just one record with the selling price of each item for sale.

The following is a summary of the database schema for the sample application:

Database Table.Field	Type
tblStudents.StuID	AutoIncrement
tblStudents.StuName	Text(25)
tblOrders.OrderID	AutoIncrement
tblOrders.StudentID	Foreign Key
tblOrders.CustName	Text(35)
tblOrders.CustAddress	Text(50)
tblOrders.CustPhone	Text(22)
tblOrders.MintCount	Integer
tblOrders.ChocolateCount	Integer
tblOrders.CaramelCount	Integer
tblOrders.LicoriceCount	Integer
tblOrders.AmountPaid	Currency
tblPrices.MintCost	Currency
tblPrices.ChocolateCost	Currency
tblPrices.CaramelCost	Currency
tblPrices.LicoriceCost	Currency

The completed database is your Database Layer.

11.2   Planning Your Data Layer

After your Database Layer is complete, the next step is to plan your Data Layer. You need to determine what data will be stored locally and how it should be organized. For this application, the following three Datasets will be needed:

- *Students:* Contains the Name and ID of all students. In this case, it contains the complete contents of tblStudents.

- *Orders:* Contains customer personal and order information for each customer of the current student. It has calculated fields for the customer total and balance due which are computed locally, not stored in the database.

- *Prices:* Contains the candy prices from the database. In this example, it will have only one record.

Notice that these Datasets are related to the database but are not merely copies of the database. They can contain data loaded from the database but can also contain data obtained from any other source. For example, the Customers Dataset in this application will contain a number of database fields but will also contain the summary calculations that are not stored in the database. A Dataset can contain all calculated fields or a mixture of calculated and database fields. Likewise, a Dataset can contain fields from any number of database tables. In this sample application, each Dataset pulls information from a single table, but this may not always be the case.

The Datasets are also related to the User Layer but are not merely copies of the fields in the User Layer. They can contain fields, such as the ID fields from the database or intermediate calculated values, that are not displayed for the user. No necessary one-to-one relationship exists between forms and Datasets. Once you disassociate the idea of a Dataset from a one-to-one relationship with database tables or application forms, then you can accomplish more versatile program designs.

The following is a summary of the Datasets for this application and the source of the information:

Dataset.Field	Source
Students.StuID	tblStudents.StuID
Students.StuName	tblStudents.StuName
Orders.OrderID	tblOrders.OrderID
Orders.StudentID	tblOrders.StudentID
Orders.CustName	tblOrders.CustName
Orders.CustAddress	tblOrders.CustAddress
Orders.CustPhone	tblOrders.CustPhone
Orders.MintsCount	tblOrders.MintsCount
Orders.ChocolateCount	tblOrders.ChocolateCount
Orders.CaramelCount	tblOrders.CaramelCount
Orders.LicoriceCount	tblOrders.LicoriceCount
Orders.AmountPaid	tblOrders.AmountPaid
Orders.Total	Calculated
Orders.Balance	Calculated
Prices.MintsCost	tblPrices.MintsCost
Prices.ChocolateCost	tblPrices.ChocolateCost
Prices.CaramelCost	tblPrices.CaramelCost
Prices.LicoriceCost	tblPrices.LicoriceCost

11.3   Mapping Your Controls

You now have three layers in progress. The Database Layer is complete. You have designed the Datasets to be stored in the Data Layer. The controls to be displayed on the User Layer are present in your prototype. Now you must connect these layers together.

The first step to tying these layers together is to map the controls in your User Layer to the Datasets in your Data Layer. It is an easy matter to do this mapping.

In your layered application, as with a bound application, it is not really necessary to individually name your controls. Since you do not reference them by name, you can use generically named control arrays. Control arrays minimize the amount of event coding required in the control events and conserve resources.

While you are not going to use the direct data binding capabilities of your controls, you still need to identify which database field will map to each control on your form. There are many ways you can map each control. The Tag property offers one ready mechanism. However, the Tag property is frequently used for other purposes. While it is possible to create named variables in your Tag string so that it can be used for multiple purposes, I recommend using a different approach.

The Datafield property provided by most controls is used to specify the field to be displayed when the control is bound. Since you are not going to bind the control in your layered application, why not use that property to map your controls? The convention we will use in this sample project is to set the Datafield property to the dataset.field of the DataSet field to display. Notice that there is no direct connection between the User Layer and the Database Layer.

The following is the expanded field mapping. It shows the control, the Datafield property setting, and the mapping from the Dataset to the database:

Control	Dataset.Field	Source
Student Combo	Students	tblStudents
Customer List	Orders	tblOrders
n/a	Orders.OrderID	tblOrders.OrderID
n/a	Orders.StudentID	tblOrders.StudentID
Name TextBox	Orders.CustName	tblOrders.CustName
Address TextBox	Orders.CustAddress	tblOrders.CustAddress
Phone TextBox	Orders.CustPhone	tblOrders.CustPhone
Mints Ordered TextBox	Orders.MintsCount	tblOrders.MintsCount

Control	Dataset.Field	Source
Mints Price Label	Prices.MintsCost	tblPrices.MintsCost
Chocolates Ordered TextBox	Orders.ChocolateCount	tblOrders.ChocolateCount
Chocolates Price Label	Prices.ChocolateCost	tblPrices.ChocolateCost
Caramels Ordered TextBox	Orders.CaramelCount	tblOrders.CaramelCount
Caramels Price Label	Prices.CaramelCost	tblPrices.CaramelCost
Licorice Ordered TextBox	Orders.LicoriceCount	tblOrders.LicoriceCount
Licorice Price Label	Prices.LicoriceCost	tblPrices.LicoriceCost
Paid TextBox	Orders.AmountPaid	tblOrders.AmountPaid
Total Label	Orders.Total	Calculated
Balance Label	Orders.Balance	Calculated

To map your User Layer, then, set the Datafield property for each control to the value shown in the Dataset.Field column. Once you have completed this, you are ready to start pseudo-coding your application.

11.4 Creating Your Layers

You already have the Database Layer. You also have the start of your User Layer in the prototype main form. There are many ways you can create the other layers. You could create DLL projects for each, or you could simply add code modules for each layer to your project. Theoretically, you could put all layers into one big module, since it is not the physical location that determines layering but the code architecture.

For this sample application, let's use separate class modules within a single project. The Project Window shown in Figure 11.2 illustrates the organization of our CandySale project:

11.5 Pseudo-Coding the User Layer

Now that you have created your project modules, it is time to start pseudo-coding the program flow and logic. The following sections will show some pseudo-code designed to demonstrate the structure of this layered program.

Note that these code listings are not intended to be complete, finished implementations. They do not include all declarations, error coding, or other code that is not essential to communicate the flow of the layering code.

11.5.1 Form_Load

A good place to start is in the Load event of your start-up form. Here is the pseudo-code in this event handler (see Listing 11.1):

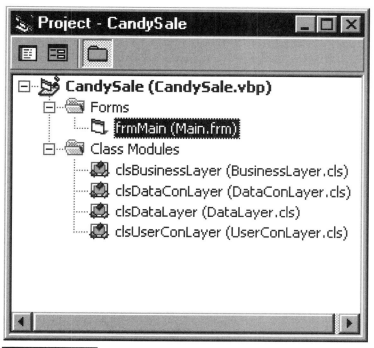

FIGURE 11.2   CandySale sample Project Window

LISTING 11.1

```
Dim mclsBL As New clsBusinessLayer

Private Sub Form_Load()

    'Get a valid database path from the user
    strSEM = sfGetDatabasePath(strDbPath)

    'Set the database path in the business layer
    strSEM = mclsBL.sfSetDbPath(strDbPath)

    'Set the current display form in the business layer
    strSEM = mclsBL.sfSetUserLayer(Me)

    'Load and display the candy prices
    strSEM = mclsBL.sfPricesShow()
```

```
'Load and display the students
strSEM = mclsBL.sfStudentsShow()

'Select the first student in the list, if any
'Note that this will trigger cboStudents_Click
strSEM = sfSelectListItem(cboStudents, 0)
```

End Sub

As you can see in Listing 11.1, the first task is to get the database path. This is a User Layer operation since it can require user interaction. The second step is to communicate the database path to the Business Layer. This step is done by passing the path to the Business Layer through a method. A property could be used, but that is not in keeping with the SPF.

After the path is set, the next step is to use a Business Layer method to set the display form. This is the form on which the underlying layers will display data. If you had multiple forms in your project, you could use this method to display any given Dataset on any form. If you are using an HTML document, you could pass this object to the Business Layer rather than a Visual Basic form.

The next code block calls the sfPricesShow method of the Business Layer. This method does many things. It creates the Prices Dataset, since it does not yet exist. It then loads the Prices Dataset from the database. It then displays the Dataset on the form that was just set as the Data Layer object. In this case, the four price fields will be populated with the fields defined by their Datafield properties.

The next step is to call the sfStudentsShow method in the Business Layer. This method is similar to the sfPricesShow method. It creates the Students Dataset, loads it, and displays all students in the combo box, since this control is mapped to the Students Dataset. After the students are displayed, sfSelectListItem is called to safely select the first student in the list.

11.5.2   *Students_Click*

In the Form_Load event, the last code block selects the first student in the combo box. This triggers a click event in the combo box. In the click event, the list of customers for the selected student is loaded. Here is the code in that event (see Listing 11.2):

LISTING 11.2

```
Private Sub cboStudents_Click()

    'Get the currently selected StudentID, if any
    strSEM = sfGetItemData(cboStudents, lngStudentID)
    If strSEM <> "" Then Exit Sub
```

```
'Load and display the Customers list for the current student
strSEM = mclsBL.sfCustomerListShow(lngStudentID)

'Select the first customer, if any, in the list
'Note that this will trigger lstCustomers_Click
strSEM = sfSelectListItem(cboStudents, 0)

End Sub
```

The first code block safely passes back the ItemData value for the currently selected student. This is the StudentID for the selected student. The next code block calls a method in the Business Layer to show the customers. The sfCustomerListShow method creates the Orders Dataset the first time this event is invoked, it will load the customers for the selected student, and it will display the Customers Dataset on the form. Since the list box is mapped to the Customers Dataset, it will be populated with the customers. The final code block selects the first customer in the list box and triggers the click event of the control.

11.5.3 Customers_Click

This event is much like the previous one. The first step is to safely obtain the Order ID of the selected customer. The second step is to call the sfOrderShow method in the business layer to display the details for that customer's order (see Listing 11.3):

LISTING 11.3

```
Private Sub lstCustomers_Click()

    'Get the currently selected OrderID, if any
    strSEM = sfGetItemData(lstCustomers, lngOrderID)
    If strSEM <> "" Then Exit Sub

    'Display the selected customer's order details
    strSEM = mclsBL.sfOrderShow(lngOrderID)

End Sub
```

At this point, the main form has loaded and displayed the initial screen of information. Not only has it shown the information from the database for the selected customer, but it has also calculated and displayed the summary figures. You will see how all this happens when we discuss the operation of the Business Layer. But first, let's finish the description of the User Layer.

11.5.4 Editing Fields

The preceding code listings handle the display of data. By clicking on a new customer, the click event will display the information for that customer. What about when the user changes editable fields? How do these changes get validated, saved, and displayed? How do dependent fields get calculated and displayed?

As with all the code in the User Layer, most of the action occurs in the Business Layer. The User Layer code is located in the KeyPress event of the text boxes. It is only one line of code. Since they are in a control array, this same line of code handles all editable fields (see Listing 11.4):

LISTING 11.4

```
Private Sub txt_KeyPress(Index As Integer, KeyAscii As Integer)

   'Update the Dataset and recalculate dependent values
   KeyAscii = mclsBL.dfValidateKey(txt(Index), KeyAscii)

End Sub
```

The dfValidateKey safe function does many things. It validates the key press according to database constraints and requirements. It also validates the key press according to any special business restrictions or logic. If the key press will not result in a value that is valid, a zero is returned and the key press is not allowed. This is a preventative approach that ensures that only valid keys can be pressed. Note that sometimes it is not possible to validate all values in the KeyPress event, since intermediate values within a valid entry may not be valid. In this case, the validation function can be placed in the LostFocus event.

Once a key is validated, the dfValidateKey function does more work. It saves the new value in the Dataset. It also recalculates and redisplays any dependent values, such as the customer and grand total fields.

11.5.5 Saving Changes

All changes are stored in their Datasets. No changes are saved to the database until the user clicks the "Save" button. When the user clicks the "Save" button, the only code required is a simple call to the Business Layer (see Listing 11.5):

LISTING 11.5

```
Private Function sfSave() As String

   'Save all dirty datasets
   strSEM = mclsBL.sfDatasetSave()

End Function
```

If no changes have been made, then the underlying layers are "smart" enough to know this and do not access the database. Since the Data Layer stores both original and working values, it determines if any changes have been made. Note that this approach cannot be fooled, for example, with a dirty flag in the Change event of the TextBox. If the user changes to a different value and back again, the dirty flag would probably be set and the data would be saved again. Using the Datasets, the original and current values can be compared to determine if they have been changed.

This storage method also makes it easy to undo any changes made prior to saving. Listing 11.6 shows the code beneath the Undo button:

LISTING 11.6

```
Private Function sfUndo() As String

   'Undo all dirty datasets
   strSEM = mclsBL.sfDatasetUndo()

End Function
```

The sdDatasetUndo method returns all current values to their original values and also redisplays all fields, including any calculated fields.

11.5.6 Adding and Deleting

Likewise, adding and deleting customer orders are simple calls to the Business Layer. Listing 11.7 shows the code beneath the "Add" and "Delete" buttons:

LISTING 11.7

```
Private Function sfCustomerAdd() As String

   'Prompt for new customer name

   'If no name is entered then exit

   'Add name to dataset and redisplay
   strSEM = mclsBL.sfCustomerAdd(strCustomerName)

End Function

Private Function sfCustomerDelete() As String

   'Get the currently selected OrderID, if any
   strSEM = sfGetItemData(lstCustomers, lngOrderID)
   If strSEM <> "" Then Exit Function
```

```
'Prompt to confirm delete

'Delete customer information from dataset and redisplay
strSEM = mclsBL.sfCustomerDelete(lngOrderID)

End Function
```

Listing 11.7 shows about all the essential pseudo-code in the User Layer. It is very light, as it should be. Even if many more controls are added on forms, little additional code need be necessary. Notice that the only other layer the User Layer sees is the Business Layer. Next you will see how the Business Layer code is structured.

11.6   Pseudo-Coding the Business Layer

The Business layer recognizes the Data Layer and the Data Connection layer. The bulk of its methods are calls to these classes.

11.6.1   Showing Datasets

Recall that the first method called in the Business Layer was the sfPricesShow method. This method was called in the Form_Load event just after the display form and the database path were set. This function displays the candy prices in the read-only label boxes on the form.

LISTING 11.8

```
Dim mclsDL as New clsDataLayer
Dim mclsUCL as New clsUserConLayer
Dim mclsDCL as New clsDataConLayer

Public Function sfPricesShow() As String
Dim strSQL As String
Dim strDataset As String

    'Set dataset name
    strDataset = "Prices"

    'Create dataset if it does not exist
    sfPricesShow = mclsDL.sfDatasetCreate(strDataset)
    If sfPricesShow <> "" Then Exit Function

    'Load dataset
    strSQL = "SELECT * FROM tblPrices"
```

```
sfPricesShow = mclsDCL.sfDatasetLoad(strDataset, strSQL)
If sfPricesShow <> "" Then Exit Function

'Display students dataset
sfPricesShow = mclsUCL.sfDatasetShow(strDataset)
If sfPricesShow <> "" Then Exit Function

End Function
```

The sfDatasetCreate method is located in the Data Layer. The Data Layer class object is created when the Business class initializes. This method does two things. First, it opens a connection to the database if none exists. It does this by calling a method in the Data Connection Layer. Next, it creates a Prices dataset if this does not already exist.

The next code block loads the Prices dataset. It does this by calling the sfDatasetLoad method of the Data Connection Layer class, passing it the dataset name to load and the SQL query string to retrieve.

The last step that the method performs is to show the dataset on the User Layer. It does this by calling the sfDatasetShow method of the Data Connection layer. Notice that all methods are safe functions.

The sfStudentsShow method is almost identical (see Listing 11.9):

LISTING 11.9

```
Public Function sfStudentsShow() As String
Dim strSQL As String
Dim strDataset As String

    'Set dataset name
    strDataset = "Students"

    'Create dataset if it does not exist
    sfStudentsShow = mclsDL.sfDatasetCreate(strDataset)
    If sfStudentsShow <> "" Then Exit Function

    'Load students dataset
    strSQL = "SELECT * FROM tblStudents ORDER BY stuName"
    sfStudentsShow = mclsDCL.sfDatasetLoad(strDataset, strSQL)
    If sfStudentsShow <> "" Then Exit Function

    'Display students dataset
    sfStudentsShow = mclsUCL.sfDatasetShow(strDataset)
    If sfStudentsShow <> "" Then Exit Function

End Function
```

Most of the Business Layer functions that display data look very similar. When the User Layer requests that database values be saved or restored to their original values, the Business Layer passes these requests along to Data Layer methods.

11.6.2   *Showing Calculated Fields*

The previous routines display database fields. When the user clicks on a customer name, the Orders Dataset that is displayed includes calculated fields as well as database fields. These fields are calculated in the Business Layer prior to display. The routine in Listing 11.10 demonstrates this process:

LISTING 11.10

```
Public Function sfOrderShow(lngOrderID As Variant) As String
Dim strSQL As String
Dim strDataset As String

    'Set dataset name
    strDataset = "Orders"

    'Create dataset if it does not exist
    sfStudentsShow = mclsDL.sfDatasetCreate(strDataset)
    If sfStudentsShow <> "" Then Exit Function

    'Load dataset
    strSQL = "SELECT * FROM tblCustomers"
    strSQL = strSQL & " Where OrderID = " & _
                    dfVntToSQL(lngOrderID)
    sfStudentsShow = mclsDCL.sfDatasetLoad(strDataset, strSQL)
    If sfStudentsShow <> "" Then Exit Function

    'Compute calculated fields
    sfStudentsShow = sfDatasetCalc(strDataset)
    If sfStudentsShow <> "" Then Exit Function

    'Display dataset
    sfStudentsShow = mclsUCL.sfDatasetShow(strDataset)
    If sfStudentsShow <> "" Then Exit Function

End Function
```

Notice that there is not much difference, except that a call is made to sfDataSetCalc. This routine located in the Business Layer computes all calculated fields. In this case, it calculates the customer total and balance due. The sample in Listing 11.11 shows the pseudo-code for this routine:

LISTING 11.11

```
Private Function sfDataSetCalc(strDataset As Variant) As String

   Select Case strDataset
      Case "Orders"
         strSEM = sfCalcValue(strDataset, "Total")
         strSEM = sfCalcValue(strDataset, "Balance")
      Case Else
         'Handle error
   End Select

End Function
```

This function computes the two calculated fields in the project. Since this function recomputes all calculated fields, the order of the calculations is important here. Notice that the Total is computed prior to the Balance, since the Total is used in the Balance calculation. If subtotals were present, they would need to be calculated before any totals.

The function sfCalcValue is called to compute each value. It is in this routine that the business calculation is performed (see Listing 11.12):

LISTING 11.12

```
Private Function sfCalcValue(strDataset As Variant, _
                  strCalcField As Variant) As String
Dim vntNew As Variant
Dim dsCalc as Dataset

   'Verify that dataset exists

   'Create a local reference to dataset
   Set dsCalc = mclsDL.Datasets("Orders")

   'Compute field - can be broken down by dataset
   Select Case strCalcField
      Case "Balance"
         vntNew = dsCalc.Field("Total").Value - _
                  dsCalc.Field("AmountPaid").Value
      Case "Total"
         'vntNew = total of candies ordered * their prices
         'For example, these are referenced as follows
         'dsCalc.Field("MintsCost").Value
         'dsCalc.Field("MintsCount").Value
   End Select
```

```
'Set calculated value in dataset
dsCalc.Field(strCalcField).Value = vntNew

End Function
```

Whereas sfDataSetCalc calculates a series of values in the correct and logical order, the sfCalcValue function performs simple calculations of a single business value. These two functions are all that are needed to accommodate most of the computations in your application, no matter how large it grows. The select statements can be expanded indefinitely without increasing the complexity of the routines. All cases will still be independent and easily maintained.

It is important to realize that in this architecture, computations are truly independent of User Layer logic. All calculations are performed in the correct order without redundancy, no matter what situation occurs in the User Layer. They can be modified and maintained without any interference from the User Layer or the Data Layer. Likewise, changes made to the business rules cannot break any other layer.

11.6.3   Changing Data in Datasets

So far, you have seen the Business Layer code required to display database fields and calculated values in the User Layer. What Business Layer code is used to handle changes that the user makes to editable fields? Remember that in Section 11.5.4 the dfValidateKey function was called in the Business Layer from the KeyPress event of the editable fields. This one function seemed to do miracles. Let's see how the function looks (see Listing 11.13):

LISTING 11.13

```
Public Function dfValidateKey(ctrl As Variant, _
              ByRef KeyAscii As Variant) As String
Dim strDataset As String
Dim strField As String

   'Get the dataset and field mapped to the control
   strSEM = mclsUCL.sfGetDatasetForControl(ctrl, strDataset)
   strSEM = mclsUCL.sfGetFieldForControl(ctrl, strField)

   'Predict the new value
   strSEM = sfPredictValue(ctrl, KeyAscii, strNew)

   'Validate new value according to Database requirements
   strSEM = mclsDL.sfValidate(strDataset, strField, strNew)
```

```
'Validate new value according to Business requirements
strSEM = sfValidate(strDataset, strField, strNew)

'Update Data Layer with new value
strSEM = mclsDL.sfSetValue(strDataset, strField, strNew)

'Recalculate any dependents
strSEM = sfDataSetCalc(strDataset)

'Rebroadcast new values
strSEM = mclsUCL.sfDatasetShow(strDataset)
```

```
End Function
```

The first code block in this routine calls a method in the User Connection Layer to return the Dataset and Field mapped to the control that was modified. It is the User Connection Layer that knows about the objects in the User Layer. Any type of control can be supported by putting code in the User Connection Layer to recognize and handle it.

The second block calls a Business Layer routine to predict the value that the field will have if the key is accepted. This is a fairly simple routine that merely adds the new key to the current value. If the key is a delete key, then the routine handles that correctly.

In the third code block, a routine in the Data Layer is called to validate the predicted value according to any database field requirements or constraints. For example, it verifies that the value can be mapped to the correct data type, that it meets length restrictions, and that it meets other constraints. In short, it verifies that the new value can be written successfully to the database. This routine is located in the Data Layer since that layer stores not only data values, but also all database schema information.

Next, the code validates the new value according to any business logic that is external to database constraints. For example, if a numeric value cannot exceed a certain limit, that value is checked in the Business Layer.

When the change has passed all data integrity and business rule checks, then the value is updated with a call to the Data Layer. After the value is changed, it may be that dependent values, such as subtotals and totals, need to be calculated. It is in the call to sfDataSetCalc that any derived values are recomputed.

After the new value is saved and any dependent values recalculated, then the sfDatasetShow method is called to redisplay all modified values in the User Layer. Notice that this single change may automatically trigger many fields to change, similar to recalculated cells in at spreadsheet. If at any point the change is rejected, KeyAscii is set to zero so that the key is filtered and not allowed in the User Layer.

11.7   Methods in the Data Layer

You may have noticed that the Business Layer makes many calls to the Data Layer. It is the Data Layer that is responsible for maintaining the Datasets that are used by the Business Layer for its computations. The following is a summary of some key methods in the Data Layer:

- *sfDatasetCreate:* Creates a new Dataset.
- *sfDatasetDelete:* Deletes a Dataset.
- *sfDatasetUndo:* Copies original values to the current values.
- *sfValueSet:* Updates a field in a Dataset with a new value.
- *sfValueGet:* Passes back the value of a field in a Dataset.
- *sfValidate:* Validates that a proposed field value meets database constraints.

11.8   Methods in the User Connection Layer

The User Connection Layer is the only layer to recognize the forms and controls in the User Layer. The primary method in this layer is the sfDatasetShow. This method displays the contents of a Dataset onto a User Layer object. Note that a User Layer object can be a Visual Basic form, an HTML document, or some other type of object. If a new type of user interface environment needs to be supported, the only application changes should be additions to this layer to support the new objects.

This method is really a critical function making layering feasible. How does this method work? Listing 11.14 shows some pseudo-code to illustrate:

LISTING 11.14

```
Public Function sfDatasetShow(strDatasetName As Variant) _
          As String

    'Verify that dataset exists

    'Determine if the User Layer object is a VB Form,
    'an HTML Document, or other

    'Step through all form controls or HTML objects

    'For each object, determine if it is mapped to a dataset
```

```
'Update each mapped object with formatted values
'from Data Layer

End Function
```

This function is really very simple to implement. You should use the TypeOf operator to determine the type of control that needs to be updated. If the control is a TextBox, you can update the Text property. If the control is a ListBox or ComboBox, you can update the list with all records in the Dataset. If the control is a grid, you can update the grid with a header and rows populated from the Data Layer.

11.9   Methods in the Data Connection Layer

Whenever data needs to be loaded from or saved to the database, the sfDatasetLoad or sfDatasetSave methods are called. These methods reside in the Data Connection Layer. This is the only layer that has any knowledge of the database object model, whether it is ADO, RDO, DAO, or something else.

11.10   Cool Features of Layered Applications

There are many cool features to try with your layered application. They illustrate the tremendous degree of maintainability achieved through layering.

- In Visual Basic, copy any one of the fields and paste the copy onto the form. When you execute the application, you will see that the new field is updated with the correct value. This occurs because the User Connection Layer automatically populates all controls.

- Edit one of the copies. Notice that the other copies stay synchronized as you type each key. This happens because all changes are broadcast to the User Layer.

- Now copy and paste one of the calculated fields. Notice that this new field is automatically updated as well. The value is only computed once, no matter how many copies you make, since the single value in the Dataset is the one recomputed.

- Now that you have a copy of a calculated field, edit the value of any dependent field. Notice that all copies of the calculated field are updated automatically. Again, no redundant computations occur in the Business Layer.

- Try deleting any field. Notice that the application does not break. The calculations are independent of the information that is or is not displayed in the user interface. Even if you delete a dependent field, the calculation is still performed properly since the calculation is based on the values in the Dataset. It makes no difference whether values appear in the User Layer.

- Delete a field from the database. As long as your SQL query selects all fields, the code will not break. The mapped field will remain blank, but the program will not fail.

- Change the type of a field in the database. The User Layer should automatically correctly display and accept input for the changed field specification.

- Remove or change a calculation in the Business Layer. The program will not fail. If a value is calculated but not displayed, that is no problem. Likewise, if a calculation fails to find the data it expects, this should be reported but should not crash the program.

You can do more operations with your layered application that you could not do with a standard application. These performance enhancements translate into improved maintainability. Improved maintainability translates into longevity. And longevity translates into higher profits.

11.11   Creating a Safe Layered Library

With this modest overview, you can go to work to create your own Safe Layered Library. Here are some notes and comments to think about as you develop your code.

When you create your User Layer, remember to keep it small. You are probably used to mixing all the layers, to some extent, in your User Layer. Resist this urge and don't include any information or logic, explicit or implicit, that should be a part of another layer. If you create your User Layer in VB, copy the same User Layer to HTML. The same code should work almost without modification if you have created a truly independent User Layer.

The Business Layer should be where all your business logic is located. It is in the Business Layer that any database queries are created or any stored procedures are selected. This is also the layer that decides which Datasets to create and when to destroy them, and it is where business rules are enforced and validated. You should be able to create two versions of the Business Layer with different business rules and interchange them without causing other layers to fail. The computations performed in this layer should be independent of any operations performed in the User Layer. The Business Layer should never need to recognize what operation or operational sequence is performed at the user level. It should not even care whether a User Layer exists. It responds to requests from the User Layer, but does not depend on it. When you construct your Business Layer calculations, you should make them robust with regard to the Data Layer. If an expected field does not exist in a Dataset, the associated calculation should not break the program.

When you create your Data Layer, you should make this layer self-maintaining. It should create Datasets and manage them without reliance on any other layer. Your choice of a strategy for storing your data is an important one. You could use simple variant arrays. You could also follow the LADS approach and use collections for Datasets and Dictionaries for data storage. A third alternative is to use disconnected ADO recordsets. This alternative may be attractive because of its simplicity and its compatibility with an ADO Data Connection layer. However, if a different interface model must be used in the Data Connection Layer, then this advantage is lost and the Data Layer will probably need to be rewritten.

Your Data Connection Layer can be built around DAO, RDO, ADO or some other technology. You can have multiple Data Connection Layers, provided that your Data Layer is generic. It is possible not only to replace Data Connection Layers without changing the other layers, but also possible to use multiple Data Connection Layers in the same application, updating a common Data Layer.

Finally, your User Connection Layer should be written to manage any type of User Layer objects. By simply changing the object, it should be feasible to write to multiple interfaces in the same application. For example, you can set a Visual Basic form as your interface object and show a Dataset on it. Then you can change the User Object to an HTML document and update it with the same Dataset.

When you package your layers, you can use modules, classes, or DLL objects. You can deploy your layer objects in a single executable or in multiple modules on different machines. You should write your layers so that they can be deployed in the most efficient manner for a particular application.

Be sure that your Data Layer, Data Connection Layer, and User Connection Layer are generic and reusable. Once you create these layers, you should be able to reuse them in every project. Also be sure to follow the Safe Programming Framework in creating your Safe Layered Library.

11.12   Using Layer-Wrapped Controls

An additional suggestion in developing safe layered applications is to use layer-wrapped controls. In Section 6, one suggestion offered was to create wrapped controls to encapsulate error prevention. Extending this, rather than use a standard TextBox, you can create a wrapped version as your own ActiveX control. This is really an extension of the philosophy of wrapping intrinsic VB functions. Why not apply this to controls as well?

As with functions, many ways exist to break standard controls. Rather than apply error prevention and handling code to each instance of a standard control, it makes sense to do this once and use the wrapped control. Not only can you include error prevention code but also many more user features that you commonly like to provide.

If you are using wrapped user input controls, why not include some additional capabilities to support layering? For example, you can expose Dataset and Field properties rather than use the standard Datafield property. You can also expose a record number property to handle Datasets with multiple records. For ListBoxes and grids, you can include properties to indicate the fields to display. You can also expose custom events to facilitate layered program flow.

Note—Wrapped Controls

One technique I use with my wrapped controls is to expose a Style property. For example, the Style property of a wrapped TextBox can be set to Numeric, Currency, Text, Phone Number, SSN, ZipCode, and others. Not only does the wrapped text box format the display of these Styles, but the Style field can be set automatically by the User Connection Layer based on the type of underlying field in the database. Thus, all of my text fields are dynamically configured by the database. The programmer does not even need to know the desired Style of the field. Most key filtering is accomplished within the control, not by the underlying layers.

11.13   Take It from Here

The purpose of this chapter was to stimulate a great many ideas for creating your own **Safe Layered Library**. Complete working code is not provided with this book because the goal is to teach you how to create safe layered code, not to teach you how to use a particular Safe Layered Library. It is up to you to take it from here. If you complete the pseudo-code provided here, you will find that the task it not difficult. Your efforts may take you in completely different directions that reach the same goals.

Accomplishing Your Mission

We have certainly covered a great deal of ground, haven't we? We started by developing a mission statement and ended with a concrete plan to accomplish that mission. The concepts, techniques, and attitudes were presented in a logical sequence, with each progressively building on the previous ones. Still, it is easy to lose the big picture when you focus on the details. It's like drawing a large mural–you quickly become engrossed in the detail. When you are finished, you need to step back to appreciate the total effect. In this chapter, we take that step back to get the big picture of our programming mural.

12.1   Getting the Panoramic View

In the beginning of the book, we drafted a mission to improve your software development effort. Now is a good time to restate that mission.

Your Mission Statement
To achieve a highly cost-effective, cumulative, and measurable improvement in both the quality and productivity of our software development process.

Remember that your mission was to improve both the quality and productivity of your software development effort. That improvement had to be cost-effective, cumulative, and measurable.

It was pointed out that software developers have a unique opportunity to retain and reuse their corporate knowledge. In this way, they can gain a cumulative benefit from their experience. This opportunity can be exploited through code reuse.

To meet the requirement of cost-effectiveness, the concept of **coding smarter** was introduced. It was pointed out that, by improving quality, you need not sacrifice productivity. In fact, with smart coding practices, both can and should improve.

The three aspects of smarter coding were identified: reuse, standardization, and error coding. It was emphasized that these three work hand-in-hand, and each supports the others. Without any one of these, the other two cannot succeed. Together these make up the **Smart Coding Triangle.** By adopting the Smart Coding Triangle, you may reasonably expect higher levels of quality and productivity.

In Chapter 2, the barriers to achieving good error coding were identified. It was pointed out that complete error coding is seldom achieved. Unique features of Visual Basic that undermine effective error coding, such as implicit behaviors, were discussed. Among the nontechnical barriers to learning and implementing error coding were space limitations in publications and management disincentives.

One of the hardest barriers to overcome in good error coding we identified as the view that code is disposable. This view causes code to be developed with strategies for short-term success. A new perspective was encouraged, a "Borg" view in which every routine is adaptable for reuse, despite changing needs of the program or its environment.

Barriers to code standardization and reuse were also discussed. Chapter 3 presented techniques for overcoming these barriers. The various techniques are encapsulated in the **Golden Rule of Error Coding.**

The Golden Rule of Error Coding
Prevent all errors that can be anticipated and prevented.
Handle all errors that can be anticipated but not prevented.
Trap all errors that cannot be anticipated.

The Golden Rule involves various error-coding strategies. These strategies include anticipating errors, preventing errors, handling errors, trapping errors, and reporting errors. We learned that complete error coding is not possible without leveraging reusable error code.

You should expect that all routines will be written for reuse, without exception, whether they will actually be reused or not. This practice imposes a consistent level of quality and standardization.

Chapter 4 tackled the problem of avoiding assumptions, which is the key to successful error coding. Many specific recommendations were presented, including the use of explicit variables, arguments, and arrays. Explicit coding was emphasized as the best discipline for achieving error-free code.

Chapter 5 presented the mechanics of error coding in detail. The On Error statement was reviewed, along with the operation of the Err object. The dangers of error suppression were discussed, as well as the risk of overusing error trapping. We saw that the most effective strategy for error coding is in-line error coding, using reusable procedures to prevent routines from becoming too long.

The Golden Rule says that all errors that can be anticipated and prevented should be prevented. Chapter 6 presented various strategies for preventing programming and user errors.

In Chapter 7, the **Safe Programming Framework** was described. The SPF provides a standardized approach for developing reusable, error-coded routines. It enforces all of the explicit programming recommendations from Chapter 4, the error-coding techniques from Chapter 5, and the preventative practices from Chapter 6. The SPF is built around a simple but powerful error reporting backbone, using **Safe Error Messages** to communicate error information. Chapter 8 provided a sampling of various SPF routines to illustrate this framework.

Chapter 9 discussed the problem of adopting the standard across a team, as well as the problem of building and using a **Safe Library.** As a strategy for creating a successful Safe Library program, the **Safe Certification Process** was offered. Certification provides a mechanism for training, code review, the enforcement of standards, quality improvement, and the dissemination of information, all in one simple process. **Recognition** of submissions to the Safe Library was identified as an important motivational force in the certification process. Various strategies for recognition were offered.

Chapter 10 considered the question of program maintainability. It was pointed out that creating quality routines only addresses a part of the mission. Even with standardized, reusable routines that are properly error-coded, programs can fail to be maintainable over the long term. The most common reason for this type of failure was identified as architectural in origin. Typical architectures create programs that become logically tangled when the operation of the controls is mixed with business logic and database coding.

To create more maintainable programs, the architectural constructs of **lobes** and **layers** were introduced. By layering your application, you not only achieve nearly flat maintenance curves, but you also create entire layers that are highly reusable and that standardize your high level architectural program structure. This strategy further contributes to the success of your mission.

As a conceptual implementation of layering, the **Universal Layered Architecture** was presented. The ULA organizes your database application into six discrete layers, each with an isolated and singular responsibility: these are the User Layer, the Business Layer, the Data Layer, the User

Connection Layer, the Data Connection Layer, and the Database Layer. A practical implementation of the ULA, called the **Layered Architecture Development System,** was provided as one example of an actual ULA architecture. LADS consists of two DLLs to provide the three reusable layers. It implements the Data Layer using a collection of Dataset objects that store data in scripting dictionaries. The LADS Datasets provide a tremendous amount of architectural flexibility within the ULA framework.

In Chapter 11, a sample application was designed using a layered architecture. It illustrated the fundamental features of layering and gave you an appreciation for its practical benefits. And that brings us to where we are now.

12.2   Assessing Your Success

Do all these recommendations and strategies, taken together, represent a plan for succeeding in your mission? I believe they do. For me, they have proved to provide dramatic increases in the quality and productivity of projects to which they have been applied. You can implement these suggestions in pieces or in phases, but the greatest benefit will not be realized until your team contributes to a Safe Library and reuses standardized, fully error-coded routines in layered applications.

When that happens, the benefits will begin to compound. Not only will your corporate knowledge be effectively retained and reapplied, but also your applications will enjoy a longer maintainable product lifetime. Your goal of a cumulative improvement of quality and productivity will steadily become realized.

The suggestions made in this book are certainly cost-effective as well. None of the suggestions costs much, if anything. All, in fact, save time and money in many ways. By emphasizing standards, the amount of time required to develop fully error-coded programs is reduced. Reuse provides a cumulative improvement in cost-effectiveness. The techniques presented in this book should take no more time to implement than standard coding. As a rule of thumb, if it takes longer to implement fully error-coded features as you go, then you need to code smarter.

The third criteria for the success of your mission is that your solution must be measurable. It is certainly possible to measure the success of your smart coding effort. I leave it up to you to find the appropriate metrics to evaluate smart coding in your particular environment. When you do, be sure to include long-term payback as well as short-term success. If you have a growing library, and if these routines are being reused, then I believe that metric will serve as a good indicator of your other measures of success.

Of course, many other factors affect the complicated process of software development. Nontechnical issues such as project planning, specifications, project team structures and roles, risk management, estimation, and motivation will also affect your success. In addition, technical tools and techniques always keep advancing in this industry. This book has tried to stay focused and not stray too far into these areas, technical or nontechnical. I do not intend to suggest that they are not vitally important. They should be considered carefully and integrated in a way that will support, not undermine, your smart coding effort.

12.3   Taking Your Next Steps

How do you proceed to implement the principles presented in this book? That partly depends on who you are. If you are an independent developer or consultant, then you can simply begin to adopt some of the general strategies in your current project. You can fully apply the standardization details in your next project.

When you interview with a new employer or client, it may be very helpful to ask the interviewer very early about the company's coding standards. Ask him or her if a coding standard exists in writing. If one does, review the standard to see if you feel you can fully comply with it. If you are not comfortable with the company's requirements, you may wish to decline the job. If the company does not have a written standard, ask the interviewer if the company would be comfortable with your programming approaches and conventions before you commit to the work. This practice makes good common sense to ensure that both parties know what to expect from each other.

If you work in a company, then you must assess which of the recommendations in this book are compatible with the approaches and standards, explicit or assumed, within your company. You may wish to discuss coding standards and issues with your supervisor before you implement any new approaches. You may find that he or she is quite interested in and excited about improving the quality and productivity of the team.

If you are in a leadership position in a software development firm, you may wish to implement some of the ideas in this book immediately, then gradually move toward others. Alternatively, you may decide to implement sweeping new standards beginning with your next project, or starting within one team immediately and later within other teams.

As you implement changes, it is important to have one or more champions. A champion is an individual with the motivation and ability to stimulate change. This person may be you, or it may be someone you recruit. The champion (or champions) should prepare a written standard and promote the use of that standard among the staff. Your standards are as important as your libraries of reusable code. The standards should not be changed lightly, but they should not be carved in stone either. They should be reviewed periodically to keep them current with technology.

If you are a supervisor, it is up to you to support your champion by providing resources and by creating an atmosphere in which his or her efforts can take root. One way to support your champion is by simply promoting this person's efforts, making it clear that you fully support him or her. Another way is by asking about the implementation of standards and expecting that they will be adopted fully by your developers.

Be sensitive to the fact that some developers may have negative reactions when you bring up standards. Some will fear that standards will entail more work and inhibit their ability to produce efficient, creative solutions. This is not necessarily the case, and well-implemented standards should reduce the amount of work required to produce creative solutions. It is your responsibility to communicate this and alleviate fears.

Giving rewards is another way that you, as a manager, can play a key role in the standards adoption process. Normally, your champion will not have the ability to grant tangible rewards, and will not be in a position to offer strong intangible recognition. Offering recognition must be up to you. Without recognition from you, the efforts of your champion have little impact.

The other task to perform at a management level is removing technical and nontechnical barriers. You must actually go beyond removing barriers and begin to create motivational catalysts that make it easy and natural for the staff to create reuse-quality code. The Safe Library and Safe Certification Process are effective catalysts that you can easily put in place.

Finally, when interviewing new employees, ask candidates about their experience with, and feelings about, following coding standards. Be certain that they are experienced enough to appreciate the benefits of coding standards, but not too rigid to adapt their previous standards to comply with those of the company.

12.4   Keep the Ball Going!

It is my sincere hope that this book has stimulated your thinking about Visual Basic program development, and that it will help to improve the quality and productivity of your efforts. We are part of a circle of Visual Basic developers. I have volleyed the ball back to you. Keep it going!

Naming Conventions

It is important to follow a standardized variable-naming convention in your code. The naming should apply to object variables as well as simple variables. The name should communicate three things. First, it should indicate the scope of the variable. Second, it should indicate the type of variable. Third, it should specify the purpose or contents of the variable.

Standard prefixes are used to indicate the scope and type. The main part of the name should be devised by you to succinctly but clearly communicate the purpose. There is no single standard convention to abide by. It seems like almost everyone recommends slightly different naming conventions. Microsoft makes naming recommendations, but Visual Basic does not follow them in default names for their standard objects. The first step is to rename every control you add to your project with a good, standardized name. It is not important exactly what prefixes you use. It is important only that you do follow some convention consistently.

The following tables show some good conventions to use for naming variables, arguments, and objects. Table A.1 shows the scope prefixes. Table A.2 shows the variable type prefixes, and Table A.3 shows the object type prefixes. Table A.4 shows the prefixes for common database objects.

These tables are not exhaustive. There are many more object types, but the ones shown are the most common.

One related naming issue that programmers need to address is the naming of third party controls. Should you use separate prefixes to indicate the particular manufacturer of, say, a grid control? Or should you use the generic "grd" prefix for any grid control, no matter which one it is?

I prefer the latter alternative. By using a generic prefix, it is more recognizable. Also, if you change controls, say to a new type of grid, then you do not need to review all your code and change every prefix.

TABLE A.1	Scope	
Scope	**Prefix**	**Example**
Global	g	gstrUserName
Module-level	m	mblnCalcInProgress
Local to procedure	None	dblVelocity

TABLE A.2	Variable prefixes	
Data Type	**Prefix**	**Example**
Boolean	bln	blnFound
Byte	byt	bytRasterData
Collection	col	colWidgets
Currency	cur	curRevenue
Date (Time)	dtm	dtmStart
Double	dbl	dblTolerance
Integer	int	intQuantity
Long	lng	lngDistance
Object	obj	objCurrent
Single	sng	sngAverage
String	str	strName
User-defined type	udt	udtEmployee
Variant	vnt	vntCheckSum

Another naming issue to consider is menu item naming. Should you include the menu name in the menu item names? For example, if you have a menu called mnuFile, should you name items as mnuFileOpen, mnuFileSave, and mnuFileQuit?

In this case, I prefer not to use this convention. During development, menu items are moved around until the menu structure is finalized. Even then, new enhancements or versions can cause menu items to be rearranged. Including the main menu name in the menu item name makes it difficult to keep the naming correct and makes it difficult to move menu items.

How do you identify a variable as a constant? One common convention is to use all uppercase letters to name a constant. For example, you would expect mintUSERCOUNT to be a constant, while mintUserCount should be a variable. The use of underscores is a source of naming controversy. I personally don't care to use the underscore in variable and object names. Underscores can be difficult to see and difficult to type. However, I do like to use underscore characters in constant naming. All uppercase letters are not used for normal names because they are difficult to read. To make constant

TABLE A.3	Control prefixes	
Control Type	**Prefix**	**Example**
Combobox	cbo	cboMemberType
Checkbox	chk	chkReadOnly
Command Button	cmd	cmdOK
Data Control	dat	datMembers
Common Dialog	dlg	dlgFileOpen
Form	frm	frmMain
Frame	fra	fraStyle
Grid	grd	grdMembers
Image Control	img	imgDarkGrey
Image List	iml	imlMain
Label	lbl	lblLabel
Line	lin	linLine
Listbox	lst	lstDates
List View	lvw	lvwBidders
Menu	mnu	mnuFileOpen
Option Button	opt	optContractType
Outline Control	out	outWorksheet
Picture	pic	picPhoto
Panel	pnl	pnlAttributes
Rich Textbox	rtb	rtbLastName
Textbox	txt	txtFirstName
Timer	tmr	tmrUdate
ToolbarBar	tbr	tbrMain
Treeview	tvw	tvwLots

TABLE A.4	Database object prefixes	
Object Name	**Prefix**	**Example**
ADO Connection	cn	gcnServer
DAO Database	db	mdbClients
Recordset	rs	rsMembers
Dynaset	ds	dsGroups
Snapshot	ss	ssPickList

names more readable, underscores make sense. Therefore, mintUSER_COUNT is a good convention for constants.

What about case and underscores in database table names? Many database developers use table and field names such as "tbl_usr_rec_dat." I find this kind of naming terribly awkward. While such naming is standardized and methodical, it is not clear or user-friendly. These names make me feel as though I am driving through a military base with signs identifying buildings called ComStatAppNav. I prefer more simple, English-sounding names such as tblUserInfo. Again, however, it is not so important exactly what conventions you use as that you do use a standardized naming convention that is clear and intuitive to others.

SPF Checklist

The following is a checklist that you can use to help ensure that your code meets all requirements for the Safe Programming Framework. Section references are shown in parentheses.

Documentation

_____ Provide a standard procedure header (7.16.1).
_____ Name variables and procedures consistently (7.11).
_____ Use standard prefixes in names (Appendix A).
_____ Describe any programming tricks that may be unclear to other programmers (7.16).
_____ Comment each code block with a clear statement of purpose (7.16).

User Interfaces (6.4)

_____ Make the user interface unambiguous for the user (6.4).
_____ Make the user interface consistent for the user (6.4).
_____ Prevent user errors as early as possible (6.4).

Procedures

_____ Use sf, df, and ds only (7.2).
_____ Return an SEM from an sf or df (7.3, 7.4).
_____ Effectively reuse other procedures (8.4).
_____ Design your procedures elegantly (6.3.6).

Variables

_____ Always use Option Explicit (4.1.1).
_____ Explicitly type variables (4.1.2).
_____ Avoid DefType statements (4.1.3).
_____ Use specific data types (4.1.4).
_____ Initialize all variables (4.1.5).
_____ Use one variable per line (4.1.6).
_____ Use TypeName, VarType, and TypeOf (4.1.7).

Arguments

_____ Always use ByVal or ByRef (4.2.1).
_____ Pass all arguments ByVal unless there is a specific reason to pass ByRef (4.2.1).
_____ Explicitly type arguments (4.2.2).
_____ Set explicit default values for optional arguments (4.2.3).
_____ Validate all arguments in the procedure in which they are used (4.2.4).
_____ Avoid using Variant data types except as arguments (4.1.4).

Arrays

_____ Never assume lower array bounds (4.3.1).
_____ Use constants for array bounds (4.3.2).
_____ Avoid using Option Base (4.3.3).

Coding Mechanics

_____ Always include an Else (4.4.1).
_____ Avoid using default properties (4.4.2).
_____ Avoid mixing data types in expressions (4.4.3).
_____ Use constants (4.4.4).
_____ Use Enumerations wherever applicable (4.1.8).
_____ Avoid operator precedence (4.4.5).
_____ Use parentheses liberally to communicate clearly to others (4.4.5).
_____ Check string lengths (4.4.6).
_____ Close all open objects as soon as possible (4.4.7).
_____ Set objects to Nothing as soon as possible (4.4.8).
_____ Always explicitly turn off error trapping (4.4.9).
_____ Never assume anything about the external world (4.4.10).
_____ Don't cut and paste code (4.4.11).
_____ Make sure each code block is like a little routine. Only one clear, complete function (5.2.5).
_____ Use & for strings and + for numerical values only (4.4.12).
_____ Pseudo-code before you code (4.4.13).
_____ Don't use clever tricks. Use slower, simpler code if it is clearer (4.4.3).

_____ Use Public and Private instead of Dim and Global (7.13).
_____ Indent consistently two to four spaces (7.2).
_____ Avoid using class properties (7.7).

Error Prevention

_____ Prevent anticipated programming errors (6.3).
_____ Prevent anticipated user errors (6.4).

Error Handling

_____ Give each procedure an independent error handler (5.15, 5.16).
_____ Use in-line error handlers (5.22, 5.23).
_____ Check for errors after each line when On Error Resume is in effect (5.10).
_____ Avoid logical operators when checking error number (5.11).
_____ Disable error handling with On Error Goto 0 after each block (5.13).
_____ Put an End Sub or End Function before any error trapping block (5.19).

Certification Rating Sheet

The following is a rating sheet you can use to evaluate Safe Procedures that are candidates for certification. It produces a rating number that can be assigned as award points if a point-based recognition system is used. This rating should be done after the routine has been reviewed and revised, if necessary, so that it meets all requirements for certification.

To complete the worksheet, rate each of the seven evaluation criteria on a scale of 0 to 10. To compile the completed worksheets:

- Add the scores on each rating sheet, but add in the square of "Size and Scope." Doing this appropriately weights the importance of "Size and Scope."
- Add the sheet totals, then divide by the number of sheets to get an overall rating.

The overall rating can be applied to the author's cumulative award total. For example, if a developer gets all 5's except for a 1 for "Size and Scope," the point award would be 31 points. For all 5's except a 10 for "Size and Scope," the point award would be 130 points. The theoretical maximum would be $(6 * 10) + (10^2)$, or 160 points. From this you can determine award levels at which you would like to offer formal acknowledgment.

Certification Rating Worksheet

For each component you certify, rate each of the following criteria on a scale of 0 to 10 and total them. The actual certification points awarded will be the average of all total ratings normalized on a 10 point scale. *A rating of 0 on any item disqualifies the component for certification.*

Component Name: _____

Reviewer Name: _____

How large is the **size and scope?**
  1 = A one-liner.
  10 = A code of epic proportions.   _____

How **innovative** is it?
  1 = My grandmother did that years ago.
  10 = Makes Relativity look like just another theory.   _____

How **useful** is it?
  1 = It will be amazing if it is ever used again.
  10 = Will be used many times in many projects.   _____

How **reusable** is it?
  1 = It will be tricky to reuse this effectively.
  10 = A no-brainer to reuse.   _____

How **standardized** is it?
  1 = Not internally consistent, let alone consistent with standards.
  10 = Follows the Safe Programming Framework fanatically. _____

How **elegant** is it?
  1 = Overly-complicated design and implementation.
  10 = Highly efficient, understandable, and maintainable. _____

How **bug-proof** is it?
  1 = A great risk of unanticipated errors.
  10 = It would take a cryptographer to break the code.   _____

Rating   _____

INDEX